PENSIONS

An Accounting
and Management Guide

FELIX POMERANZ, C.P.A.

PARTNER, COOPERS & LYBRAND

GORDON P. RAMSEY

PRINCIPAL, COOPERS & LYBRAND

RICHARD M. STEINBERG, C.P.A.

MANAGER, COOPERS & LYBRAND

A RONALD PRESS PUBLICATION

JOHN WILEY & SONS, New York • Chichester • Brisbane • Toronto

ISBN 0 471 06548 X

Library of Congress Catalog Card Number: 75–35288

PRINTED IN THE UNITED STATES OF AMERICA

10 9 8 7 6 5 4 3

To

PHILIP L. DEFLIESE

who, by example, has set the standard
of professional responsibility
to which we all aspire

PREFACE

With the passage of the Employee Retirement Income Security Act, the entire area of accounting, auditing, and financial reporting for pension plans has become the subject of much discussion and uncertainty. Accountants, auditors, plan trustees, sponsors, and administrators, and others involved with pension plans are raising questions regarding implications of the Act for generally accepted accounting principles, reporting and disclosure requirements, generally accepted auditing standards, and various aspects of plan management.

It will undoubtedly be years before the clouded picture of pension accounting, auditing, and reporting becomes clear. In addition to clarification of vague or contradictory provisions of the law via forthcoming regulations of the Secretaries of Labor and the Treasury, authoritative accounting and auditing professional bodies will be taking steps to revise and clarify standards with the aim of improving the utility of financial statements to shareholders, plan participants and beneficiaries, and other users of employers' and pension funds' financial statements. The Financial Accounting Standards Board, senior committees of the American Institute of Certified Public Accountants, and the Securities and Exchange Commission have all indicated that they will be comprehensively reviewing the various issues involved.

This book is designed to provide a frame of reference for the major accounting, auditing, and financial reporting issues related to pension plans in light of the new law. It attempts to answer many questions and, where no answer is presently available, to point out the ramifications of the problem. While the conclusions set forth herein are necessarily tentative, pending issuance of regulations and accounting and auditing pronouncements, it is the authors' intent that this book will stimulate discussion of the issues within the profession and will enable those involved with pension plans to cope with the requirements and implications of the new law during the transitional period.

We would like to gratefully acknowledge the contributions of our associates in Coopers & Lybrand. William J. McHugh and Ronald J. Murray, in addition to providing valuable advice and counsel, reviewed numerous drafts of the manuscript with great care; their comments and suggestions were most constructive. We also acknowledge the valuable counsel of Kenneth P. Johnson and the helpful comments of John J. Fox, Martin Abrahams, and James J. Walsh. Sections dealing with actuarial and benefits matters were critically reviewed by Ferne R. Goldman, whose advice and suggestions were most useful. Daniel S. Harris and William J. Stephan also provided advice with respect to actuarial matters.

Particular credit must go to Gerald W. Ackerman, whose unlimited cooperation and efforts in researching and in helping develop the manuscript played an important role in the completion of this work. Finally, we express appreciation to Morton Meyerson, for his role in visualizing and initiating development of this book, and to Norman E. Auerbach, Associate Managing Partner of Coopers & Lybrand, for his constant support and encouragement.

FELIX POMERANZ
GORDON P. RAMSEY
RICHARD M. STEINBERG

New York, New York
November 17, 1975

CONTENTS

Dates. *Limits on Benefits and Contributions.* Penalties. Effective Dates. *Back-Loaded Benefits.* Penalties. Effective Dates. *Joint and Survivor Annuities.* Penalties. Effective Dates. *Plan Termination Insurance.* Penalties. Effective Dates. *Fiduciary Responsibilities.* Definition. Exemptions. Penalties. Effective Dates. *Enforcement.* How Penalties Apply. *Annual Registration.*

Accountants and Actuaries. Material Covered by Accountant's Opinion. Material Covered by Actuary's Opinion. *Rejection of Filings. Other Waivers. Penalties. Effective Dates.*

II. Employer Company Accounting, Auditing, and Financial Reporting

Historical Background. Statements of the American Institute of Certified Public Accountants (AICPA). APB Opinion No. 8. Applicability of APB Opinion No. 8. *Annual Provision for Pension Cost.* Minimum Provision. Maximum Provision. Calculation of Annual Provision. Valuing Vested Benefits. *Actuarial Factors.* Actuarial Cost Method. Actuarial Assumptions. Actuarial Gains and Losses. Actuarial Valuation Date. Differences Between Funding and Accounting. *Defined Contribution Plans. Disclosures.* Comparison With SEC Requirements. *Special Situations.* Regulated Companies. Nonprofit Organizations. Deferred Compensation Contracts. Death and Disability Benefits. *Accounting Effects of ERISA.* Liability for Unfunded Prior Service Cost. Liability for Unfunded Vested Benefits. Pension Expense. Disclosures. Liability to Acquiring Company.

Basic Objectives and Audit Procedures. Auditing Actuarial Information. Insured Plans. *Audit Procedures Directly Related to ERISA.* Accounting-Related Impact. Compliance With ERISA. *Reporting Considerations.* Comparability and Consistency. Departures from the Opinion and Interpretation.

III. Pension Fund Accounting, Auditing,
and Financial Reporting

IV. Plan Management Under ERISA

Appendixes

PART I

Pension Fundamentals
and Provisions
of ERISA

1

INTRODUCTION AND BACKGROUND ON PENSIONS

The Employee Retirement Income Security Act of 1974, commonly known as "ERISA," was the culmination of a decade or more of consideration and review by various government entities and others. It is the most complex and far-reaching legislation affecting pensions in over thirty years, and substantially changes the way in which employers and pension funds are required to operate. ERISA:

- Establishes funding requirements for some plans which have not previously been funded and increases minimum funding requirements for others;
- Makes vesting mandatory for the first time;
- Requires payment of insurance premiums to the newly established Pension Benefit Guaranty Corporation, which guarantees vested benefits;

- Increases substantially the disclosures and reporting required of pension funds;
- Imposes substantial restrictions upon the manner in which pension fund assets may be invested;
- Requires pension funds for the first time to provide financial statements audited by qualified independent public accountants.

These are only a few of the many requirements that are imposed by ERISA.

HISTORICAL BACKGROUND

Payments have probably been made to retired employees ever since commerce and industry began. At first, payments were granted on an informal, almost casual, basis; their amounts and the persons to whom they were given depended entirely upon the will of the employer. Early pensions were probably granted in recognition of past employee loyalty. Undoubtedly, though, an important consideration was the removal of superannuated employees from the payroll.

This informal basis of dealing with pensions carried into the present century, in the early part of which formal pension plans were largely confined to government employees and employees of railroads and utilities. Even formal plans did not generally provide for advance funding, and pensions invariably were accounted for on a pay-as-you-go basis. The prevailing opinion was that the granting of a pension to a particular employee was a specific decision related to the circumstances of that employee at the time of the grant, rather than to an established general policy.

As time went on, however, the granting of pensions gradually became a permanent part of employment policy. A pension grant came to imply that payments would continue to the employee throughout his retirement, and that similar consideration would be given to other employees. Managements began to recognize the desirability of making some advance provisions, during the active service lives of employees, for pensions they expected to pay those employees upon retirement. Such provisions often took the form of contractual arrangements with insurance companies. Self-administered funding arrangements were also instituted. Enactment of Internal Revenue Code provisions under which contributions to a qualified pension plan fund were made immediately deductible by an employer (but with the resultant benefits not becoming taxable income to the employees until actual pension payments were made) gave considerable impetus to the formation of self-administered funded plans.

Institution of wage and price controls during World War II resulted in the establishment or improvement of many pension plans as a means of increasing total employee compensation while staying within the wage guidelines.

PENSION PLANS

A pension plan is an arrangement whereby an employer can provide retirement benefits for employees in recognition of their service to the company before their retirement. The arrangement may be informal, calling for voluntary payments to the retired employee in amounts and under conditions more or less at the discretion of the employer, or it may be a formal plan with the benefit payments and other features explicitly stated, susceptible to ready computation, or otherwise determined. A formal plan is usually set forth in a written document, but an established policy with regard to pension payments may be sufficiently definitive to constitute a formal plan.

One consequence of ERISA is that previously informal plans may, under certain circumstances, become subject to federal regulation. Plans subject to ERISA must now be established and maintained pursuant to a written instrument.

An employer may establish a pension plan unilaterally (referred to as a *conventional* or *voluntary* plan) or as a result of collective bargaining between employer(s) and employees (referred to as a *negotiated* plan). A plan established by bargaining between a labor union and one or more companies is sometimes referred to as a *pattern* plan, where terms of the plan are adopted, perhaps with variations, by companies in the same or allied industries.

All plans are either those of a single employer or a group of affiliated employers (*single-employer* plans) or of several employers in one or more industries (*multi-employer* plans). Some single-employer plans are unilaterally established, whereas others are collectively established; multi-employer plans are usually established pursuant to collective bargaining agreements and jointly managed by representatives of labor and management.

A *qualified* pension plan is a plan that conforms with Internal Revenue Service requirements. It provides certain tax advantages, including the deductibility of employer contributions to the plan as a business expense, deferment of taxes upon the employee for those contributions and the income therefrom until he actually receives retirement payments (or until such payments are made available to him), exemption of the pension fund's investment income from taxation, and taxation of certain lump-sum retirement payments at more favorable (capital gains, 10-year forward averaging) rates.

A *contributory* pension plan is one in which both the employer and the employees make contributions. Employee contributions in a contributory plan may be mandatory or voluntary. A *noncontributory* pension plan is one in which only the employer makes contributions.

Employer contributions are usually based either upon actuarial calculations (*defined benefit* plan) or upon amounts or rates stipulated under the terms of the plan (*defined contribution* plan).* A defined benefit plan is one in which benefits are defined, and actuarial calculations are used to establish the amount of contributions required to meet those benefits. In a defined contribution plan, contributions are defined and the benefits which can be paid must be calculated. (For certain types of plans such calculations must be made by an actuary.)

It should be noted, however, that a plan that is called a defined contribution plan may be, in fact, a defined benefit plan. A common characteristic of the defined contribution plan is the requirement that the employer contribute to the plan pursuant to a stated formula (for example, a fixed amount for each ton produced, so many cents per hour worked, or a fixed percentage of compensation). In most such cases the benefits for each employee are the amount which can be provided by the sums contributed for him, and it is clear that such a plan is a defined contribution plan. Where a contribution formula also provides for a contemplated scale of benefits, however, careful analysis is required to ascertain whether the plan should be considered to be substantively a defined benefit

---

* A common example of a defined contribution plan is the money-purchase plan (see "Normal Retirement Benefits," later in this chapter). Under ERISA, profit-sharing and similar plans, which were heretofore not normally considered to be pension plans, would fall into the defined contribution category.

plan rather than a defined contribution plan. This determination may be important for accounting and auditing purposes.

PENSION FUNDS

A pension fund is the entity which receives contributions, accumulates assets, makes benefit payments, and performs other functions in accordance with the provisions of a pension plan. ERISA generally requires that assets of a pension fund be held in trust by one or more trustees or held in the form of insurance policies or contracts.

PLAN VERSUS FUND

The above descriptions of the terms pension "plan" and pension "fund" are, in the authors' view, both realistic and convenient. ERISA does not distinguish between the two terms; it defines a pension plan as "any plan, fund, or program. . . ." This lack of distinction has created uncertainty with respect to important accounting and auditing matters, particularly with respect to whether financial statements of a "plan" required by ERISA should relate to a plan or to a fund. Some observers believe that this distinction is significant. In their view, financial statements of a plan should contain data regarding future pension benefit payments and related data and these data should be audited, while financial statements of a fund should not include such data but rather should be restricted primarily to accountability for the assets managed by the fund trustees.

We believe that the matter of semantics is not as important as the question of which data should be contained in the financial statements and which data must be audited. In our view the financial statements, in order to be meaningful, should contain appropriate data regarding future benefit payments and related data, and such data should be audited (as discussed in Chapters 8–10). Thus, while the entity for which financial statements are to be prepared and audited is referred to herein as the *fund*, it must be understood that those statements should be prepared, and the audit procedures performed, in light of the provisions of the *plan*.

PROVISIONS OF PENSION PLANS

Eligibility Requirements

The earliest date or age when an employee can become a participant in a plan and begin to accumulate pension credits is determined by the plan's eligibility provisions. Some plans provide that employees may become eligible immediately upon being hired, regardless of age or lack of prior service. Most plans, however, have required a period of service or a combination of age and period of service (e.g., 30 years of age with at least two years of service). ERISA has generally shortened the waiting period which a plan may require before employees can become eligible to participate. (See "Participation" in Chapter 4.)

Retirement Dates

A designated retirement age at which an employee may receive the normal pension is termed the *normal retirement date* or *age* (for example, age 65, or age 58 with 30 years of service). *Mandatory retirement date,* also referred to as *compulsory* retirement date or *automatic* retirement date, is the date at which an employee must retire. The mandatory date may be the same as, or later than, the normal retirement age.

Most plans provide for an *early retirement date* prior to the normal retirement age, at the election of either the employee or the employer. Benefits paid upon early retirement are usually less than normal retirement benefits (see Figure 2–1 for discussion).

A plan may permit an employee to postpone his retirement from the normal retirement date to a *deferred retirement date*, also referred to as a *delayed* retirement date or *late* retirement date. Such late retirement may be at the employer's or the employee's election, and may or may not involve higher than normal benefits.

Some plans also contain disability provisions which allow early retirement (at full or reduced rate) when a qualifying plan participant must terminate employment because of disability.

Vesting

When an employee's entitlement to benefits arising from employer contributions is not contingent on his continuing in the service of the employer until he is eligible to retire, he is said to have a *vested interest*. The applicable provision in the plan is described as a *vesting provision*. The vested benefits to which the employee would be entitled upon termination of employment are usually in the form of a deferred annuity income, with payments commencing at the normal (or early) retirement date. If the vested benefits are in an amount equal to the accrued pension rights determined up to the date his employment ends, the plan is said to provide for *full vesting*. If a portion of the accrued benefits is forfeitable, the term *partial vesting* is used.

Under ERISA, plans are required for the first time* to vest accrued benefits of employees with specified years of service and/or age, even if those employees do not remain until retirement (or qualifying early retirement) age. (See "Vesting" in Chapter 4.)

In addition to any vested interest in employer contributions, employees generally have the option, at termination of employment, to receive a refund of their own contributions under contributory plans, usually with accrued interest. If the employee chooses such a refund of his own contributions, however, he usually forfeits any vested interest that he would otherwise have. This kind of vesting is called *conditional vesting*. (The use of conditional vesting will be restricted as ERISA becomes effective, as discussed in Chapter 4.)

Normal Retirement Benefits

A variety of methods is used for determining the amount of retirement benefits. Benefits may be the same for all participants with a specified period of service, e.g., $300 per month for participants with 20 or more years of service; this is known as a *flat benefit*. A variation of a flat benefit is a benefit based on years of service, e.g., $10 per month for each year of service. In many instances, however, benefits are specified in terms of percentages of each year's compensation, sometimes with fixed minimum and maximum amounts. The total benefit so accumulated is said to be on a *career average* compensation basis. Alternatively, the compensation base may be determined by average earnings during a certain specified period such as the final three or five years of service (*final average pay* or *final pay* plan).

---

* Qualified profit-sharing plans have historically been required by the IRS to provide vesting comparable to or more favorable than requirements of ERISA.

Many plans correlate or integrate retirement payments with federal social security retirement benefits. This may be provided for in the benefit formula by the application of a lower percentage to the part of earnings covered by social security or by reducing the benefit amount by a portion of the social security benefit.

In some cases, pension payments are determined as the amount of a retirement annuity purchasable by the contributions specified in the plan. This type of plan is referred to as a *money-purchase* plan. This method usually produces decreasing benefit units with advancing years of service because the period of investment of contributions diminishes and the probability of the employee's living to retirement age becomes greater.

Death Benefits

Some pension plans provide a *death benefit*, which is any benefit payable upon the death of an employee. In a contributory plan, the minimum death benefit would necessarily be the total contributions made by the employee, together with accumulated interest. In some plans, however, death benefits are related to the employee's anticipated pension benefits or the value of his accumulated pension credits, and hence may be substantial.

Duration of Retirement Benefits

A pension plan's retirement benefits may be either for the annuitant's remaining lifetime or for a longer period if the plan so provides. The annuity provided for the employee's lifetime is called a *life* (or *straight life*) *annuity*.

Annuities which may extend beyond the annuitant's lifetime are, generally, either:

- Period certain and life or
- Joint and survivorship.*

The former provide that if the annuitant dies before the end of a stipulated guaranteed period, payments (reduced from the straight life amount) will continue to the end of the guaranteed period to a named beneficiary (usually the annuitant's spouse). For example, if the annuity is a five-year certain and life annuity, the named beneficiary would receive benefits for two years if the annuitant dies

---

* ERISA modifies the use of joint and survivorship option provisions somewhat, as discussed in Chapter 4.

three years after retirement and would receive nothing if the annuitant lived beyond five years.

Under joint and survivorship options, the employee may elect to receive reduced retirement benefits with provision for a continuation of all or a portion of benefits to a named beneficiary (usually a spouse), whereby the named beneficiary receives benefits for the rest of his or her life.

With respect to both period certain and life and joint and survivorship options, the option is elected prior to retirement, and the benefit amount is usually (but not always) the actuarial equivalent of the normal benefit, based generally, in the case of joint and survivorship options, upon the ages of the annuitants and the percentage reduction to the named beneficiary (*joint annuitant* or *contingent annuitant.*)

In contributory plans, the annuitant is usually entitled to receive the full amount of his own accumulated contributions and interest thereon. Therefore, contributory plans commonly contain a *modified cash refund* annuity provision under which a deceased annuitant's named beneficiary receives any difference between the cash amount that would have been payable at retirement date and pension benefits paid between retirement date and death.

FEDERAL INCOME TAX CONSIDERATIONS

Although ERISA made various changes to the Internal Revenue Code (generally to conform it with certain other ERISA provisions, such as those related to participation, vesting, funding, etc.), the Code's requirements for qualifying plans for tax deductibility are otherwise generally unchanged. These requirements include the following:

- A plan must not discriminate in favor of employees who are officers or shareholders or are highly compensated;
- Benefits under the plan must be reasonable in amount when considered with other forms of compensation;
- The plan must be permanent;
- Contributions to the fund must be exclusively for the benefit of participants.

If a plan qualifies, contributions by the employer are currently deductible, income on accumulated funds held for a qualified plan is not subject to tax, and the employees will be subject to income tax on the resulting benefits only as payments are received or made available. In addition, certain distributions receive favorable tax treatment, e.g., capital gains and forward averaging.

It is customary to obtain a determination from the Internal Revenue Service that a plan is qualified, to avoid later difficulties in interpreting the technical qualification requirements.

PENSION FUND ADMINISTRATION

A pension fund is generally administered under a declaration of trust that sets forth the duties and responsibilities of the trustee(s), or in accordance with a contract between an employer and an insurance company.

ERISA requires that the pension plan ". . . instrument shall provide for one or more named fiduciaries who jointly or severally shall have authority to control and manage the operations of the plan." It further specifies that one or more administrators shall have full responsibility for the operation of the plan, and defines the term "administrator" to mean:

1. the person specifically designated by the terms of the instrument under which the plan is operated;
2. the plan sponsor, if the plan instrument does not designate an administrator; or
3. such other person as the Secretary of Labor may by regulation prescribe (where the plan does not designate an administrator and a plan sponsor cannot be identified).

The term "plan sponsor" is defined to mean:

1. the employer in the case of a pension plan established or maintained by a single employer;
2. the employee organization in the case of a plan established or maintained by an employee organization; or
3. the association, committee, joint board of trustees, or other similar group of representatives of the parties who establish or maintain the plan, where the plan is established or maintained either by two or more employers or jointly by one or more employers and one or more employee organizations.

Fund Policy and Operation

Responsibility for operation of a pension fund in accordance with the plan, trust instrument, insurance contract, policies (e.g., as set forth in minutes of board or administrative committee meetings), and all applicable laws is normally held in a single-employer plan by an administrative committee and in a multi-employer plan by a joint board of trustees. The administrative committee usually consists of three or more officers or other responsible employees of the employer company acting for—and reporting to—the company's board of directors in matters pertaining to the plan. The joint board of trustees is generally comprised of an equal number of employer and employee representatives.

The day-to-day administration of a single-employer pension plan, e.g., determination of eligibility, payment of benefits, employee record maintenance, and so forth, is usually undertaken by the employer company. The benefits to be received, the conditions of eligibility for benefits, and other participants' rights are set forth in the plan documents. Broad policy decisions concerning the operation and interpretation of the plan are generally made by the administrative committee.

The joint board of trustees in a multi-employer plan generally has broad responsibility for determining benefits and other participant rights under the plan, and such trustees are responsible for: (1) collection of contributions, (2) payment of benefits, (3) management of the fund's assets, (4) maintenance of the fund's records, and (5) preparation of reports.

While retaining responsibility for the overall supervision of the fund's activities, the administrative committee or the board of trustees usually delegates the fund's day-to-day administration to one or more of the following:

- The employer company;
- A bank trust department;
- An insurance company;
- An independent contractual administrator;
- An employed administrator.

Administrative Expenses and Fees

Administrative expenses of a single-employer plan are generally borne by the employer company. This may vary from year to year under some plans that call for expenses to be paid by the fund unless the employer elects to pay them. Administrative fees of a multi-employer fund may be based on a percentage of contributions received, on a specified amount per participant per month, or on

some other basis. Such fees and/or expenses are usually approved
by the board of trustees. Where an administrative office manages
several multi-employer trust funds for a single industry, appropriate
provision must be made for an equitable allocation of administrative
expenses among the several funds, since such funds are independent
entities having their own assets, records, and reporting requirements.

Accounting Records

The basic accounting records for a pension fund should produce
information necessary for effective management of the fund and
provide the detailed information needed for financial reporting. In
the case of single-employer funds, pertinent information is obtained
from records similar to those used by other organizations; in the
case of multi-employer funds, the following additional records are
generally required:

- *Employers' Contribution Reports.* Under collective bargaining
  agreements, employers must submit periodic contributions with
  an accompanying report listing the participants for whom contributions are submitted.
- *Contribution Records.* The funds must maintain contribution records for each employer, showing all payments and accumulating
  the total annual contributions to be reported to the Department of Labor under ERISA [see Figure 5–2, item (b)]. The
  contribution record is also used for determining delinquencies in
  employer contributions, and records are maintained to follow up
  on delinquent contributions or reports.
- *Participants' Eligibility Records.* To ensure that each plan participant is properly credited with benefits earned (whether based
  upon hours worked, dollars earned or contributed, etc.), the fund
  must maintain separate records for each participant, to record and
  accumulate all pension credits earned. It is important that proper
  record retrieval and retention systems are in effect, since the ac-
  cumulation of pension credits usually covers a long period of time.
  (In the case of a single-employer plan, the eligibility records are
  generally part of the employer's payroll and personnel records.)

ERISA provides for specific information on vesting to be included in participants' eligibility records. (See "Vesting" in
Chapter 4.)

ACTUARIAL CONCEPTS, ASSUMPTIONS, AND METHODS

In defined benefit pension plans, pension costs must be ascertained by an actuary using various statistical, financial, and other techniques for computing the value of plan benefits, assigning costs to particular periods, evaluating and projecting actuarial experience under a plan, and periodically determining unfunded amounts.

In defined contribution plans, actuarial computations are usually needed for determining the amount of benefits the specified contributions will provide.

This chapter discusses the general nature of pension costs, actuarial cost methods, actuarial assumptions, and actuarial gains and losses.

THE GENERAL NATURE OF PENSION COSTS

The ultimate cost of any pension plan is determined primarily by the total pension benefits that will actually be paid to retired employees over their lives. This cost cannot be exactly determined so long as the plan continues to operate, since benefits for active employees are unknown and, once retired, the duration of benefit payments is also unknown. Therefore, pension cost determinations are based upon *actuarial assumptions* and *actuarial cost methods,* which are used to establish total cost and assign that cost to periods of time. The portion of cost assigned to employee service in each year after the inception of the plan is called *normal cost.* The portion of cost assigned to years of service prior to the inception of the plan is called *past service cost.* At any later valuation date, the portion of cost assigned to prior years is called *prior service cost,* which includes as of the particular valuation date, past service cost, normal cost to date, and increases or decreases in plan cost arising as a result of any amendments to the plan (e.g., to increase benefit levels.)* Although most cost methods identify past service cost for separate amortization, some cost methods do not differentiate past service cost and instead assign all costs to years subsequent to the inception of the plan.

Basic to actuarial determinations of pension cost is the concept of *present value.* Actuarial applications of the present value concept are described in Figure 2–1. Actuarial assumptions and actuarial gains or losses are discussed in the section following actuarial cost methods.

ACTUARIAL COST METHODS

Actuarial cost methods fall into two general categories:

- The accrued benefit cost method, sometimes called "unit credit," "unit purchase," "step-rate," or "single premium" method, and
- Projected benefit cost methods, sometimes called "level cost" or "level premium" cost methods.

---

* Since amounts of increases or decreases in prior service cost arising from plan amendments are normally treated like past service cost, the term "past service cost" is sometimes used in this discussion to refer to both past service cost (arising on adoption of a plan) and the amounts of any increases or decreases in prior service cost arising on plan amendments.

FIGURE 2-1

Present Value Applications to Actuarial Determinations

The present value (PV) principle permits the value at any future point in time to be expressed as the equivalent value at the present time under a given set of conditions. It also permits the computation of a series of financial transactions over a period of time to be expressed as a single value at any point of time. The principle is particularly useful in dealing with financial transactions involving a time series, such as periodic contributions and retirement annuities.

The present value concept is frequently used for business purposes. For example, the present value of a debt of Y dollars payable X years hence is the amount that, with accumulated compound interest thereon for X years, would accrue to Y dollars. This illustration has a single assumption and is quite precise.

In contrast, actuarial use of the present value concept normally involves several factors, and little of the certainty entailed in present value determinations in the preceding example. Actuarial determinations are based upon the interaction of various assumptions, such as mortality and severance of employment.

A general statement of a company's prospective pension obli-gation at any given time with respect to then covered employees, i.e., the present value of future contributions required to meet retirement payments, may be expressed by the following formula:

$$\frac{PV}{\text{contributions}} = \frac{PV}{\text{benefits}} + \frac{PV}{\text{expenses}} - \frac{\text{Funds}}{\text{on hand}}$$

While many assumptions are normally involved when determining the present value of contributions as set forth in the preceding equation, actuaries' use of the present value concept may in other instances require the use of relatively few assumptions. For example, where a plan provides that the benefit at early retirement is to be the actuarial equivalent of the amount otherwise payable at normal retirement age, only the assumptions concerning income yield and mortality usually need be considered. The actuarial equivalent concept is used in any situation in which the value of a retirement benefit under one set of conditions is equated to one under a different set of conditions, e.g., the conversion from a normal benefit to a joint and survivorship optional benefit.

The accrued benefit cost method considers as cost for a period (which may be a definite time interval such as a fiscal year) the present value of an annuity for each employee that would provide for retirement payments applicable to pension credits related to that period. Other things being equal, costs so calculated will increase with the advancing age of an employee because of the shorter time remaining for income accretions before retirement age and the greater likelihood of survival to retirement. Because of this ascending characteristic, this method is often referred to as *step-rate*.

Under the projected benefit cost methods of calculating periodic pension costs, the effect of the ascending characteristics of the accrued benefit cost method is counteracted. Actuarial costs are based on providing for the present value of total projected benefits by level amounts or level percentages of compensation. Costs so calculated will, under normal circumstances, remain at a uniform rate unless pension benefits are revised.

The actuarial cost methods are used both for determining costs and as a basis for the advance funding of benefits, as discussed in Figure 2–2.* The following descriptions of actuarial cost methods include information on funding and funding agencies where deemed useful.

Accrued Benefit Cost Method

The accrued benefit cost method operates on the principle that the retirement pension is or may be divided into units of benefits, each unit being related to a year of employment service. The normal cost for each year of service is the amount needed to provide in full for the benefit unit or units assigned to that year.

The benefit units related to the various years of an employee's credited service are usually equal in amount or equal as a percentage of earnings. The normal cost applicable to an individual employee, however, increases with each advancing year, since it is increasingly probable that he will live, and will work for the employer, until retirement age, and there is less time to earn interest on the amount funded. The total annual cost for the group as a whole usually

---

* The terminal funding method and the pay-as-you-go method (described in Figure 2–2) have been used in certain instances as actuarial cost methods for funding and even accounting purposes. The pay-as-you-go method is not an actuarial cost method, and neither of these methods is acceptable under ERISA (for funding) or under APB Opinion No. 8 (for accounting).

FIGURE 2–2

Funding

Where there is a separate determination of past service cost, a plan's funding rate is commonly based upon normal cost plus some portion of past service cost; and plans commonly set the funding rate at a level which will amortize past service cost over a specified period of years ranging from as few as 10 * to as many as 40. Where there is no separate determination of past service cost, as is normally the case when the individual level cost method or aggregate method is used, there is a built-in funding of past service cost over employees' remaining service lives. Many plans differentiating between past service cost and normal cost previously delayed the funding of past service cost indefinitely by setting the funding rate at normal cost plus the equivalent of interest on past ser-

vice cost—the minimum previously required by the Internal Revenue Service for qualified plans. Not funding past service cost is generally no longer allowed under ERISA, which provides specific periods for amortizing past service cost.

Some plans in the past did not pre-fund benefits; in such cases, plan sponsors either used *terminal funding* or followed a pay-as-you-go policy. Under terminal funding, pensions are not funded until the date of an employee's retirement. At that time, a fund is established that is actuarially equivalent to all payments expected to be made to the retiree under the pension plan. Under a pay-as-you-go policy, benefits are paid to retired employees as due, with no advance funding. Under a variation of terminal funding, contributions are made in installments, giving such terminal funding some aspects of a pay-as-you-go method. Under ERISA, most pension plans must use some form of advance funding.

* ERISA has increased the deduction limitation from 10% of past service cost (12- to 14-year funding) to 10-year funding (12% to 14% of past service cost).

does not reflect the same pronounced step-up effect because of the effect of replacement, generally, of older employees upon their death or retirement by younger employees. For a mature population, therefore, the normal cost may be relatively uniform, while for an initially immature group, the normal cost will rise before ultimately leveling off.

The past service cost under the accrued benefit cost method is the single sum necessary at the inception of a plan to provide for retirement benefit units for credited service for the years before inception. Stated in present value terms, past service cost is the amount determined at the plan's inception date to be the present value of the units of benefit credited to employees for all years of service prior to the inception of the plan.

Past service cost may be funded in a variety of ways. A common method is to fund it on the basis of a series of uniform payments (which recognize interest) over a specified term. (Some insured plans using the unit credit funding method provide that the initial past service cost for any individual must be fully funded by his normal retirement date.) The group annuity type of insured plan frequently makes use of the accrued benefit cost method for funding, but the method is also used in self-administered (trusteed) or deposit administration plans.

Projected Benefit Cost Methods

The step-rate increases in normal costs which would occur under the accrued benefit cost method as an employee gets older can be avoided by using one of the projected benefit cost methods which assign costs in level amounts to each year of service, resulting in higher cost in the earlier plan years than under the accrued benefit cost method, and thus lower cost in later years. A level-cost method may use rates that are level in dollar amounts or a level percentage of earnings. If level cost is determined as of an employee's current age to cover the benefits for all subsequent years, it is known as the *attained-age normal method.* If level cost is determined as of the age the employee could have entered the plan had it been in existence, it is known as the *entry-age normal cost method.*

Entry-Age Normal Cost Method. Normal cost under this method is the annual amount which would have been needed to fund pension benefits over the entire service life or lives of an employee or group of employees had the current pension plan always been in effect.* Past service cost is separately determined.

Past service cost under this method is sometimes defined as the "fund" that would have been accumulated at the inception of a

---

* The term "entry-age" derives from the fact that cost is determined on the assumption that the plan had always been in effect, and contributions commenced when the employee entered the plan.

plan if annual contributions had, in fact, been made over the entire credited service lives of employees up to that time. This is known as a retrospective method.

Past service cost is usually determined, however, by a prospective method in which the present value of the future normal cost is subtracted from the present value of all expected benefit payments, with the difference being the past service cost. If all elements were in accordance with the actuarial assumptions, this would equal the amount that would have been on hand if the plan had always been in effect. For any subsequent valuation, the value of all expected benefits is determined by the same procedure. The amount so determined, less the value of future normal cost and less the funds accumulated under the plan, would represent the then unfunded past service cost.

A modification of this method is often used, referred to as an "entry-age normal method with frozen initial liability." The first-year costs are determined in the same way as under the entry-age normal method. Past service cost is not adjusted at any future time to recognize actual experience, and it is thus termed "frozen initial liability." As a result, actuarial gains and losses are recognized in determinations of future normal cost amounts. In each year after the first, normal cost is computed as under the aggregate method (see below), except that the portion of the total liability represented by the unfunded part of the frozen initial liability is amortized by separate amounts.

The entry-age normal cost method is used in self-administered trusteed plans and for insured plans such as the deposit administration group annuity.

Individual Level Cost Method. This method uses the level cost approach, but fixes the level cost or level rate of compensation for each employee at an amount that would spread future pension costs over the remaining future service of each employee, thus including past service cost in normal cost, rather than treating it separately. This method is also termed the *individual level premium method* or the *individual funding to normal retirement age method.*

Under this method, past service cost (not separately identified) is in effect amortized over the remaining service lives of employees. This usually results in very high costs in the early years because the

past service cost associated with participants retiring in those years
is amortized over a very short period. In later years, however, this
method gives costs similar to those determined under the entry-age
normal cost method.

The individual level cost method is used in insured individual
policy or group permanent plans and can be adopted for self-administered trusteed or insured plans.

Aggregate Method. This method is similar to the individual
level cost method, except that calculations are made on a collective
basis. The total cost of future pension benefits for all employees
covered at the inception of the plan is spread over their average
future service lives. Costs are normally computed as a percentage
of payroll.

Because cost is determined on a collective rather than an individual basis, past service cost, though not separately determined, is
amortized over the average future service lives of all employees,
thus avoiding the particularly heavy early-year costs involved under
the individual level cost method.

The aggregate method is used in self-administered trusteed plans
and may also be used in an insured deposit administration plan.

Attained-Age Normal Method. This method's name derives
from the view of normal cost as the annual amount necessary to
fund future service benefits over the period beginning with the age
the employee has attained at the date of the plan's inception (or
at the date of initial coverage if he is employed thereafter). The
attained-age normal method combines some features of the accrued
benefit cost method and others of the aggregate method. As under
the accrued benefit cost method, benefits are divided into units
applicable to past and future service, and all units applicable to
years prior to the inception of the plan are treated as past service
cost. The cost of service in years after the inception of the plan,
however, is spread over employees' future service lives in a manner
similar to that of the aggregate method. Normal cost is usually
determined as a percentage of payroll.

Although normal costs tend to decline over a period of time, costs
in the early plan years are generally not as high as under the aggregate method or individual level cost method.

The attained-age normal method is used both in trusteed plans
and in deposit administration contracts.

ACTUARIAL ASSUMPTIONS

Actual pension costs depend upon future occurrences, such as total years of employee service, mortality, compensation, and earnings on funds set aside for the future payment of benefits; therefore, pension cost estimates are predicated on assumptions concerning those future occurrences.

Actuaries make these assumptions when evaluating the financial impact of pension plan benefits, suggesting appropriate funding arrangements, and determining pension costs. Some significant factors for which actuarial assumptions must be made are described in the following sections.

Mortality

Since pension benefits are not paid unless the employee lives to retirement, and may cease with the death of a retired employee, an actuarial assumption about expected mortality rates of covered employees (and of their co-annuitants in the case of joint and survivorship options) is a major consideration in the determination of pension costs. Making allowances for future mortality is sometimes referred to as *discounting for mortality.* The value of any included death benefits also depends on the mortality assumptions.

Employee Turnover

An assumption is also made about the rates of future employee turnover, since termination of employment before retirement age generally reduces or eliminates benefits that would otherwise accrue, thereby reducing pension costs. Studies made of turnover rates usually involve recognition of the effects of age, sex, length of employment, and type of work. Making allowance for future employment severance is called *discounting for turnover.*

Retirement Age

When plans permit retirement at a date other than the normal retirement age, i.e., at either an early retirement date or a deferred retirement date, assumptions about the number of employees who will retire at various ages may be needed. However, in many plans the benefits for early retirement are adjusted to amounts that are equivalent, actuarially, to those at normal age. It is then frequently assumed that all employees will retire at normal retirement age.

Salary Scales

When benefits are keyed to future salary rates, as in a percentage-of-compensation formula, assumptions may be made about future salary levels. This is essential in the case of a final-pay plan, where all benefits are related to earnings for a limited period of years immediately before retirement.

Interest Rate

Monies available to provide benefits result not only from contributions but from the income earned on investments in, and net gains or losses of, fund assets. The term *income yield* is sometimes used to describe all types of income. Recognition of future fund income is called *discounting for interest*.

Other Assumptions

Additional actuarial assumptions may have to be made, depending on the provisions of the plan. Thus, where plans provide for disability retirement or death benefits, or contain features dependent on marital status or changes in a cost-of-living index or social security benefits, appropriate assumptions are needed as to future events or status changes with respect to these conditions.

ACTUARIAL GAINS AND LOSSES

To the extent that actual experience after an actuarial valuation differs from the actuarial assumptions used in the valuation, actuarial gains or losses will arise. For example, if the actual experience is such that the contributions to the plan, as previously determined on the basis of assumptions at a particular valuation date, turn out to be larger than necessary, an actuarial gain would have occurred. If the contributions turn out to be smaller than necessary, an actuarial loss would have occurred. For example, if more employees die prior to retirement or soon after retiring than had been anticipated, total benefits payable will be smaller than anticipated, creating an actuarial gain and reducing the otherwise required contributions. The opposite situation would involve an actuarial loss.

When a plan's costs are computed, the effect of the difference between actual experience to date and the actuarial assumptions is automatically reflected in the new cost computation. From the valuation date on, however, the present value of projected benefits and other elements in the valuation may again be based on the same actuarial assumptions. It is thus necessary to determine when experience indicates that the actuarial assumptions themselves should be changed.

Actual experience may differ from the actuarial assumptions merely because of fluctuations occurring when the group is not extensive enough for averages to work out. On the other hand, the differences may arise because the assumptions used are no longer applicable to the group. For example, many plans that were started in the 1950's used an interest assumption of $2\frac{1}{2}$ per cent, which at that time seemed as high as could be reasonably expected on a conservative basis. The investment returns have been above this for many years, and this rate is usually no longer applicable.

As indicated in Figure 2–1, the following formula is used in connection with determining the present value (PV) of future contributions required to meet retirement benefits:

$$\begin{array}{c} \text{PV} \\ \text{contributions} \end{array} = \begin{array}{c} \text{PV} \\ \text{benefits} \end{array} + \begin{array}{c} \text{PV} \\ \text{expenses} \end{array} - \begin{array}{c} \text{Funds} \\ \text{on hand} \end{array}$$

This formula can also be used to illustrate the nature of actuarial gains and losses. Anything that reduces the present value of contributions more than anticipated by the assumptions can be considered a gain. Thus, such a gain would result if the following were greater than expected: (1) reduction in the present value of benefits, (2) reduction in the present value of expenses, or (3) increase in the funds on hand. A gain would arise as a result of experience more favorable than the underlying actuarial assumptions would produce; e.g., if investment income to date has been greater than assumed, the funds on hand will be larger than assumed, and the present value of contributions will be smaller. Similarly, if mortality to date has been greater than expected, fewer employees will survive to retirement, and the present value of benefits will be reduced. And, if employee turnover is higher than expected, the number of employees included in the present value of benefits will be lower, creating an actuarial gain. Conversely, differences between actual experience and assumptions that increase the present value of contributions would be termed actuarial losses.

Changes that occur from causes outside the experience under the plan, however, would not be considered gains or losses. An example would be a change in the present value of benefits arising from a change in the benefit formula.

When a change is made in the actuarial assumptions, it affects the present value of benefits and therefore the present value of contributions.

Computing Actuarial Gain or Loss

Analyzing and computing the amount of gain or loss attributable to each actuarial assumption is more difficult than calculating aggregate net gain or loss on an overall basis. As part of the annual actuarial valuation of a plan, however, the actuary will frequently make the technical computations necessary to determine the sources of gains or losses, to compare actual experience with assumed experience. It is necessary to make these analyses from time to time in order to decide when adjustments should be made in the assumptions to be used in the future.

In the case of actuarial cost methods that reflect gains and losses as adjustments to past service cost, the aggregate gain or loss can be determined by comparing the actual unfunded past service cost at the valuation date with the unfunded past service cost that would have existed if experience had followed the actuarial assumptions used, taking into account the actual contributions made to the fund. In the case of actuarial cost methods that reflect gains and losses in future normal costs, the aggregate gain or loss can be determined by comparing the actual unfunded future normal costs with the unfunded future normal costs that would have existed if experience had followed the actuarial assumptions, again taking into account the actual contributions made. If the expected unfunded amount exceeds the actual unfunded amount, the difference is an actuarial gain; the opposite is an actuarial loss. See Figure 2–3 for an example of such a computation.

Actuarial Gain or Loss Adjustment

Actuarial gains or losses may be used as adjustments to costs immediately, or averaged or spread over a period of years. The

FIGURE 2–3

Illustrative Computation of Actuarial Gains and Losses

1. Expected Unfunded Past Service Cost

Unfunded past service cost at beginning of period	$100,000
Plus interest on above to end of period (at the assumed interest rate)	5,000
Total	105,000
Less contributions during period toward past service cost, and	10,000
Less interest on above from contribution dates to end of period at assumed rate	250
Expected unfunded past service cost at end of period	$ 94,750

2. Gain or Loss Determination

Present value of future benefit payments to employees for credited service to end of period	$300,000
Less actual fund at end of period	206,000
Actual unfunded past service cost at end of period	94,000
Less expected unfunded past service cost at end of period	94,750
Actuarial loss (gain)	($ 750)

methods by which pension costs are adjusted for actuarial gains or losses are discussed below.

Immediate Method. The first method, called the *immediate* method,* entails the immediate addition of an amount equal to the loss to (or subtraction of an amount equal to the gain from) the current or following year's normal cost. Where there is a significant loss, however, it can be added to the unfunded past service cost, which is almost always done when the accrued benefit (step-rate) cost method is used.

Averaging Method. The second method, called the *averaging* method, involves averaging gains or losses over future periods. Under this method, an average of net gains and losses developed

---

* See "Funding" in Chapter 4 regarding recognition of actuarial gains and losses for funding purposes, and see "Actuarial Gains and Losses" in Chapter 6 regarding restrictions on use of the immediate method for accounting purposes.

from those that have occurred in the past, with consideration of those expected to occur in the future, is applied to normal cost.

Spread Method. The third adjustment method, called the *spread* method, spreads the adjustment over future periods and is almost always used with the projected benefit cost methods (level funding). The gain or loss is spread by the basic actuarial cost method over the same future period over which other remaining unfunded costs are spread. If the actuarial assumptions are being modified, the adjustment for prior actuarial gains and losses may be added to the effects of the new actuarial assumptions in order to arrive at a modified cost rate for future periods. Although the adjustment usually affects only future normal costs, in some situations it may be apportioned to the unfunded past service cost.

In either the individual level cost method or the aggregate cost method, the spread technique is automatically used because costs are based on the present value of all unfunded future benefits. Thus, a revised cost rate at any valuation date automatically spreads the adjustment over future periods. Since the past service cost is not separately determined in the computation of the cost rate, either of these two methods, in effect, applies the actuarial gain or loss to all future costs.

VALUATION OF FUND ASSETS

The valuation of fund assets is a principal factor in the calculation of a plan's costs and actuarial gains and losses, and in the determination of any underfunding or overfunding. Thus, it is important to use an acceptable method of valuing the fund's assets.

In performing actuarial valuations, pension fund investment portfolios had traditionally been valued at cost, thus excluding unrealized gains or losses from the calculation until realized through sales.

Since APB Opinion No. 8 specified that unrealized appreciation and depreciation should be recognized in the determination of pension cost for accounting purposes, employers have departed from the use of the cost basis for such purposes where the effect would be material. As a result, several techniques are in use for the gradual recognition of unrealized appreciation (depreciation).

The most direct method would be to use market value in valuing fund assets, but the effects of short-term fluctuations often make this undesirable. The various techniques now used seek to smooth out these short-term effects. Such techniques include recognition of a portion of unrealized appreciation (depreciation) each period, and recognition of an average of unrealized appreciation (depreciation) over a number of years.

3

AGENCIES FOR FUNDING PENSION PLANS

Pension plans may be funded either on a trusteed basis or an insured basis. This chapter describes the principles of trusteed plans and the various categories of insured plans commonly used.

Although the funding agencies discussed in this chapter are referred to as "plans," in conformity with terminology commonly used by insurance specialists, actuaries, and others, such funding arrangements should not be confused with types of plans discussed in Chapter 1.

TRUSTEED PLANS

A pension plan that uses a trust as its funding agency is called a *trusteed* pension plan. Other terms used for such a plan are *self-administered* pension plan, *self-insured* pension plan, and *uninsured* (or *noninsured*) pension plan. Trusteed plans are generally set up under an agreement between an employer and a bank or one or more individual trustees; the agreement prescribes the terms under which the trust is to be created and administered. Subject to the provisions of the trust agreement, investment decisions may be made by the bank, by the employer company, or by others designated by the administrative committee or joint board of trustees. Cash and securities, the collection of income, and disbursements are frequently handled by the bank.

Under a trusteed plan, contributions are made to the pension trust, and the fund so established is invested according to the terms of the trust agreement. Earnings serve to increase the fund, and the fund's assets are used to provide pensions or other benefits for employees. Retirement benefits may be paid out by the trust during the period of retirement, or an annuity may be purchased for the employee upon his retirement, thus transferring the obligation at that date to an insurance company (see "Split Funding" at the end of this chapter).

Retirement benefits to be paid are based upon the stipulations in the plan. Trustees assume responsibility for the proper administration of the trust, but do not guarantee actuarial adequacy, rate of income, or sufficiency of assets to pay benefits.

The majority of large and medium-sized funded pension plans currently in effect are of the self-administered trusteed type.

INSURED PLANS

An arrangement with an insurance company may be used as a medium for the receipt of pension contributions, administration of a pension fund, and payment of benefits. A plan that uses only an insurance company as a funding agency is called an *insured* plan. Under some insured plans, insurance companies contract to pay specific retirement benefits in return for certain set premium payments. Under others, the insurance companies receive and accumulate funds for use at subsequent dates, either to pay specified retirement benefits in return for certain set premium payments taken from the accumulated funds, or to pay benefits directly from the accumulated funds. The retirement benefits and eligibility for such benefits are established on the basis of the provisions of the pension plan.

Insured plans may provide either for individual policy contracts or for master group contracts. Under some insured group plans, segregated accounts may be used which accumulate funds separately from the insurance company's general assets. This procedure differs little from funding through a trust fund. Some of the more common types of insured plans are described below.

Individual Policy Plan

As the name implies, this type of plan involves the purchase by the employer of a separate life insurance or annuity policy in the name of each covered employee. The premiums paid under such a policy are referred to as *level annual premiums* because they remain uniform for each employee through the period of coverage to retirement date. The premium is determined by reference to annuity benefits the employee will receive. When benefits are revised for any reason, such as changes in compensation, additional policies are issued and total premiums are changed accordingly. An annuity policy is sometimes referred to as a *level premium deferred annuity* or an *annual premium retirement annuity*.

Individual policy plans frequently use insurance policies that provide, for an additional premium, life insurance protection in addition to the annuity benefits. A policy that combines annuity and life insurance features is called, variously, a *retirement income policy*, an *insurance income policy*, or an *income endowment policy*. Such an individual policy provides for a death benefit before retirement equal to a specified sum related to monthly retirement income or to the cash value of the policy, whichever is greater. For an employee who is uninsurable, there is usually issued a policy with a death benefit limited to the gross premiums paid or, if greater, cash value of the policy. A slightly different arrangement utilizes an *ordinary life policy* which provides death benefits and only a part of the retirement income. The balance of the retirement income is provided by a separate fund normally referred to as a "side fund," which is maintained either by the insurance company or in a trust. Although death benefits after retirement vary depending on a particular plan's provisions, a common practice is to provide a period certain and life annuity, the period usually being 10 years.

Individual policy premiums do not involve discounting for either mortality or severance of employment before retirement age. In the event of severance, the employer is entitled to a refund, but this is considerably less than the amount credited for severance under a group annuity plan.

Because of the possible adverse tax consequences of direct owner-ship of the policies by either the employer or the employee, indi-vidual policy plans provide for a trust under which the trustee holds title to the individual policies and administers the plan in accord-ance with the formal plan document or a separate trust instrument.

Group Annuity Plan

Under this type of insured plan, the employer enters into a mas-ter contract with the insurance company which covers the entire group of eligible employees. The contract calls for the purchase each year of a fully paid-up deferred annuity in an amount equal to the benefit accrued in that year for each participating employee. (This method of funding is the conceptual basis of the accrued benefit cost method for computing contributions.) When an em-ployee retires, the total amount of his benefits will be equal to the sum of the separately purchased units of deferred annuity. This plan is also referred to as a *deferred annuity group annuity plan*. Because there is a direct correspondence between the premium and the amount of deferred annuity that is purchased by a given *single premium*, the group annuity plan is also said to employ the single premium method of funding.

The premium rates applicable to the various ages under a group annuity plan are guaranteed by the insurance company for a fixed period, usually five years, after which a new premium structure may be established and guaranteed for a future fixed period.

Since group annuity contracts usually do not provide a refund of employer contributions upon an employee's death, premium rates related to these contributions reflect a discount for mortality prior to retirement. The employee's contributions, usually with added interest, are paid as a death benefit if the employee dies before his retirement date. Therefore, the premium rates used to determine the annuity available from employee contributions are set at a higher level because they do not involve a discount for mortality prior to retirement. Group annuity plans do not discount for turnover; past employer's contributions which have been made for the account of those separated employees who do not receive vested benefits are credited against the employer's next premium payment, less a portion retained by the insurance company as a *surrender charge* to provide for applicable administrative expenses. Employees' contributions are returned, usually with interest.

The premium payment schedule for a given employee is usually of the step-rate type, i.e., premiums increase each year with advancing age. However, the stability of the overall average cost for all employees depends upon the current and future age distribution of the group or its degree of maturity.

Although not common, some group annuity plans may use a money purchase basis for computing benefits. In such instances, the annual contribution applicable to each employee is determined by the plan. The amount of the deferred annuity that can be purchased for an individual each year with a constant amount of annual contribution will become progressively smaller as his age increases.

The provisions of a group annuity plan are ordinarily set forth in a master contract and individual employees receive *certificates* as evidence of participation.

At one time most insured plans were of the group annuity plan type. This type is now used primarily for small groups or special situations.

Deposit Administration Group Annuity Plan

Under this plan, as in the case of a group annuity plan, a master contract is drawn between the employer and the insurance company. This contract may be referred to as a *deposit administration contract*, a *deposit administration group annuity contract*, or, in abbreviated form, a *DA contract*.

Contrary to what is done under a group annuity plan, under a DA contract no annuity units are purchased for the individual employee before the date he retires. Instead, the employer's periodic contributions are deposited with the insurance company in an unallocated fund, to which the insurance company adds interest at a rate usually guaranteed for five years but subject to change thereafter. The rate, when changed, applies to funds deposited from the date of change, but the initial rate often continues to apply to previously deposited funds. When an employee retires, the amount required to buy an *immediate* annuity to provide for his pension is applied by the insurance company as a single premium from the unallocated fund. The premium rates for such annuities to be purchased in the future are also guaranteed by the insurance company on a five-year basis. The insurance company guarantees the pension payments on purchased annuities, but does not guarantee that the unallocated fund will necessarily be adequate to meet the cost of annuities to be purchased. The contract provides for periodic dividends (rate credits, if the company is a stock company) determined by the insurance company, at its discretion, on the basis of its experience under the contract. In effect, these dividends represent an adjustment of past premiums. Contributions to the unallocated fund may be determined by the use of any one of several actuarial cost methods.

Immediate Participation Guarantee Contract

This contract is an outgrowth of the DA contract, and strongly resembles aspects of a trusteed plan. The master contract, if it is with a mutual insurance company, is called an *immediate participation guarantee contract* or, in abbreviated form, an *IPG contract*. If it is with a stock insurance company, it is called a *direct rerating contract*.

As in the case of a DA contract, the employer makes periodic payments into a fund maintained by the insurance company, and the insurance company credits interest to the fund and pays annuity benefits on employees' retirement. However, unlike the DA contract, which guarantees interest, the IPG contract calls for interest credits to be based essentially on the rate of the insurance company's earnings for the year on its investment portfolio after investment profits and losses are reflected. The insurance company charges expenses directly to the fund, whereas under DA contracts expenses are charged only in the determination of dividends or rate credits. Essentially, the IPG contract is intended to give the employer the immediate effect of experience under the contract, including the insurance company's investment results; at the same time the insurance company makes fewer guarantees under such a contract.

The IPG contract is written in two forms with the same ultimate result. One form, like the DA plan, may provide for the actual purchase of single-premium annuities as employees retire. There is an adjustment each year for actual experience under the annuities, based upon the insurance company's analysis of mortality, benefits

paid, and earnings. The annual adjustment for favorable or unfavorable experience is reflected by an addition to, or a deduction
from, the fund.

In the other form, the IPG contract may achieve the same result
through a different technique. When an employee retires, the retirement income payments to him are made directly out of the fund
without the purchase of an annuity. However, the fund on deposit
with the insurance company must be maintained at the amount
required, according to a premium schedule in the contract, to provide for the remaining retirement benefits for all those on retirement
at any time. Thus, if necessary, the fund could always be applied
to buy all annuities in force. Under either form of IPG contract,
the insurance company guarantees lifetime benefit payments to retired employees.

Separate Accounts

Legislation permitting an insurance company to offer separate
accounts as an adjunct to one of the other insured plan contracts is
now in effect in most states. The investments in these accounts
are not restricted by insurance laws; they are used primarily for
investing pension plan funds in equity securities. Such an account
may be established solely for use in conjunction with the contract
for one policyholder. Usually, however, the account is pooled with
funds of various policyholders. The availability of separate accounts with DA or IPG contracts has resulted in a considerable
increase in the number of plans using insurance company funding
facilities.

The separate account facility is sometimes used as a basis for
the insurance company to offer investment services only, without
necessarily being involved in the payment of plan benefits. This
is the same as the investment service of a bank under a trusteed plan.

Split Funding

Many employers use both a trust fund and an insurance contract
in an effort to get some of the expected advantages of each method.
If this is done, the annuities to retired employees would usually be
paid under the insurance contract, and all or part of the funds for
active employees would be accumulated in the trust fund. The DA

or IPG insurance contract is usually used for this purpose. If the contract calls for only the purchase of immediate annuities as employees retire, with all funds for active employees being accumulated in a trust fund, it is similar to the portion of the DA contract used to purchase annuities as employees retire.

4

PRINCIPAL ERISA PROVISIONS

In changing the requirements for private pension plans, ERISA affects both employer company financial statements and financial statements of pension funds.

This chapter summarizes * principal provisions of ERISA rele-

---

* As a summary, this material cannot serve as a substitute for full reading of the Act itself and pertinent regulations, and advice of legal counsel.

vant to accounting and auditing (see Table 4–1 for a comparison of ERISA requirements with prior requirements). Reporting and disclosure requirements are held for separate discussion in Chapter 5. Certain other matters which might be material for plan design, tax planning, and other purposes are omitted here; significant questions outside the scope of this and the following chapter should be considered in light of the law itself and whatever rules and regulations may pertain.

GENERAL COVERAGE OF ERISA

ERISA repeals provisions of the Welfare and Pension Plans Disclosure Act of 1958 (as amended), which previously governed private pension plans; it will ultimately replace all provisions of the 1958 Act, as of the various dates on which ERISA provisions become effective. With respect to the ERISA provisions discussed herein, the effective dates range from as early as July 1, 1974 to as late as June 30, 1984 (see Table 4–2 for a summary of such effective dates). Title II of ERISA amends pertinent sections of the Internal Revenue Code. And, inasmuch as ERISA supersedes all state laws insofar as they relate to plans covered by ERISA as of January 1, 1975, pension funds are now generally exempt from state requirements.

PLANS COVERED AND EXCLUDED

Generally, the law applies to all plans established by sponsors engaged in interstate commerce except:

- Government plans, including state and local governments.
- Church plans, unless they elect to be covered by ERISA.
- Plans established and maintained solely for the purpose of complying with applicable workmen's compensation, disability insurance, or unemployment compensation laws.
- Plans maintained outside the United States for persons substantially all of whom are non-resident aliens.
- Unfunded excess benefit plans, i.e., plans that are unfunded *and* are maintained solely for the purpose of providing benefits for certain employees in excess of the maximum benefit limitations imposed by the Internal Revenue Code.

TABLE 4–1. Comparison of Prior Requirements for Select Plan Provisions with Requirements of ERISA

	Prior Requirements	ERISA
Eligibility	No specific requirements	(a) One year of service or age 25, whichever is later; or (b) After three years of service and attainment of age 25 if after that time the employee is 100% vested in his accrued benefits Defined benefit and target benefit plans may exclude new employees hired within five years of normal retirement age
Coverage (for purposes of discrimination tests)	(a) 70% or more of all the employees, or 80% or more of all the employees who are eligible to benefit under a plan if 70% or more of all the employees are eligible to benefit under the plan (b) A classification or group of employees acceptable to the IRS	Same as prior law with two significant differences: (a) Union employees who have collectively bargained *not* to be covered under plan may be excluded in applying the coverage test, and (b) All employees of all corporations that are members of a controlled group of corporations shall be treated as employed by a single employer
Vesting (accrued benefits derived from employer contributions upon termination of employment other than for death or attainment of retirement age)	At normal retirement age, or upon termination of plan	Same as prior law, plus: (a) 25% after five years of service, 5% additional for each of next five years, 10% additional for each of the next five years (100% after 15 years), or (b) 100% vesting after 10 years of service (no vesting required before 10 years), or

(c) "Rule of 45"—50% vesting when, after five years of service, age plus service equals 45. 10% additional for each of the following five years of service. An employee with 10 years of service must be 50% vested, with 10% additional for each of the following five years

Note: "Class year" plans—special five-year rule

Minimum Funding Standards (for defined benefit plans)

An accumulative test of meeting normal cost plus interest on initial unfunded past service cost

Normal cost plus amortization of unfunded past service cost over no more than 30 years for new plans and no more than 40 years for existing plans

Amounts from plan amendments that increase or decrease unfunded past service cost must be separately amortized over no more than 30 years

Experience losses or gains amortized over no more than 15 years

Longer periods would apply under multiemployer plans; variances permitted for substantial hardship situations

Maximum Deductible Contributions (for defined benefit plans)

Normal cost plus 10% of initial past service cost

Normal cost plus an amount sufficient to amortize initial past service cost over 10 years

TABLE 4–2. Effective Dates of Various Requirements of ERISA

Requirement	Effective Date		Defined Benefit Plans	Defined Contribution Plans [2]
	Existing Plans	New Plans [1]		
Minimum participation and vesting standard	1–1–76	9–3–74	X	X
Limitations on benefits and/ or contributions	1–1–76	1–1–76	X	X
Back-loaded benefits prohibition	1–1–76 [3]	9–3–74	X	
Minimum funding requirement	1–1–76 [3]	9–3–74	X [4]	[4]
Termination insurance Single-employer	7–1–74	7–1–74	X	
Multi-employer	1–1–78	1–1–78	X	
Annual report	1–1–75 [5]	1–1–75 [5]	X [6]	X [6]
Actuarial statement	1–1–75 [5]	1–1–75 [5]	X [4]	[4]
Fiduciary standards	1–1–75 [7]	1–1–75 [7]	X	X
Limitation on investment in employer securities and real property	1–1–75	1–1–75	X	X [8]
	+ 10-yr. transition			

Notes on Effective Dates: Underscored dates are actual, others are plan years beginning on or after indicated dates.

1. Generally, plans established after January 1, 1974.
2. Includes money-purchase pension plans, profit-sharing plans, and other individual account plans such as individual annuity contracts, thrift and savings plans, etc.
3. For certain collective bargaining plans, at expiration of contract but no later than a plan year beginning on or after January 1, 1981.
4. Does not apply to certain tax-qualified or insured defined benefit plans, but does apply to money-purchase plans and target benefit plans.
5. Secretary of Labor has, by regulations, postponed to the first plan year beginning after January 1, 1975 (for other than calendar year plans).
6. Reporting requirement is the only Act requirement that is applicable to unfunded deferred compensation plans for key executives.
7. Certain transactions are exempted from prohibited transaction rules until as late as June 30, 1984.
8. Except for plans which meet specified requirements for exemption from limitation.

PARTICIPATION

Under ERISA, a plan may not require stricter age and service standards for participation than one year of service and the attainment of age 25. Alternatively, the plan may provide the age 25 requirement and a three-year waiting period provided that a participant's accrued benefits vest 100% thereafter. Defined benefit plans and target benefit plans may exclude employees who are employed for the first time within five years of the normal retirement age under the plan (usually 65).

Penalties

Failure to conform to ERISA's participation requirements (as well as to vesting, funding, limits on benefits, and certain other requirements described in this chapter) may cause the imposition of various penalties. These include possible civil actions by plan participants or beneficiaries to recover lost benefits and to clarify rights as to future benefits, and disqualification of the plan with concomitant loss of tax benefits. For a discussion of how these penalties may affect the plan administrator, employer company, and fund, see the section "How Penalties Apply," later in this chapter.

Effective Dates

For plans established after January 1, 1974, these requirements are generally effective for plan years beginning after September 2, 1974. For plans in existence on January 1, 1974, these requirements generally apply for plan years beginning after December 31, 1975.

VESTING

ERISA allows three alternatives for vesting benefits derived from employer contributions. (Under prior law, generally, and in all cases under the new law, an employee's right to receive benefits derived from his own contributions is nonforfeitable.) The three alternatives are:

1. Graded vesting of accrued benefits, with at least 25% after five years of service, at least 5% each year thereafter for five years, and 10% each year thereafter, so that the employee's accrued benefits would be 100% vested after 15 years.
2. One hundred per cent of accrued benefits after 10 years of service, with no vesting required before the end of the 10-year period.
3. A "rule of 45," under which accrued benefits of an employee with five or more years of service must be at least 50% vested when

the sum of his age and service equals 45, with 10% additional vesting for each year of service thereafter, provided that a participant with 10 years of service must be at least 50% vested and vest thereafter at a rate of not less than 10% per year of service.

A special minimum vesting schedule applies to class–year plans (i.e., profit-sharing, stock bonus, or money-purchase plans providing separate vesting of contributions made in each plan year, or of the rights derived from them, and the withdrawal of these amounts on a class-by-class basis as they mature). Such plans must provide 100% vesting of benefits derived from employer contributions within five years after the end of the plan year for which the contribution was made.

Employee service before age 22 may generally be ignored unless the plan uses the "rule of 45," in which case such service may be ignored only if the employee was not a participant in the plan during the years before age 22.

While the prescribed vesting requirements will prevail in a substantial majority of cases, it should be noted that more stringent vesting could be required administratively in some cases. For example, the Internal Revenue Service, particularly with small companies, usually requires 100% vesting in profit-sharing plans three to five years after participation. Similarly, where discrimination in favor of "highly paid" employees would occur under ERISA's vesting schedules, the IRS could require the use of stricter vesting standards to the extent needed to eliminate discrimination. As a general rule, however, unless (1) there has been a pattern of abuse under the plan (e.g., dismissal of employees before their accrued benefits become vested) tending to discriminate in favor of employees who are officers, shareholders, or highly compensated or (2) there have been, "or there is reason to believe there will be," an accrual of benefits or forfeitures tending to discriminate in favor of such employees, adherence to one of the prescribed minimum vesting schedules should suffice.

The rules for computing years of service are complex. Generally, an employee is considered to have a year of service if he has worked 1,000 hours in a 12-month period, subject to special provisions for breaks in service, covering when, and under what circumstances, service before and after a break must be included.

If at least 50% of a participant's accrued benefits derived from employer contribution is vested, the withdrawal of his own required contributions will not cause him to forfeit his employer-financed benefits.

Record-Keeping Requirements

The employer is required to maintain records of each employee's years of service (including breaks in service) and vesting percentage. In the case of a multi-employer plan, the data are to be submitted to the plan administrator, to the extent practicable. Multi-employer plans are expected to meet the same requirements as single-employer plans. ERISA provides that the employer (or plan administrator) maintain such further records as may be needed to determine each employee's benefits. In most cases, data such as age, hours worked, salary, and employee contributions will be needed.

The Department of Labor has indicated that it is aware that many employers, especially those with high turnover rates, lack adequate records of employee service before passage of ERISA, which are necessary to enable them to comply with the record-keeping requirements. Arrangements are being made for a study of this problem, with priority to be given to records of participants retiring in the next three to five years.

Penalties

Failure to comply with the record-keeping requirements can result in penalties imposed upon the plan administrator and/or employer of $10 for *each* employee with respect to whom such failure occurs.

Some of the other penalties which may be imposed for failure to conform to the vesting requirements summarized herein are described under "Participation."

Effective Dates

The vesting requirements become effective as described under "Participation."

FUNDING

For most defined benefit plans, employers' contributions must include (1) normal cost, (2) interest on unfunded amounts, and (3) a portion of unfunded original past service liability (and of unfunded additional past service liability arising from plan amendments).

In determining the funding requirements, ERISA contains certain specifications, including the following:

- The value of the plan's assets shall be determined on the basis of any reasonable actuarial method of valuation which takes into account fair market value and which is permitted under regulations to be prescribed by the Secretary of the Treasury (except that, at the election of the plan administrator, bonds or other evidence of indebtedness not in default may be valued at amortized cost);
- Normal costs, accrued liability, past service liability, and experience gains or losses shall be determined under the method used to determine costs under the plan;
- All costs, liabilities, rates of interest, and other factors under the plan shall be determined on the basis of actuarial assumptions and methods which, in the aggregate, are reasonable (taking into account the experience of the plan and reasonable expectations) and which, in combination, offer the actuary's best estimate of anticipated experience under the plan; and
- If the funding method (or the plan year) for a plan is changed, the new method (or plan year) can be used only if the change is approved by the Secretary of the Treasury.

It should be noted that the Conference Committee Joint Explanation states: ". . . a single set of actuarial assumptions will be required for all purposes (e.g., for the minimum funding standard, reporting to the Department of Labor and to participants and beneficiaries, financial reporting to stockholders, etc.)." If such a requirement is included in forthcoming regulations, it is apparent that the same set of assumptions will have to be used with respect to funding requirements and financial statements of both the fund and the employer company. Also, it would not be considered unlikely, if such regulations are issued, for them to require that the same actuarial cost method and possibly asset valuation method be used for all purposes.

Amortization Periods

Unfunded past service liability on the first day of the first plan year to which the minimum funding rules apply must be funded in equal annual installments as follows:

- For plans in existence on January 1, 1974, over a period of no more than 40 years,
- For single-employer plans established after January 1, 1974, over a period of no more than 30 years, and
- For multi-employer plans established after January 1, 1974, over a period of no more than 40 years.

Where unfunded past service liability increases as a result of plan amendments adopted in a plan year, single-employer plans must fund the increases over a period of no more than 30 years, and multi-employer plans must fund the increases over a period of no more than 40 years. Where unfunded past service liability decreases as a result of plan amendments adopted in a plan year, the amount of the decrease is amortized over the same number of years to reduce the amount otherwise required to be funded.

In addition, experience losses must be funded over a period of no more than 15 years by single-employer plans and 20 years by multi-employer plans, with gains amortized to reduce the amount otherwise required to be funded.

Funding must also reflect losses resulting from changes in actuarial assumptions. Such losses must be funded over a period of no more than 30 years, with gains amortized to reduce the amount otherwise required to be funded.

Funding Standard Account(s)

For the purpose of determining whether a defined benefit plan is meeting the minimum funding requirements, ERISA requires the plan to maintain a (memorandum) funding standard account and allows the use of an alternative account under specified circumstances. Requirements for maintenance of such accounts and examples of their operation are summarized in Tables 4–3, 4–4, and 4–5. (The difference in the two illustrations in Table 4–4 is in the total value of plan assets, based on the plan's normal valuation method: in the illustration in column A the value is $28,500,000;

TABLE 4–3. ERISA Requirements for

	Amortization Period (in Years)	
Annual Charges	**Single-Employer Plans**	**Multi-Employer Plans**
Normal cost of the plan for the plan year	—	—
Amortization of (see Note 1):		
Unfunded past service liability under plan on first day of first plan year subject to ERISA:		
In existence on 1/1/74	40	40
Comes into existence after 1/1/74	30	40
Separately, with respect to each plan year:		
Net increase (if any) in unfunded past service liability under the plan arising from plan amendments adopted in such year	30	40
Net experience loss (if any) under the plan	15	20
Net loss (if any) resulting from changes in actuarial assumptions used under the plan	30	30
Waived funding deficiency for each prior plan year	15	15
Any amount credited to this account as an excess of any debit balance in this account over any debit balance in the alternative minimum funding standard account (as described contra)	5	5
Total for year	—	—
Debit balance (if any) from prior year	—	—
Adjusted total	—	—

Notes:
1. Amounts required to be amortized may be combined or offset against each other, with the resulting amount amortized over a period determined on the basis of the remaining amortization periods for the appropriate items entering into such combined or offset amounts, pursuant to regulations to be issued by the Secretary of the Treasury.

Maintenance of Funding Standard Account

Annual Credits	Amortization Period (in Years)	
	Single-Employer Plans	Multi-Employer Plans
Employer contribution considered made for the plan year	—	—
Amortization of (see Note 1):		
Separately, with respect to each plan year:		
Net decrease (if any) in unfunded past service liability under the plan arising from plan amendments adopted in such year	30	40
Net experience gain (if any) under the plan	15	20
Net gain (if any) resulting from changes in actuarial assumptions used under the plan	30	30
Waived funding deficiency for the plan year	—	—
Excess (if any) of any debit balance in this account (prior to this credit) over any debit balance in the alternative minimum funding standard account (applies only where the accumulated funding deficiency was determined under the alternative minimum funding standard in the preceding plan year)	—	—
Amount of accumulated funding deficiency (prior to this credit) in excess of full funding limitation (see page 53)	—	—
Total for year	—	—
Credit balance (if any) from prior year	—	—
Adjusted total	—	—

2. ERISA requires that the account (and items therein) be charged or credited, as determined under regulations to be prescribed by the Secretary of the Treasury, with interest at the appropriate rate consistent with the rate or rates of interest used under the plan to determine costs.

TABLE 4–4. Examples of Funding Standard Account Operation

Description	A Full Funding Limitation Inapplicable		B Full Funding Limitation Applies	
	Charges	Credits	Charges	Credits
Normal cost of the plan for the plan year	$1,000,000	NA	$1,000,000	NA
Amortization of:				
Unfunded past service liability	100,000	NA	100,000	NA
Net increase or decrease in unfunded past service liability arising from plan amendments	25,000	$ 30,000	25,000	$ 30,000
Net experience loss or gain	15,000	25,000	15,000	25,000
Net loss or gain resulting from changes in actuarial assumptions	10,000	45,000	10,000	45,000
Waived funding deficiency for each prior plan year	50,000	NA	50,000	NA
Any amount credited to this account as an excess of any debit balance in this account over any debit balance in the alternative minimum funding standard account	20,000	NA	20,000	NA
Waived funding deficiency for the plan year	NA	—	NA	—
Excess of debit balance in this account over any debit balance in the alternative minimum funding standard account	NA	—	NA	—
Employer contribution *	NA	1,120,000	NA	200,000
Amount of accumulated funding deficiency in excess of full funding limitation **	NA	—	NA	920,000
Debit or credit balance from prior year	—	—	—	—
Totals (nets to zero balance)	$1,220,000	$1,220,000	$1,220,000	$1,220,000

* Difference between total charges and total credits (before this amount).

** Accumulated funding deficiency (before contribution and full funding limitation credit)		$1,120,000		$1,120,000
Plan's accrued liability, etc.	$30,000,000		$30,000,000	
Total value of plan assets	28,500,000	(1,500,000)	29,800,000	(200,000)
Amount of accumulated funding deficiency in excess of full funding limitation		NA		$ 920,000

NA = Not applicable.

TABLE 4–5.   ERISA Requirements for Maintenance of Alternative Minimum Funding Standard Account and Example of Its Operation

Annual Charges:

Lesser of the following:

Normal cost under the funding method used under the plan ($1,000,000; see Table 4–4)	
Normal cost determined under the unit credit method ($900,000)	$ 900,000

Excess, if any, of the present value of accrued benefits under the plan ($28,900,000) over the fair market value of the assets ($28,600,000)   300,000

An amount equal to the excess, if any, of credits to this account for all prior plan years over charges to this account for all such years (applies only where this account was used in determining the accumulated funding deficiency)   —

Total	1,200,000

Annual Credits:

Employer contribution considered made for the plan year (see Table 4–4, Column A)	1,120,000
Net balance—debit (credit)	80,000
Debit or credit balance from prior year	—
Adjusted net balance	$ 80,000

Notes:

1. It can be seen that the contribution required to avoid an accumulated funding deficiency (before the contribution) under the funding standard account ($1,120,000) is less than the amount that would have been required under the alternative minimum funding standard account ($1,200,000).
2. ERISA requires that the account (and items therein) be charged or credited, as determined under regulations (to be) prescribed by the Secretary of the Treasury, with interest at the appropriate rate consistent with the rate or rates of interest used under the plan to determine costs.

in the illustration in column B the value is $29,800,000. Table 4–5 is based on the illustration in column A of Table 4–4.)

Such accounts are not required to be maintained by profit-sharing and stock bonus plans, certain other tax-qualified plans, and insured plans funded exclusively by individual insurance contracts or group insurance contracts having the characteristics of individual insurance contracts.

For money-purchase plans and target benefit plans, a funding standard account is generally required only to the extent that the employer is charged each year for the amount that must be contributed under the plan formula and credited with the amount actually paid.

Annual charges to the funding standard account are generally the following:

- The normal cost for that year, and
- Amounts necessary to amortize:
    Initial unfunded past service liability;
    Increases in plan liabilities;
    Experience losses; and
    Waived funding deficiencies for prior plan years, if any.

Annual credits to the funding standard account are generally the following:

- Employer contributions made for that year;
- Amounts necessary to amortize portions of plan cost decreases resulting from plan amendments, experience gains, and gains resulting from changes in actuarial assumptions; and
- The amount of any waived funding deficiency for the plan year.

If the funding standard account has an accumulated funding deficiency in a plan year following a year for which such deficiency was determined under the alternative minimum funding standard (see discussion below), any excess of the debit balance in the funding standard account over any debit balance in the alternative minimum funding standard account must be amortized as charges in the funding standard account over a five-year period.

In addition, the funding standard account (and items therein) shall be charged or credited (as determined under regulations prescribed by the Secretary of the Treasury) with interest at the appropriate rate consistent with the rate or rates of interest used under the plan to determine costs.

Waivers. The waiver item referred to in the credits to the funding standard account is based upon ERISA's provision that the Secretary of the Treasury may waive all or part of the minimum funding requirements for a plan year in which the minimum funding standard cannot be met without imposing substantial business hardship upon the employer(s), but only if failure to give the waiver would be adverse to participants' interests. The Secretary of the Treasury determines whether such hardship would occur, based upon various factors including certain factors stated in ERISA. ERISA limits waivers on all or part of the funding requirements to not more than five years out of any consecutive 15 years.

The amount of any waived funding deficiency is to be amortized as a charge over 15 years, beginning in the following year; such amounts being amortized may not themselves be waived.

Full Funding Limitation. To prevent contributions in excess of full funding (i.e., which would result in total plan asset values in excess of the plan's total accrued liability), ERISA provides that the funding standard account be credited with the excess of:

1. The accumulated funding deficiency (determined without regard to the alternative minimum funding standard account)

    over

2. The excess of the plan's accrued liability (including normal cost) over the total value of plan assets.

This effectively limits the year's contribution to the amount that would fund 100% of the plan's accrued liability. The plan's accrued liability referred to herein is determined either by the plan's funding method or, if the liability cannot be directly calculated thereunder, by the entry-age normal funding method. Asset values are to be based upon the lesser of fair market value or the valuation method normally used by the plan.

In a plan year to which the full funding limitation credit applies, all "amortization period" items described in this section shall be considered fully amortized for purposes of all future years' calculations. If the plan is amended in later years to increase plan liabilities, however, a new amortization schedule would be established with respect to that increase in liabilities.

Alternative Minimum Funding Standard Account. Plans using a funding method which requires contributions in all years not less than those required under the entry-age normal funding method are permitted to use an alternative minimum funding standard account.

This alternative account is to be charged each year with the sum of the following:

- The lesser of normal cost under the plan's funding method or under the unit credit method,
- Any excess of the present value of the plan's accrued benefits over the fair market value of plan assets, and
- Any excess of credits over charges to the alternative minimum funding standard account for all prior years.

The annual credit to the account is the amount the employer has contributed for the plan year.

A plan that elects to use the alternative minimum funding standard account must also maintain the funding standard account. The basis for electing its use is that the year's minimum contribution may be lower than when the funding standard account is used alone.

If both accounts have debit balances at the end of a plan year, a funding deficiency exists in the amount of either the debit balance in the funding standard account or the debit balance in the alternative minimum funding standard account if less. No deficiency exists where either the funding standard account or the alternative minimum funding standard account contains a zero or a credit balance.

Penalties

Unless a contribution is made within two and one half months after the plan year end (or by the filing date of the federal income tax return with extensions, but in no event later than eight and one half months after the plan year end) in at least the amount of the accumulated funding deficiency, an excise tax of 5% of the accumulated funding deficiency is levied upon the company. An additional tax of 100% of the accumulated funding deficiency is similarly levied where the initial 5% tax is imposed and the accumulated funding deficiency is not corrected within 90 days from mailing of a deficiency notice (or such other period allowed by the Internal

Revenue Service). Payment of the tax alone does *not* correct an accumulated funding deficiency.

Some of the other penalties which may be imposed for failure to conform to the funding requirements summarized herein are described under "Participation."

Effective Dates

The minimum funding standards are generally effective for plan years beginning after September 2, 1974, except as follows: For plans in existence on January 1, 1974, funding standards apply to plan years beginning after December 31, 1975; for certain plans in existence on January 1, 1974 and maintained under a collective bargaining agreement, funding standards apply to plan years beginning after December 31, 1980, unless the agreement terminates earlier, in which case standards apply to the first plan year beginning after the termination date (but not earlier than December 31, 1975).

MAXIMUM DEDUCTIBLE CONTRIBUTION

For qualified defined benefit plans, the maximum annual deduction, formerly based on normal cost plus 10% of past service cost, is now based on normal cost plus the amount necessary to amortize past service cost over 10 years (approximately 12% to 14% of past service cost, depending upon actuarial investment yield assumption). The maximum annual deduction based on 5% of covered compensation has been eliminated, but the deduction based on level funding is still available. If the minimum funding rules require a larger dollar amount than the above, the larger amount would be deductible. The 15% limitation on covered compensation with respect to profit-sharing and stock bonus plans remains unchanged, except that where a profit-sharing or stock bonus plan is maintained together with another type of defined contribution plan or with a defined benefit plan the maximum limitation is 25% of covered compensation.

Effective Dates

The effective dates for the maximum deduction limits generally are the same as those for the funding rules.

LIMITS ON BENEFITS AND CONTRIBUTIONS

For qualified defined benefit plans, ERISA provides that the maximum annual benefit derived from employer contributions may not exceed the lesser of (a) $75,000 or (b) 100% of the participant's average compensation during his highest three years. The $75,000 limit is adjusted upward for cost-of-living increases and is not reduced for early retirement unless the participant retires before age 55. Regardless of the foregoing, the limit is generally not less than $10,000 if the employee has never participated in a defined contribution plan of the employer.

For qualified defined contribution plans, ERISA provides that a participant may be credited with no more than the lesser of 25% of compensation or $25,000 per year. For purposes of calculating the limit, the individual's share of forfeitures (and in some cases a portion of employee contributions, if any) are to be included. Upward adjustments in the $25,000 limit for cost-of-living increases are allowed under ERISA.

If a participant is covered by both a defined benefit plan and a defined contribution plan of the same employer (multiple plans of the same type, e.g., two defined benefit plans of a single employer, are considered as a single plan), the total benefits permitted to accrue under the defined benefit plan and the contributions permitted to be made under the defined contribution plan with respect to a participant are limited as follows: The sum of (a) the accrued benefit (projected to normal retirement age) under the defined benefit plan as a percentage of the maximum amount permitted under ERISA plus (b) the amounts contributed to the defined contribution plan as a percentage of the maximum amounts permitted to be contributed under ERISA cannot exceed 140%. For example, if 60% of the maximum amount permitted to be contributed each year was contributed for a participant under the defined contribution plan, the maximum amount of benefit that could be accrued under the defined benefit plan would be limited to 80% of the maximum permitted under ERISA for defined benefit plans.

Penalties

Some of the penalties which may be imposed for failure to conform to the summarized requirements are described under "Participation."

Effective Dates

These limits are generally effective for contributions made and benefits accrued in years beginning after December 31, 1975.

BACK-LOADED BENEFITS

ERISA contains provisions applicable to defined benefit plans which restrict so-called "back-loaded" benefits, a term which denotes a higher rate of benefit accrued during an employee's later years of service than during his early years. An example of back-loading is a formula that provides for benefits to accrue at the rate of 1½% of compensation for each year of service until age 55 and 2½% thereafter. Other examples may include: (a) final-pay plans that provide for reductions for social security benefits where the offset is subject to a maximum amount and (b) plans that provide for a minimum benefit after a specified number of years of service.

ERISA limits back-loading by prescribing that benefits provided must accrue at a rate which meets any one of three specified back-loading rules. The first rule basically requires accrual in each year of at least 3% of the maximum normal retirement benefit. The second rule generally prohibits accruals in later years which exceed 133⅓% of the annual rate of accrual in any previous year. The third rule requires a service-based proration of the projected normal retirement benefit.

Penalties

Some of the penalties which may be imposed for failure to conform to these requirements are described under "Participation."

Effective Dates

The effective dates are the same as those described under "Funding."

JOINT AND SURVIVOR ANNUITIES

ERISA requires that when a plan provides for a retirement benefit in the form of an annuity, the plan must provide for a joint and survivor annuity for married participants. The survivor annuity must be not less than one half of the annuity payable to the participant during the joint lives of the participant and his spouse.

In the case of an employee who retires, or who attains the normal retirement age, the joint and survivor provision is to apply unless the employee has elected otherwise.

In the case of an employee who is eligible to retire prior to the normal retirement age under the plan but who continues in active employment, the plan must offer a survivor's annuity but may require an affirmative election by the employee. Moreover, the plan need not make this option available until the employee is within 10 years of normal retirement age. (Of course, a plan may provide that a joint and survivor annuity is to be the only form of benefit payable under the plan, and in this case, no election need be provided.)

The employee is to be afforded a reasonable opportunity to exercise his election *out of* (or, before normal retirement age, possibly *into*) the joint and survivor provision before the annuity starting date (or before he becomes eligible for early retirement). The employee is to be supplied with a written explanation of the joint and survivor provision, in layman's language, as well as the practical (dollars-and-cents) effect on him (and his or her spouse) of making an election either to take or not to take the provision.

The plan may provide that any election, or revocation of an election, is not to become effective if the participant dies within a certain period of time (not in excess of two years) of the election or revocation (except in the case of accidental death where the accident which causes death occurs after the election).

The plan may provide that the joint and survivor benefit is to be the actuarial equivalent of the participant's accrued benefit, in which case there would be no additional cost to the employer for the joint and survivor provisions.

Penalties

Some of the penalties which may be imposed for failure to conform to these requirements are described under "Participation."

Effective Dates

These requirements generally apply for plan years beginning after December 31, 1975.

PLAN TERMINATION INSURANCE

ERISA requires plan administrators to pay annual termination insurance premiums to a new Pension Benefit Guaranty Corporation (PBGC) within the Department of Labor. Premiums were initially set at $1 per participant for single-employer plans and 50 cents per participant for multi-employer plans, for the first plan year or fraction thereof after September 2, 1974.

Premium rates for later years will be such "as may be necessary" to provide the PBGC with sufficient revenue to carry out its functions. The PBGC, in turn, will insure the benefits vested according to the plan's terms at the time the plan is terminated (other than those benefits arising solely because the plan was terminated). The limit on the benefits to be guaranteed by the PBGC under ERISA is generally the lesser of (a) 100% of the average wages paid to a participant during his five highest years of participation, or (b) $750 per month (adjusted upward for cost-of-living increases). A phase-in rule provides that the amount actually paid to the employee will depend on the length of time the plan (or amendments thereto) was in effect. Benefit coverage is to be phased in at 20% per year until the plan or benefit is fully covered after it has been in effect for five years.

ERISA establishes an employer liability of up to 30% of its net worth for losses the PBGC sustains as a result of payments made due to a plan terminated by the sponsoring employer.

Net worth is to be determined as of a date (not more than 120 days prior to the date of termination) selected by the PBGC and on whatever basis the PBGC regards as best reflecting the current status of the employer's operations, and the resultant liability thus imposed may be enforced by a priority lien on the employer's assets. As written, it appears that the law provides that this liability applies for each plan terminated, even where an employer has multiple plans terminated at the same time. PBGC counsel has indicated, however, that it is likely that if more than one plan terminates on the same date, the 30% would apply only once, whereas if terminations are two or more years apart, the 30% would apply to each termination. The PBGC has not yet closely examined the question of how the 30% would apply where more than one plan is terminated within a two-year period but not on the same date. Forthcoming regulations should clarify this.

Employers are allowed to insure this "contingent liability," as ERISA calls it, either with the PBGC itself or through private insurance carriers.

ERISA requires that certain events related to a potential plan termination be reported to the PBGC by the plan administrator.

The plan termination insurance provisions generally pertain only to qualified plans, and generally do not apply to defined contribution plans.

Penalties

Failure to pay the termination insurance premiums when due can result in the imposition of a civil penalty of up to 100% of the premium which was not timely paid, plus interest. Nonpayment of such premiums does not result in loss of coverage.

Effective Dates

Generally, the plan termination insurance provisions became effective upon ERISA's passage (September 2, 1974) except that, for single-employer plans, the provisions relating to benefit payments are effective for plans terminated after June 30, 1974. For multi-employer plans, benefits generally are not payable for plans terminating before January 1, 1978. Premiums for both single- and multi-employer plans are payable for fractional years beginning with the date ERISA became law.

FIDUCIARY RESPONSIBILITIES

ERISA contains detailed provisions for the fiduciary's responsibilities and transactions prohibited to him in fulfilling his responsibilities, as summarized in Figures 4–1 and 4–2.

These provisions include prohibitions against a plan fiduciary's engaging the plan in certain transactions with a party in interest. The term "party in interest" is defined broadly in ERISA and includes employers of plan participants, persons rendering services to the plan, unions whose members are plan participants (and their officers and agents), officers, fiduciaries and employees of a plan, and relatives, agents, and joint venturers of any of the foregoing.

Definition

ERISA defines the term "fiduciary" as any person who:

FIGURE 4-1

Duties of, and Restrictions Upon, Pension Fund Fiduciaries Established by ERISA

(a)   Must manage assets solely in the interest of participants and beneficiaries;

(b)   Must act with the care that a prudent man in like circumstances would exercise;

(c)   Must diversify investments in order to minimize the risk of large losses (unless clearly not prudent to do so);

(d)   May invest no more than 10% (less than 10%, if required by the diversification and prudence rules) of the fair market value of plan assets (as defined) in a combination of qualifying employer securities (stock and marketable obligations, as defined) and qualifying employer real property (see Notes);

(e)   May not transfer assets outside the United States unless specifically permitted by the Secretary of Labor; and

(f)   Are liable for those acts or omissions of co-fiduciaries which constitute breaches of their fiduciary responsibilities in specified circumstances.

Notes:

1. Qualifying employer real property is defined as parcels of real property and related personal property which are leased to an employer or its affiliate and (a) a substantial number of the parcels are dispersed geographically and (b) each parcel of real property and the improvements thereon are suitable (or adaptable without excessive cost) for more than one use.

2. This provision is effective January 1, 1975, but the plan is allowed a 10-year transition period within which to comply with this requirement. Further, until June 30, 1984, under certain circumstances, this provision will be complied with even when employer securities or real property that is not considered "qualifying" employer securities or real property is held or acquired. Acquisition or holding by a plan of certain employer debt securities such as bonds, notes, etc., is limited to certain percentages.

3. An exception to this requirement exists for "individual account plans" that are, in general, (a) profit-sharing plans, (b) thrift and savings plans, (c) money-purchase pension plans in existence on September 2, 1974 which held investments primarily in qualifying employer securities as of that date, and (d) stock bonus plans (including employee stock ownership trusts, commonly known as "ESOTs"), where such individual account plans are designed primarily to make, and specifically provide for, investments in qualifying employer securities or real property.

FIGURE 4–2

Transactions Prohibited to Pension Fund Fiduciaries by ERISA

TRANSACTIONS PROHIBITED WHEN INVOLVING A PARTY IN INTEREST

(a) A sale, exchange, or lease of property, except as noted in Figure 4–1, item (d), to the extent allowed.

(b) A loan or other extension of credit.

(c) The furnishing of goods, services, or facilities.

(d) A transfer of plan assets to a party in interest for the use or benefit of a party in interest.

(e) An acquisition of employer securities or real property, except as noted in Figure 4–1, item (d), to the extent allowed.

OTHER PROHIBITED TRANSACTIONS

(a) Dealing with the plan assets in his own interest or for his own account.

(b) Acting in any transaction involving the plan on behalf of a party whose interests are adverse to the interests of the plan or its participants or beneficiaries.

(c) Receiving consideration for his own account from a party dealing with the plan in connection with a transaction involving the plan assets.

(d) With respect to fiduciaries who have authority or discretion to control or manage plan assets, permitting the plan to hold employer securities or real property, except as noted in Figure 4–1, item (d), to the extent allowed.

1. Exercises any discretionary authority or discretionary control over management of the plan or exercises any authority or control respecting management or disposition of plan assets;
2. Renders investment advice for a fee or other compensation, direct or indirect, with respect to any monies or other property of such plan, or has any authority or responsibility to do so; or
3. Has any discretionary authority or discretionary responsibility in the administration of such plan.

Additionally, ERISA provides that a pension plan must have a "named fiduciary" or provide a procedure for identifying the "named fiduciary," and it continues the requirements of prior law that fiduciaries be bonded. The fiduciary standards do not apply, generally, to unfunded plans for top executives, nor to an insurance company to the extent that the policy provides payments guaranteed by the insurer. Similarly, a mutual fund is not deemed a fiduciary merely because a pension fund holds shares in the mutual fund.

Exemptions

Despite the rules on prohibited transactions summarized in Figure 4–2, ERISA provides various exemptions to prevent undue restriction of the fiduciary's flexibility in managing fund assets.

Services. Banks and similar financial institutions are permitted to perform "ancillary services" for a plan, under specified circumstances. Payments to parties in interest for reasonable compensation for services necessary to operate the plan are also permitted.

Investments. ERISA permits investment of plan assets in interest-bearing deposits in a bank or similar financial institution, if such bank or other institution is a fiduciary of such plan and if (1) the plan covers only employees of the bank or institution and employees of affiliates of the bank or institution, or (2) such investment is expressly authorized by a provision of the plan or by a fiduciary (other than the bank or institution or affiliate thereof) who is expressly so empowered.

Loans. The plan may make loans to parties in interest who are plan participants or beneficiaries if the plan expressly allows such loans, if they are made on a nondiscriminatory basis at reasonable rates, and if they are adequately collateralized. Under certain circumstances, a party in interest may make a loan to an employee stock-ownership plan.

Pooled Funds. The prohibitions of party-in-interest transactions do not apply to pooled funds under certain circumstances.

Life Insurance Companies. A life insurance company can use its own contracts to fund a pension plan for its employees.

Other. The exercise of a privilege to convert securities is permitted, subject to regulations to be issued by the Secretary of Labor.

Furthermore, the rules on prohibited transactions do not prevent a plan fiduciary from:

1. Receiving reasonable compensation for services to the plan unless he receives full-time pay from the employer or employee organization;

2. Receiving benefits from the plan as a participant or beneficiary, as long as these are consistent with the terms of the plan as applied to other participants and beneficiaries;
3. Receiving reimbursement for expenses; or
4. Being an officer, employee, agent, or other representative of a party in interest.

Penalties

A plan fiduciary is liable to make good any losses to the plan resulting from a breach of fiduciary duties and to restore to the plan any profits which he made through the use of the plan's assets. In addition, parties in interest who participate in certain prohibited transactions are subject to an excise tax, for the year of the transaction *and* for each subsequent year for which it is not corrected, equal to 5% of the amount of the transaction, plus a tax of 100% of the amount of any such transaction if it is not corrected after notice from the Internal Revenue Service.

Some of the other penalties which may be imposed for failure to conform to the fiduciary requirements summarized herein are described under "Participation."

Effective Dates

The described fiduciary standards generally became effective January 1, 1975, with the exception of certain restrictions and limitations on holding or acquiring employer securities or employer real property, for which certain transitional rules apply.

ENFORCEMENT

The law gives both the Internal Revenue Service and the Labor Department many methods of enforcing ERISA's requirements, providing both criminal and civil penalties as well as direct remedies for plan participants. In general, the Labor Department is charged with the responsibility of looking after individuals' rights, while the IRS is responsible for overseeing whether funding, vesting, and other requirements are met by particular plans. ERISA provides many remedies and sanctions for its enforcement, including the opening of the federal court system to plan participants and the provision of assistance from the Labor Department in enforcing their rights.

How Penalties Apply

Some of the penalties which may be imposed for failure to conform to ERISA requirements (as cited in earlier sections of this chapter, and also in Chapter 5) include possible civil actions by plan participants or beneficiaries to recover lost benefits and to clarify rights as to future benefits, and disqualification of the plan with concomitant loss of tax benefits.*

Although ERISA specifies that certain penalties are levied against the plan (which could be interpreted to mean the fund) or against the plan administrator, the administrator is often the employer company and, even where that is not the case, it is likely that penalties would fall not upon the fund but rather upon the employer company. This evaluation is based upon the fact that Congress, in drafting the various provisions of ERISA, sought to protect fund assets for participants and beneficiaries, not to insulate the employer company from liability. In the case of a defined benefit plan, most penalties will in any event ultimately fall upon the employer company, if not directly, then indirectly via increased future contributions. The provisions of ERISA described in this chapter (and also in Chapter 5) are nevertheless important to the auditor of the fund (as well as to the auditor of the employer company).

ANNUAL REGISTRATION

ERISA requires that all plans subject to the vesting standards file an annual registration statement with the Secretary of the Treasury, effective with respect to plan years beginning after December 31, 1975. The statement must contain, among other things, the names and taxpayer identification numbers of the participants who separated from service and who are entitled to deferred vested benefits. This information is to be transmitted by the Treasury Department to the Department of Health, Education, and Welfare, which will notify claimants for social security benefits of their rights to benefits under the employer's pension plan.

---

* Past experience has shown that a company failing to comply with provisions of the Internal Revenue Code is normally allowed a period of time to take the necessary steps so as to be in compliance and thereby avoid disqualification of the plan.

5

ERISA PROVISIONS RELATING TO REPORTING AND DISCLOSURE

ERISA requires significantly more reports and disclosures than were required under the 1958 law. Reports are to be submitted to plan participants and/or beneficiaries and to various governmental agencies. A summary of reporting and disclosure requirements under ERISA is provided later in this chapter (Table 5–2, pages 76–79). Information to be reported to the Secretary of Labor and to participants and/or beneficiaries is summarized in greater detail in Figure 5–1.

FIGURE 5-1

Summary of Reports and Disclosures To Be Made to the Secretary of Labor and to Plan Participants and/or Beneficiaries Under ERISA

To the Secretary of Labor

1. Plan Information

(a) A plan description [by April 30, 1975 for most existing plans, or within 120 days from the establishment of a new plan (see Note 1)], and an updated plan description no more frequently than once every five years, as the Secretary of Labor may require.

(b) A copy of the summary plan description as described in (l) below [by April 30, 1975 for most existing plans or within 120 days from the establishment of a new plan (see Note 2)].

(c) Any material modification in the terms of the plan and any change in certain required information included in the plan description (within 60 days after such modification or change is adopted or occurs, as the case may be; see Note 3).

2. Annual Report—Financial and Other Information (Note 4)

(d) Financial statements and supporting schedules, examined by an independent qualified public accountant, including his opinion as to whether such financial statements and supporting schedules are presented fairly in conformity with generally accepted accounting principles applied on a basis consistent with that of the preceding year, and also his opinion as to whether the separate schedules and summary material required to be furnished to participants and/or beneficiaries [see (n) below] present fairly and in all material respects the information contained therein when considered in conjunction with the financial statements taken as a whole. (See Table 5-1.)

(e) An actuarial statement (with respect to most pension plans, but generally not profit-sharing, savings, and similar types of plans) prepared by an actuary, with his opinion as to whether the contents of the matters reported in the actuarial statement (see Figure 5-2) are in the aggregate reasonably related to the experience of the plan and to reasonable expectations, and represent his best estimate of anticipated experience under the plan.

(f) The number of employees covered by the plan.

(g) The name and address of each fiduciary.

(h) Detailed statement of salaries, fees, and commissions charged to the plan.

(i) An explanation of the reason for any change in appointment of trustee, accountant, insurance carrier, actuary, administrator, investment manager, or custodian.

(j) Such financial and actuarial information including but not

FIGURE 5–1

Continued

limited to material described in (d) and (e) above as the Secretary of Labor may find necessary or appropriate.

(k) Where some or all plan benefits are purchased from and guaranteed by an insurance company or similar organization, a statement from such organization enumerating (1) total premiums received, (2) total benefits paid, (3) administrative expenses charged, (4) commissions or other specific acquisition costs paid, (5) amounts held to pay future benefits, and (6) other specified information.

To Plan Participants and/or Beneficiaries

(l) A summary description of the plan (including any material modification in the terms of the plan and any change in certain required information included in the summary description of the plan), in layman's language, covering matters such as eligibility requirements, schedule of benefits, source of financing, and claims procedures [by April 30, 1975 for most existing plans or within 120 days from the establishment of a new plan (see Note 2), or, if later, within 90 days from employee's participation or beneficiary's first receipt of benefits—also see (p) below].

(m) When material plan modifications, or changes, have occurred, a summary thereof (within 210 days after the end of the plan year in which the change is adopted; see Note 3).

(n) A summary of the annual report [see (d) to (k) above], and the supplemental schedules of (1) assets and liabilities by categories, and (2) the year's receipts and disbursements aggregated by general sources and applications (within 210 days after the close of the plan's fiscal year).

(o) When requested in writing by participants or beneficiaries, or when a participant either terminates his service with the employer or has a one-year break in service (as defined in ERISA), a statement showing the individual's accrued and vested benefits (see Note 5).

(p) At least every five years (or ten years if there have been no plan amendments), an update of the summary description of the plan, reflecting all amendments prior to its publication.

Notes:

1. The form to be used in filing the plan description is Form EBS–1; the filing deadline date has been postponed by regulation to May 30, 1976, except that the first two pages of Form EBS–1 (but not the schedules referred to in those pages) and the signature page (item 38 only) must be filed by August 31, 1975.
2. The filing deadline date has been postponed by regulation to May 30, 1976.
3. Not required if information is included in the summary plan description filed on or before May 30, 1976.

FIGURE 5-1

Continued

4. While ERISA provides that the annual report is, generally, to be filed within 210 days after the close of the plan year, proposed Form 5500 provides that it is to be filed on or before (a) the 15th day of the 5th month following the close of the employer's taxable year, for a single-employer plan whose plan year ends either with the employer's taxable year or within 4 months before the end of such taxable year, or (b) 135 days following the close of the plan year, for all other plans;

effective with plan years beginning on or after January 1, 1975. Thus, the first due date is May 15, 1976 for a calendar-year plan of a calendar-year employer.

5. Where the anticipated or actual number of requests is large, the authors suggest that the plan administrator consider the desirability of providing this information annually to *all* employees so as to minimize the information retrieval and processing cost of complying with this requirement.

ACCOUNTANTS AND ACTUARIES

ERISA requires plan administrators to retain both "qualified public accountants" and "enrolled actuaries" on behalf of the plan's participants and beneficiaries. ERISA defines the term "qualified public accountant" as:

1. a person who is a certified public accountant, certified by a regulatory authority of a State;
2. a person who is a licensed public accountant, licensed by a regulatory authority of a State; or
3. a person certified by the Secretary of Labor as a qualified public accountant in accordance with regulations published by him for a person who practices in any State where there is no certification or licensing procedure for accountants.

The term "enrolled actuary" is defined in ERISA as an actuary enrolled by a Joint Board for the Enrollment of Actuaries (established jointly by the Secretary of Labor and the Secretary of the Treasury under ERISA's requirement for such establishment). ERISA further requires that the Joint Board shall, by regulations, establish reasonable standards and qualifications for persons performing actuarial services with respect to plans to which ERISA applies and, upon application by an individual, shall enroll such individual if the Joint Board finds that such individual satisfies such standards and qualifications. Different standards are specified for persons applying for enrollment (1) before January 1, 1976 and (2) on or after January 1, 1976. Proposed regulations for individuals applying before January 1, 1976 require the applicant to have (1) qualifying experience within the prior 15 years of (a) at least 36 months of "responsible pension actuarial experience" (as defined) or (b) at least 60 months of "total responsible actuarial experience" (as defined) including at least 18 months of responsible pension actuarial experience and (2) other qualifications as follows: (a) specified educational degree or (b) specified organizational qualifications or (c) satisfactory completion of an examination prescribed by the Joint Board.

In offering his opinion upon the financial statements, schedules, and summary material [see Figure 5–1, item (d)], the accountant is allowed by ERISA to rely on the correctness of any actuarial matter certified to by an enrolled actuary, if he states his reliance. Accountants differ, however, on whether an accountant should refer in his report to an actuary, as discussed in Chapter 10.

In making his certification to the items summarized in Figure 5–1, item (e), the enrolled actuary may rely on the correctness of any accounting matter as to which any qualified public accountant has expressed an opinion, if he states his reliance.

Material Covered by Accountant's Opinion

Because the accountant's opinion is to cover specified information in the annual report to be filed with the Secretary of Labor, and the separate schedules and summary of that report to be furnished to participants and/or beneficiaries, one needs to identify those items which are required to be covered by the accountant's opinion, and which of them must be included on Department of Labor forms.

Table 5–1 identifies those items which must be covered by the accountant's opinion, and indicates whether they may be required to be submitted on forms to be prescribed by the Secretary of Labor. [The accountant's opinion is required to be made a part of the annual report, but is not required to be furnished to participants and beneficiaries as part of the material mentioned in Figure 5–1, item (n), nor to be submitted on forms.] Column A describes the item, column B indicates whether the item is required to be included in the annual report, column C indicates whether the item is required to be furnished to plan participants and/or beneficiaries, and column D indicates whether the item may be required to be submitted on a form to be prescribed by the Secretary of Labor.

Although ERISA states that financial statements shall not be required to be submitted *on forms,* indications are that the Department of Labor is likely to prescribe financial statement *format and content,* based upon ERISA's provisions allowing the Secretary of Labor to prescribe the format and content of reports, statements, or certain other documents which are required to be furnished or made available to plan participants and beneficiaries. In apparent support of this interpretation of this ERISA provision is the following passage from the Congressional Committee Report (Conference Committee Joint Explanation): "The financial statement prepared [sic] by the independent qualified accountant and the actuarial statement prepared by the enrolled actuary . . . are not required to be submitted on forms. However, the Secretary [of Labor] may prescribe the *format and content of the accountant's and actuary's statements* . . . and other *statements* or reports required . . . to be furnished or *made available* to participants and beneficiaries." [Emphasis added.] It seems clear that such *statements* would include the financial statements, inasmuch as ERISA provides (separately from the "format and content" provision) that financial statements are to be "made available" to participants and beneficiaries.

A combined annual report form has been proposed by the Department of Labor and the Department of the Treasury. The proposed annual report, Form 5500, "Annual Return/Report of Employee Benefit Plan," indicates that information on which the accountant is to express an opinion may be modified somewhat from that called for in ERISA. The proposed annual report contains forms for a statement of assets and liabilities and a statement of income and expenditures, and it is not clear from the proposed form whether those statements relate to the basic financial statements (i.e., statement of assets and liabilities and statement of changes in net assets available for plan benefits) or to the supplemental schedules (i.e., statement of assets and liabilities and statement of receipts and disbursements) called for in ERISA. One might assume either that the annual report combines the supplemental schedules with the basic financial statements or that the basic financial statements must be attached to the annual report. A discussion with staff of the Department of Labor, however, revealed that it is the intention of the Department that the forms for

TABLE 5–1.   Items Required To Be Covered by the Accountant's Opinion and Which May Be Required To Be Reported on Department of Labor Forms

A Description	B Included in Annual Report	C Furnished To Partici- pants and/or Beneficiaries	D Labor Dept. Form
Financial Statements			
Assets and liabilities	x		
Changes in net assets available for plan benefits, to include details of revenues and expenses and other changes aggregated by general source and application	x		
Notes to Financial Statements (Note 1)			
Description of plan including any significant changes in plan made during the period and impact of such changes on benefits	x		
Funding policy (including policy with respect to prior service cost), and any changes in such policy during the year	x		
Description of any significant changes in plan benefits made during the period	x		
Material lease commitments	x		
Other commitments	x		
Contingent liabilities	x		
Description of agreements and transactions with parties in interest	x		
General description of priorities upon termination of plan	x		
Information concerning whether a tax ruling or determination letter has been obtained	x		
Any other matters necessary to present fully and fairly the financial statements of the plan	x		
Supplemental Schedules			
Assets and liabilities aggregated by categories and valued at their current value, in comparative form with the prior year's figures	x	x	x
Receipts and disbursements during year, aggregated by general sources and applications	x	x	x
Assets held for investment purposes aggregated by issuer, borrower, or lessor, or similar party to the transaction, together with specified disclosures (including cost and current value)	x		x

TABLE 5–1. Continued.

A Description	B Included in Annual Report	C Furnished To Partici- pants and/or Beneficiaries	D Labor Dept. Form
Transactions with parties in interest	x		x
Loans or fixed income obligations in default or uncollectible	x		x
Leases in default or uncollectible	x		x
Most recent annual statement of assets and liabilities of a common or collective trust, or, in the case of a separate account or trust, certain other information, where plan assets are held by a bank or similar institution or insurance carrier (Note 2)	x (Note 3)		x
Reportable transactions, generally those exceeding 3% of the current value (generally fair market value) of the plan's assets (Note 4)	x		x
Other Material			
Summary of annual report		x	x

Notes:
1. Disclosures concerning these items shall be *considered* by the accountant. (ERISA does not *require* that these disclosures be made in all instances.)
2. The accountant's opinion need not cover the annual statement of assets and liabilities of a common or collective trust, or, in the case of a separate account or trust, certain other information, if the bank or similar institution or insurance carrier is regulated and supervised and subject to periodic examination by a state or federal agency and such statement or other information is certified as accurate by such bank, etc., and is made a part of the annual report (see page 74 for further discussion).
3. Annual statement of assets and liabilities of a common or collective trust, or, in the case of a separate account or trust, certain other information, need not be filed with the annual report in those instances where the Secretary of Labor permits such omission, and such statement or other information is filed with the Secretary of Labor by the bank or insurance carrier which maintains the common or collective trust or separate account.
4. ERISA is unclear whether the 3% criterion should be measured against the value of the plan's assets at the close of the plan's fiscal year or at some other date. Proposed Form 5500, however, states that the 3% should be based on the value of plan assets at the beginning of the year.
5. See the discussion on pages 71 and 73 regarding format and content of financial statements.
6. Proposed Form 5500 does not require the accountant's opinion for plans with fewer than 100 participants, but see page 80 for later developments.

the statement of assets and liabilities and the statement of income and expenditures in the proposed annual report are to serve as supplemental schedules and that the basic financial statements called for in ERISA would be attached to the annual report. A final annual report form or final regulations should clarify this point.

Concerning Table 5–1, Note 2, on exceptions for trusts and separate accounts of certain state or federally supervised banks or similar institutions or insurance carriers, accountants and others disagree about whether the allowed omission of the accountant's opinion applies to all financial statements and all schedules required to be filed under ERISA, or only to the specified supplemental schedule. This disagreement is complicated by the fact that the proposed annual report (Form 5500) contains no exception for filing when assets are held by a bank or insurance carrier, yet it does not contain a form for the annual statement of assets and liabilities of the common or collective trust or for related information. This question will require resolution, presumably by the Secretary of Labor.

Proposed Form 5500 also provides for the inclusion of Schedule A, "Insurance Information" (not called for in ERISA) when any benefits under the plan are provided by an insurance company, insurance service, or similar organization. It does not appear, however, that the proposed form requires the information contained therein to be covered by the accountant's opinion.

Material Covered by Actuary's Opinion

ERISA requires that an actuarial statement (with respect to most pension plans), and the actuary's opinion thereon, be filed with the Secretary of Labor as part of the annual report. Figure 5–2 summarizes ERISA's requirements for information needed for the actuarial statement that must be included in the annual report filed with the Secretary of Labor and covered by the actuary's opinion. The actuary's opinion shall be based on his making an actuarial valuation of the plan for every third plan year, unless he determines that a more frequent valuation is necessary to support his opinion. The Department of Labor (and the Internal Revenue Service) has proposed Schedule B to Form 5500, "Actuarial Information," to be used in filing the actuarial statement.

REJECTION OF FILINGS

The Secretary of Labor may reject any filing under ERISA if he determines that there is any material qualification by an accountant or actuary contained in an opinion submitted pursuant to requirements of ERISA. In certain instances where the annual report is deemed inadequate, the Labor Department may retain an inde-

FIGURE 5–2

Information Required To Be Covered by the Actuary's Opinion

(a)   The date of the plan year, and the date of the actuarial valuation applicable to the plan for which the report is filed.

(b)   The date and amount of the contribution (or contributions) received by the plan for the plan year for which the report is filed and contributions for prior plan years not previously reported.

(c)   The following information applicable to the plan year for which the report is filed: the normal costs, the accrued liabilities, an identification of benefits not included in the calculation, a statement of the other facts and actuarial assumptions and methods used to determine costs, a justification for any change in actuarial assumptions or cost methods, and the minimum contribution required under Section 302 (minimum funding standards).

(d)   The number of participants and beneficiaries, both retired and nonretired, covered by the plan.

(e)   The current value of the assets accumulated in the plan, the present value of the assets of the plan used by the actuary in any computation of the amount of contributions to the plan required under Section 302, and a statement explaining the basis of such valuation of present value of assets.

(f)   The present value of all of the plan's liabilities for nonforfeitable pension benefits allocated by the termination priority categories as set forth in Section 4044, and the actuarial assump-

tions used in these computations. The Secretary of Labor shall establish regulations defining (for purposes of this section) "termination priority categories" and acceptable methods, including approximate methods, for allocating the plan's liabilities to such termination priority categories. [*Note:* The Secretary of Labor may waive or modify these requirements in cases where he thinks that (1) the interests of the plan participants are not harmed thereby and (2) the expense of compliance with these specific requirements is not justified by the needs of the participants, the Pension Benefit Guaranty Corporation, and the Department of Labor for some portion or all of the information otherwise required herein.]

(g)   A certification of the contribution necessary to reduce the accumulated funding deficiency to zero.

(h)   A statement by the enrolled actuary that:

(1)   to the best of his knowledge the report is complete and accurate, and

(2)   the requirements of Section 302(c)(3) (relating to reasonable actuarial assumptions and methods) have been complied with.

(i)   Such other information regarding the plan as the Secretary of Labor may by regulation require.

(j)   Such other information as may be necessary to disclose fully and fairly the actuarial position of the plan.

TABLE 5-2. Summary of Reporting and Disclosure Requirements Under ERISA

Filing Date and Applicable Section of Law	Type of Report and/or Disclosure	Contents of Report and/or Disclosure	Person(s) to Whom Report and/or Disclosure Furnished
After September 1, 1974, first premium payment due by December 1, 1974. Next premium due within 30 days after new plan year begins. [ERISA Sec. 4007(a)]	Premium payment declaration (Form PBGC–1).[1]	Declaration of estimated premium, premium payment, plan name, identification number, administrator, type of plan.	Pension Benefit Guaranty Corporation
After September 1, 1974 (10 days' notice must be given). [ERISA Sec. 4041(a)]	Notice of plan termination.[1]	Notice.	Pension Benefit Guaranty Corporation
After September 1, 1974 (must notify within 30 days). [ERISA Sec. 4043(a)]	Reportable event.[1]	A reportable event, as specified in Sec. 4043, e.g., (1) loss of qualified status, (2) failure to meet minimum funding standards, (3) inability to pay benefits, etc.	Pension Benefit Guaranty Corporation
After September 1, 1974 (30 days prior to merger, consolidation, or transfer of plan assets or liabilities. [IRC Sec. 6058(b)]	Actuarial statement of valuation.[1,2]	State that benefits will not be decreased.	Secretary of Treasury Secretary of Labor
After September 1, 1974, to be prescribed by regulations. [ERISA Secs. 111(c) and 503]	Claims procedure.[1,2]	Written and adequate notice of reasons for denial of benefit claim.	Participants and beneficiaries
For plan years beginning after September 2, 1974. [IRC Sec. 6058(a); filing date to be prescribed][6]	Annual return.[1,2]	Information as to qualification, financial condition, and operation of plan. Extent of such information may be prescribed by regulations.	Secretary of Treasury

After September 1, 1974 (within six months after end of plan year). (ERISA Sec. 4065)[3]	Annual report to PBGC.[1]	Statement as to whether any reportable event in ERISA Sec. 4043 occurred during plan year.	Pension Benefit Guaranty Corporation
For plan years beginning after December 31, 1975. [IRC Sec. 6057(b); filing date to be prescribed]	Notification of change of status.[1,2]	Change in name of plan or administrator, plan termination, merger, consolidation, or division.	Secretary of Treasury
Effective January 1, 1975, after written request. Plan administrator can make a reasonable charge (no more than once a year). [ERISA Sec. 104(b)(4)]. Penalty of $100 a day if requested information not supplied within 30 days. [ERISA Sec. 502(c)]	Copies of plan description, summary of plan description, annual report, bargaining agreement, trust instrument, or other documents under which plan is established or is operated.[1,2]	See prior column.	Participants and beneficiaries; shall also be available in principal office of administrator and other places that may be prescribed by regulation
Effective January 1, 1975, after written request (no more than once a year). [ERISA Sec. 106(a) and (b)]. Penalty of $100 a day if information not supplied within 30 days. [ERISA Sec. 502(c)]	Statement of total benefits accrued and nonforfeitable pension benefits accrued or when such benefits will become nonforfeitable.[1,2]	Based on latest available information as to accrual and nonforfeitability.	Participants and beneficiaries
After December 31, 1974 (within 60 days after change is adopted or occurs). [ERISA Sec. 104(a)(1)(D)][4]	Description of modifications and changes.[1,2]	Changes occurring in plan as enumerated in ERISA Sec. 102(b).	Secretary of Labor
After December 31, 1974 (by April 30, 1975, or 90 days after individual becomes a participant or beneficiary). [ERISA Sec. 104(a)(1)(C) and (b)(1)][4]	Summary plan description.[1,2]	Information called for in ERISA Sec. 102(b), which includes major plan provisions, names and addresses of plan officials, and claims procedures.	Secretary of Labor, participants, and beneficiaries

TABLE 5-2. Continued.

Filing Date and Applicable Section of Law	Type of Report and/or Disclosure	Contents of Report and/or Disclosure	Person(s) to Whom Report and/or Disclosure Furnished
After December 31, 1974 (by April 30, 1975, or 120 days after adoption of new plan). [ERISA Sec. 104(a)(1)(B)] [5]	Plan description.[1,2]	Same information as immediately above, but on prescribed forms.	Secretary of Labor
After December 31, 1974 (within 210 days after end of plan year.) [ERISA Sec. 104(a)(1)(A)].[7]	Annual report.[1,2]	Audited financial statements, certified actuarial report, and other items enumerated in ERISA Sec. 104.	Secretary of Labor
Same as above. [ERISA Sec. 104(b)(3)]	Summary of annual report.[1,2]	Statements of assets and liabilities and of receipts and disbursements, and other materials necessary to fairly summarize the annual report.	Participants and beneficiaries
Same as "Summary plan description" above. [ERISA Sec. 104(b)(1)]	Summary description of any material modification of the plan.[1,2]	Modification description.	Participants and beneficiaries
For plan years beginning after December 31, 1975, for existing plans; effective immediately for plans not in existence on January 1, 1974. [IRC Sec. 6059(a); filing date to be prescribed]	Periodic report of actuary (for first and every third year thereafter).[1]	Description of funding method, actuarial assumptions, contributions necessary to reduce accumulated funding deficiency to zero, and other information to fully and fairly disclose actuarial position of plan.	Secretary of Treasury

Report	Information required	Filed with
Annual registration.[1,2] Effective for plan years beginning after December 31, 1975. [IRC Sec. 6057(a); filing date to be prescribed]	Names of separated participants entitled to deferred vested benefits and form and amount of such deferred benefits.	Secretary of Treasury, who in turn shall transmit to Secretary of Health, Education, and Welfare
Statement of terminated vested participants' benefits.[1,2] Same as above. [IRC Sec. 6057(e)]	Deferred vested benefits and form and amount.	Terminated vested participants or beneficiaries
Updated summary plan description.[1,2] Every fifth year. [ERISA Sec. 104(b)(1)]	Information called for in ERISA Sec. 102(b).	Secretary of Labor; participants and beneficiaries
Updated plan description.[1,2] Every fifth year. [ERISA Sec. 104(a)(1)(B)]	Same information as immediately above, but on prescribed forms.	Secretary of Labor

Notes:

1. Applies to defined benefit plans.
2. Applies to defined contribution plans, which include money-purchase pension plans, profit-sharing plans, and other individual account plans such as individual annuity contracts, thrift and savings plans, etc.
3. Indications are that this date may be delayed until six months after the end of the first full plan year beginning after September 2, 1974.
4. Regulations delay initial reporting date to May 30, 1976.
5. Regulations delay initial reporting date to (a) August 31, 1975 for a portion of the reporting form (EBS-1) and (b) May 30, 1976 for the balance.
6. Proposed Form 5500 provides that it is to be filed with the Secretary of Treasury on or before the 15th day of the 5th month following the close of (a) the employer's taxable year, in the case of a single-employer plan, or (b) the plan year, in the case of a plan with more than one employer; effective with plan years ending in taxable years ending on or after December 31, 1975 (except for industry- or area-wide union-negotiated plans for which the effective date is for plan years ending on or after December 31, 1975).
7. Proposed Form 5500 provides that it is to be filed with the Secretary of Labor on or before (a) the 15th day of the 5th month following the close of the employer's taxable year, for a single-employer plan whose plan year ends either with the employer's taxable year or within 4 months before the end of such taxable year, or (b) 135 days following the close of the plan year, for all other plans; effective with plan years beginning on or after January 1, 1975. Thus, the first due date is May 15, 1976 for a calendar-year plan of a calendar-year employer.

All reports and/or disclosures, save one, are to be filed by the plan administrator. The claims procedure report shall be filed by the employee benefit plan. IRC Sec. 414(g) defines plan administrator as "(1) the person specifically so designated by the terms of the instrument under which the plan is operated, (2) in the absence of a designation . . . (A) in the case of a plan maintained by a single employer, such employer, (B) in the case of a plan maintained by two or more employers or jointly by one or more employers and one or more employee organizations, the association, committee, joint board of trustees, or other similar group of representatives of the parties who maintained the plan, or (C) in any case in which . . . (A) or (B) does not apply, such other person as the Secretary [of Treasury] or his delegate may, by regulations, prescribe." ERISA Sec. 3(16) provides a similar definition. ERISA Sec. 3(3) defines an employee benefit plan to mean an employee welfare benefit plan and/or an employee pension benefit plan. It is likely that such obligation will, in practice, fall upon the administrator.

pendent accountant to perform an audit and/or an enrolled actuary to prepare an actuarial statement, with their expenses to be paid by the sponsoring plan.

OTHER WAIVERS

Even though a pension plan is otherwise covered by ERISA, the Secretary of Labor has the power to:

1. Prescribe simplified annual reports for any pension plan which covers fewer than 100 participants, and
2. Waive the actuarial statement and opinion, and the opinion of the independent accountant, for such pension plan.

The Secretary is considering utilizing such power since instructions to the proposed annual report form state that (1) a simplified form (Form 5500-K) must be filed, in lieu of Form 5500, for owner–employee (Keogh) plans that have fewer than 100 participants and at least one owner–employee participant and (2) an accountant's opinion is waived for all pension plans with fewer than 100 participants. Subsequent reports indicate, however, that the Secretary is proposing that all plans, regardless of size, engage an independent accountant to express an opinion on the financial statements.

PENALTIES

Failure to comply with the reporting and disclosure requirements may lead to fines of up to $100,000, and fines of up to $100 *per day per participant or beneficiary* for failure to comply with the requests for information. As is the case with certain other penalties which may be imposed under the law, the penalties related to reporting and disclosure are imposed upon the plan administrator; but, in many cases, the employer company may ultimately become liable for such penalties, as discussed in Chapter 4. Other penalties which may be imposed for failure to conform to reporting and disclosure requirements are also discussed therein.

EFFECTIVE DATES

The effective date for these reporting requirements generally is January 1, 1975; in the case of a plan year beginning in 1974 and ending in 1975, the Secretary of Labor has issued proposed regulations postponing the effective date until the beginning of the first plan year beginning after January 1, 1975.

PART II

Employer Company Accounting, Auditing, and Financial Reporting

ACCOUNTING FOR EMPLOYER'S PENSION COSTS

As indicated in Chapter 1, in the early part of this century pensions were invariably accounted for on a pay-as-you-go basis. The only charge to income for the cost of pensions was the amount of benefits paid to retired employees during the accounting period.

The adoption of formalized funded pension plans and the consequent need for determining the amounts of contributions to the related funds led to recognition of the concept of past service cost as an element in determining the amount of funding contributions. For accountants, this gave rise to considerable uncertainty, and some difference of opinion, about the nature of contributions made for past service. Since these contributions were for past services, the question arose whether they should be charged to retained earnings at the time they were made, or to current expense, which was the generally accepted procedure for contributions for current services.

This chapter discusses the manner in which companies account for the cost of their pension plans.

HISTORICAL BACKGROUND

Statements of the American Institute of Certified Public Accountants (AICPA)

The AICPA's first pronouncement on accounting for pension plan costs was issued by the Committee on Accounting Procedure in Accounting Research Bulletin (ARB) No. 36, published in 1948. In this bulletin the Committee expressed the belief that costs of annuities based upon past service were generally incurred in contemplation of present and future services, not necessarily of the individual affected, but of the organization as a whole, and that such costs should be allocated to current and future services and not charged to retained earnings. It did not, however, specify how pension costs should be recognized in the accounts.

In September 1956, ARB No. 47 was issued. In this bulletin the Committee specified how past service cost should be accounted for, and also recognized the concept of vested benefits. It expressed a preference for full accrual of pension costs over the remaining service lives of employees covered by a plan, generally on the basis of actuarial calculations. It regarded as being acceptable "for the present," however, minimum accruals whereby "the accounts and financial statements should reflect the accruals which equal the present worth, actuarially calculated, of pension commitments to employees to the extent that pension rights have vested in the employees . . . ." The Committee stated that these accruals should not necessarily depend on funding arrangements, or on strict legal interpretations of a plan, and indicated a view that past service cost should be charged off over a reasonable period on a systematic and rational basis that would not distort the operating results of any one year.

Following the issuance of ARB No. 47, divergent accounting practices continued. During 1958, several companies that had previously followed the practice of accruing the full amount of current service costs (which coincided with contributions to the funds) either eliminated or drastically reduced pension costs charged to income. The supporters of these actions justified them on the grounds that funds provided in the past were enough to afford reasonable assurance of the continuance of pension payments, and more than enough to meet the company's liabilities for the then vested rights of employees; thus, the minimum requirements of ARB No. 47 were satisfied.

It was against this background that the Accounting Principles Board (APB), which succeeded the Committee on Accounting Procedure, decided that the subject needed further study, and authorized an accounting research study. This study, published in 1965, detailed the accounting complexities of pension plans. In November 1966, after lengthy consideration, the APB promulgated its Opinion No. 8, "Accounting for the Cost of Pension Plans," whose major objective was to eliminate inappropriate fluctuations in the amount of annual provisions for pension costs.

APB Opinion No. 8

Opinion No. 8 provided that, effective with fiscal periods beginning after December 31, 1966, costs charged to income should be determined in accordance with the guidelines expressed in the Opinion. The Opinion states that the provision for pension cost should be based on an actuarial cost method that gives effect, in a consistent manner, to pension benefits, pension fund earnings, investment gains or losses (including unrealized gains and losses), and other assumptions regarding future events. The method selected should result in a systematic and rational allocation of the total cost of pensions among the employees' years of active service. If the method selected includes past service cost as an integral part of normal cost, the provision for pension cost should be normal cost adjusted for the effect on pension fund earnings of differences between amounts accrued and amounts funded. If the actuarial cost method deals with past service cost separately from normal cost, the provision for pension cost should include normal cost, an amount for past service cost, and an adjustment for the effect on pension fund earnings of differences between amounts accrued and amounts funded. Provisions for pension cost should not necessarily be based on contributions to the pension fund, be limited to the amounts for which the company has a legal liability, or fluctuate widely as a result of pension fund investment gains and losses or other causes unrelated to the size and composition of the employee group.

The Opinion narrowed the limits within which the annual provision for pension costs must fall by:

- Increasing the minimum required annual provision for pension costs to include a supplementary provision for vested benefits, if applicable;
- Requiring that actuarial gains and losses and unrealized appreciation and depreciation be recognized in the computation of the annual provision for pension cost in a consistent manner that reflects the long-range nature of pension cost and avoids giving undue weight to short-term market fluctuations; and
- Eliminating pay-as-you-go and terminal funding as acceptable methods of computing the annual provision for pension costs, except in the rare instances where their application would not result in amounts materially different from amounts obtained by the application of acceptable actuarial cost methods.

The APB concluded that all employees who can reasonably be expected to receive benefits under a pension plan should be included in pension cost determination. It also concluded that any change made in the method of accounting for pension cost should not be applied retroactively. The Opinion set forth disclosure requirements for accounting method changes as well as for other pertinent pension cost data.

Applicability of APB Opinion No. 8

APB Opinion No. 8 applies "both to written plans and to plans whose existence may be implied from a well-defined, although perhaps unwritten, company policy." Where a company has been providing its retired employees with benefits that can be determined or estimated in advance, there is generally a presumption that a pension plan exists within the meaning contemplated by the Opinion.

ANNUAL PROVISION FOR PENSION COST

The determination of the annual provision for pension cost requires consideration of the minimum and maximum provisions under Opinion No. 8.

Minimum Provision

Opinion No. 8 provides for a minimum annual provision for pension cost equal to the total of (1) normal cost, (2) an amount equivalent to interest on unfunded prior service cost,* and (3) a supplemental provision for vested benefits, ** if required. The supplemental provision for vested benefits is required if the unfunded or otherwise unprovided-for value of vested benefits † at the end of the year is not at least 5% less than the comparable amount at the beginning of the year. When the supplemental provision is required, it may be the lesser of:

1. An amount, if any, by which 5% of the value of unfunded vested benefits at the beginning of the year exceeds the reduction in the comparable value of unfunded vested benefits at the end of the year; or
2. An amount sufficient to make the aggregate annual provision for pension cost equal to the sum of (a) the normal cost, (b) amortization of prior service cost on a 40-year basis (including interest), and (c) interest equivalents on differences between provisions and amounts funded.

In comparing the value of unfunded vested benefits at the end of the year with the comparable amount at the beginning of the

* The term "unfunded prior service cost," as used herein, includes unfunded past service cost and unfunded increases in past service cost arising from plan amendments. Normal cost is generally funded on a current basis, in conformance with past and present Internal Revenue Code requirements for qualified plans; in such cases normal cost is not included in unfunded prior service cost.

** Vested benefits are defined as benefits "that are not contingent on the employee's continuing in the employer's service."

† The term "unfunded or otherwise unprovided-for value of vested benefits" means an excess of the present value of vested benefits over the total of (a) the pension fund, (b) any balance sheet pension accruals, less (c) any balance sheet prepayments or deferred charges. For convenience, the term "unfunded vested benefits" is used in this discussion in place of the longer term.

year, the amount at the end of the year should be measured exclusive of any net change occurring during the year resulting from changes in benefits due to plan amendments.

The first provision described above is equal to 5% of the value of unfunded vested benefits at the beginning of the year to the extent that such 5% is not covered by a net reduction in such amounts due to plan experience during the year (e.g., contributions to the fund, fund earnings, actuarial gains). The 5% is a declining balance type of provision; assuming no change in unfunded vested benefits other than through the provision, it would take about 45 years to reduce the unfunded vested benefits to 10 percent of the original amount.

Within the general framework of these "minimum" provisions, a company may adopt, as a single accounting policy, one of three procedures regarding unfunded or otherwise unprovided-for prior service cost. It may provide for such cost on the basis of (1) the first method above, commonly referred to as the interest only plus vesting method, (2) the second method described above, commonly referred to as the 40-year amortization method, or (3) the lower of the two determined on an annual basis, even though either method may call for a larger amount than the other in a particular year. The 40-year amortization procedure has the practical advantage of avoiding the need for separately determining the annual change in unfunded vested benefits. The current amount of such unfunded vested benefits, however, will have to be determined for the disclosure requirements of the Opinion, unless it can be determined that there are none. The 40-year basis of amortization is computed as a level annual amount, including the equivalent of interest; thus, if a 4% interest factor is assumed in the actuarial calculations, the amortization rate would be approximately 5% and a 3½% interest assumption would result in an amortization rate of about 4.7%.

Maximum Provision

The maximum annual provision for pension cost is stated as being the total of (1) normal cost, (2) 10% of past service cost at inception of the plan and of increases or decreases in prior service cost arising from plan amendments (in each case until fully amortized), and (3) interest equivalents on differences between provisions and amounts funded. The 10% includes an interest factor and, assuming interest rates of between 4% and 6%, the maximum provision therefore requires from about 13 to slightly over 15 years to fully amortize such past service cost and increases or decreases in prior service cost. Past service cost and increases or decreases in prior service cost as used in this paragraph refer to costs unreduced by amounts previously amortized.

Calculation of Annual Provision

The annual provision for pension expense must be within the range of minimum and maximum limits established by APB Opinion No. 8. Illustrations of the calculation of the annual provision and comparison with the limits are provided in Figure 6–1. Assumptions are the same for both computations. In practice, computing both limits is usually not necessary because the determination is being made only for that limit which may be exceeded in the particular situation.

Valuing Vested Benefits

The valuation of vested benefits is generally required for determining the annual pension expense provision, as discussed earlier, and/or for disclosure (see "Disclosures" on pages 97–99).

The value * of vested benefits at a particular date includes not only the value of the amounts of benefits payable or to become payable to retired employees and to ex-employees with vested benefits, but also the value of benefits that would remain to the credit of those employees in active service if they were to terminate service as of the valuation date. Vested benefits do not accrue ratably between valuation dates, but reflect the vesting percentage in effect for the individual employee on the valuation date.

As indicated in an interpretation of APB Opinion No. 8 published by the AICPA, the accrued benefit cost (unit credit) method of calculation should be used to determine the value of vested benefits, even though a different method may be used for other purposes. In the determination of the amount of unfunded or unprovided-for value of vested benefits, the method of valuing the pension fund assets should preferably be consistent with that employed in

---

* I.e., the present value, at a particular actuarial valuation date, of future expected payments as determined actuarially.

FIGURE 6–1

Computation of Limits of Provision for Annual Pension Expense as Provided in APB Opinion No. 8

ASSUMPTIONS

Normal cost	$ 200,000
Employee contributions	25,000
Prior service cost:	
Unfunded at beginning of year	1,500,000
Funded in prior years	1,000,000
Amortization of actuarial gains	3,500
Amortization of unrealized appreciation	1,500
Unfunded pension accruals	50,000
Actuarial value of vested benefits:	
Beginning of year	5,000,000
End of year	5,300,000
Fund assets:	
Beginning of year	2,000,000
End of year	2,400,000
Interest rate	4%

OVERALL COMPUTATION

	Minimum		Maximum
	I	II	III
1. Normal cost	$ 200,000	$ 200,000	$ 200,000
2. Employee contributions, if not considered in arriving at normal cost	(25,000)	(25,000)	(25,000)
3. Interest on unfunded, unprovided-for prior service cost	58,000 [1]		
4. Supplemental provision for vested benefits (see following computation)	47,500		
5. Amortization of prior service cost:			
(a) on a 40-year basis, including interest		126,250 [2]	
(b) at 10% per year			250,000
6. Interest on excess of prior years' accounting provisions over amounts funded (or on excess of amounts funded over provisions)	2,000	2,000	2,000
7. Provision for actuarial (gains) or losses	(3,500)	(3,500)	(3,500)
8. Provision for unrealized (appreciation) or depreciation	(1,500)	(1,500)	(1,500)
9. Total	$ 277,500	$ 298,250	$ 422,000

FIGURE 6–1

Continued

Pension expense for the year must be an amount between Column III and the lesser (in any one year) of Columns I and II based upon an acceptable actuarial cost method consistently applied.

Notes:

1. Unfunded, unprovided-for prior service cost equals $1,500,000 less $50,000, or $1,450,000.
2. Level annual charge which will amortize total prior service cost of $2,500,000 (with interest) on a 40-year basis; amortization will cease when the unfunded amount of $1,500,000 has been amortized.

COMPUTATION OF SUPPLEMENTAL PROVISION FOR VESTED BENEFITS (PARAGRAPH 17a OF OPINION NO. 8)

	At Date of Most Recent Valuation	At Date of Preceding Valuation
1. Actuarial value of vested benefits	$5,300,000	$5,000,000
2. Amount of pension fund (Note)	2,400,000	2,000,000
3. Unfunded amount (Item 1 minus Item 2)	2,900,000	3,000,000
4. Amount of balance sheet pension accruals less pension deferred charges (Note)	50,000	50,000
5. Actuarial value of unfunded or unprovided-for vested benefits (Item 3 minus Item 4)	$2,850,000	$2,950,000
6. 5% of Item 5 for the prior year	$ 147,500	
7. Excess of Item 5 for the prior year over Item 5 for the current year	100,000	
8. Excess of Item 6 over Item 7 (provision for vested benefits—to Item 4, Overall Computation)	$ 47,500	

Note: The dates for Items 2 and 4 may be the end of the company's fiscal year or the actuarial valuation date. Consistency is the primary consideration.

periodic actuarial valuations in use for accounting purposes, except that the use of full market value may not be desirable because its use might cause wide fluctuations in the unfunded vested benefit figure. Nonetheless, the use of full market value is acceptable pursuant to the aforementioned interpretation of APB Opinion No. 8, even where the full amount of appreciation has not been recognized in the cost provision.*

ACTUARIAL FACTORS

The determination of the annual provision for pension cost and amounts to be disclosed under APB Opinion No. 8 involves the use of actuarial cost methods, actuarial assumptions, and methods of treating actuarial gains and losses.

Actuarial Cost Method

APB Opinion No. 8 defines five actuarial cost methods whose application would result in an appropriate annual provision foi pension cost; these methods are discussed in Chapter 2. In addition, variations of those methods may be used (e.g., the aggregate method with frozen, separately amortized, past service cost). For accounting purposes, many accountants prefer the entry-age normal cost (or entry-age level cost) method, the aggregate method, or the variation referred to in the preceding sentence. On the other hand, the accrued benefit method may initially result in lesser charges to income than the other methods.

Terminal Funding and Pay-As-You-Go. The Opinion regards these methods of accounting (the latter of which is not an actuarial cost method) as unacceptable because they give no recognition to pension cost until the employees retire. There may be, however, circumstances where the use of pay-as-you-go or terminal funding as a basis of accounting for a portion of total pension benefits for employees would not have the effect of a material departure from the Opinion. For example, if pay-as-you-go is used for employees already retired at the effective date of the Opinion, its application would be limited to a diminishing class of employee and the difference between use of pay-as-you-go and an acceptable actuarial cost

---

* See "Funding" in Chapter 4 for discussion of forthcoming regulations to ERISA which may require use of one set of actuarial assumptions, and possibly of one actuarial cost method and one asset valuation method, for all purposes.

method might not be material. Somewhat the same considerations may be relevant with regard to supplementary pension benefits (other than payments pursuant to deferred compensation contracts, discussed later in this chapter) for a limited number of mature employees who are approaching retirement age (say, within five years) at the time a pension plan is adopted or amended.

Interest Component. Paragraph 23 of the Opinion refers to the fact that "the equivalent of interest . . . may be stated separately or it may be included in the amortization." This statement pertains only to computation and should not be construed to allow any so-called interest component of pension cost to be classified in financial statements or treated for any other accounting purpose as interest rather than pension cost.

Interest on Unfunded Plans. Costs under unfunded pension plans should be determined under an accepted actuarial method including the use of interest equivalents. Suggested bases for determination of an appropriate interest rate include rates used by funded pension plans of the company or generally used by other companies, or the borrowing rate paid by the company. Use of an assumed rate of return on the employment of additional capital would generally not be appropriate.

Actuarial Assumptions

Actuarial assumptions should be reasonable in relation to current conditions and consistently applied.* They should ordinarily be based upon the current conditions of the pension plan. Although an uncommon practice, there may be instances where actuarial assumptions are not based on current plan conditions or provisions. For example, actuarial assumptions in some instances include a factor for anticipated increased benefit levels where they are reasonable in the light of either the company's past policy of bettering pension benefits or the company's reasonable expectation of increasing pension benefits in the future. When anticipated increased benefit levels are considered in the determination of normal cost, they should also be considered in the determination of prior service cost (where separately computed).

---

* See "Funding" in Chapter 4 for discussion of forthcoming regulations to ERISA which may require use of one set of actuarial assumptions, and possibly of one actuarial cost method and one asset valuation method, for all purposes.

Actuarial Gains and Losses

Actuarial gains and losses arise from the need to use assumptions concerning future events. Under APB Opinion No. 8, adjustments required from time to time to reflect actual experience must be recognized in a consistent manner that reflects the long-range nature of pension cost. Except in specified circumstances relative to plant closings, acquisitions, etc., actuarial gains and losses are to be spread or averaged rather than accorded immediate recognition; the latter course is considered undesirable because of the possibility of wide fluctuations in annual pension expense. From 10 to 20 years is considered a reasonable period over which to spread actuarial gains and losses when spreading is accomplished by separate adjustment rather than by the routine application of the actuarial cost method used.

The averaging method of dealing with actuarial gains and losses involves determining an average annual amount of such gains or losses, e.g., a five-year moving average might be used. Results under averaging may be appropriate for gains and losses which tend to be repetitive but may be inappropriate for unusual gains or losses. In certain instances, a combination of methods may be desirable; for example, spreading might be applied to gains or losses that are not expected to recur frequently, while averaging may be applied to recurring items. When actuarial assumptions have been changed, past experience regarding actuarial gains and losses may not be an appropriate basis for averaging. The averaging method, when suitable, has the advantage of avoiding a possible cumulative effect that could result from use of the spread method. For example, if actuarial gains were to occur at the rate of $1,000 a year, spreading over 10 years would result in recognition of $100 in the first year, $200 in the second year ($\frac{1}{10}$ of the prior year's gain and $\frac{1}{10}$ of the current year's gain), $300 in the third year, etc.

APB Opinion No. 8 recognized that "an effect similar to spreading or averaging may be obtained by applying net actuarial gains as a reduction of prior service cost in a manner that reduces the annual amount equivalent to interest on, or the annual amount of amortization of, such prior service cost and does not reduce the period of amortization." For example, the application of a $100,000 gain to prior service cost would, assuming a 4% rate, reduce the "interest" charge by $4,000 annually. As a period of 10 to 20 years is considered reasonable for spreading, the authors believe that net actuarial gains should not be applied to prior service cost if the remaining amortization period of such prior service cost is less than 10 years. While the Opinion does not discuss applying a net actuarial loss to prior service, this would appear to be acceptable, provided prior service cost is being amortized over a remaining period of between 10 and 20 years, the period over which actuarial losses could otherwise be separately spread.

Unrealized Investment Appreciation and Depreciation. APB Opinion No. 8 requires recognition of unrealized appreciation or depreciation in the value of equity investments in the determination of pension cost on a rational and systematic basis that avoids giving undue weight to short-term market fluctuations. (Appreciation and depreciation need not be recognized for debt securities expected to be held to maturity and redeemed at face value.) Adopting a consistent method for according recognition to unrealized appreciation and depreciation is particularly important.

It should be noted that in certain cases, e.g., when investments are valued by the actuary at fair market value, unrealized appreciation or depreciation is recognized in the determination of actuarial gains and losses. In other cases, e.g., when investments are valued by the actuary at cost, the amount of unrealized appreciation or depreciation is not recognized in the determination of actuarial gains and losses and thus must be treated separately.

Actuarial Valuation Date

The date as of which the actuarial valuation is made will generally not coincide with the end of a company's fiscal year. In the absence of any substantially changed conditions that would render obsolete the data on which the actuarial valuation was made (e.g., acquisition or disposal of a significant division or product line or segment of the business, or significant change in the level of benefits), valuations made as of a date within 12 months from the end of the fiscal year should be suitable for accounting determinations. A valuation made as of an earlier date may also be suitable, but its use could present problems in some areas—value of vested benefits, for example. Technical problems concerning the use of the valuation date should be discussed with actuaries.

Differences Between Funding and Accounting

As pointed out in the Opinion, the actuarial cost method used for accounting need not be the same as the actuarial method used for funding.* It follows that different actuarial assumptions may also be used for each of these purposes even though the same general actuarial method may be used; obviously, all relevant factors should be given proper recognition in the assumptions used for accounting. It is likely that, in most instances, the actuarial cost method and actuarial assumptions used for funding purposes will also be appropriate for accounting use but this will not always be so (e.g., for funding purposes, no consideration may be given to unrealized appreciation or depreciation of investments, or actuarial gains or losses may be given immediate recognition); accordingly, actuarial methods and assumptions should be carefully considered from the standpoint of their appropriateness for accounting.

DEFINED CONTRIBUTION PLANS

As noted under "Pension Plans" in Chapter 1, some plans referred to as defined contribution plans provide a contemplated scale of benefits and thus may need to be treated for accounting purposes as defined benefit plans.

APB Opinion No. 8 states that the periodic cost of a defined contribution plan is usually appropriately measured by the amount of contribution determined by the formula specified in the plan. It would appear that where the employer's liability is limited to the amount of the pension fund, the amount of the defined contribution can be presumed to be the proper amount of the current charge to expense. This is often the case with bilateral plans negotiated by either an employer or a group of employers—such as an industry group—with a union or other employee representatives.

Where a plan provides both a formula for plan contributions and a scale for plan benefits, however, and the contributions are found to be inadequate or excessive for the purpose of funding the scale of benefits, subsequent adjustment of either the contributions or the benefits, or both, is necessary. If the plan history indicates that only the scale of benefits is adjusted, the plan presumably should be treated as a defined contribution plan. If, however, the plan history indicates (and/or the current employer policy contemplates) the maintenance of benefit levels regardless of the amount of defined contribution or legal limitation of the employer's liability for such

* See "Funding" in Chapter 4 for discussion of forthcoming regulations to ERISA which may require use of one set of actuarial assumptions, and possibly of one actuarial cost method and one asset valuation method, for all purposes.

benefits, the plan should be treated as a defined benefit plan, with the current charge to expense computed actuarially. If a company's liability for benefit levels is not limited by the amount of the pension fund, minimum current charges to expense should generally be not less than an amount actuarially computed on the basis of specified benefit levels.

DISCLOSURES

APB Opinion No. 8 calls for specific disclosures in financial statements or notes. The disclosures required by the Opinion are shown in the left column of Figure 6–2.

In computing unfunded vested benefits, as described in item 4 (left column), it has been the practice of some companies to perform the computation on an aggregate basis for all the company's plans, i.e., the total assets of all plans are compared with the total vested benefits of all plans. Such netting is permitted, pursuant to paragraph 37 of APB Opinion No. 8, only in instances in which a company has two or more plans covering the same employee classes and the assets in any one of the plans ultimately can be used in paying present or future benefits of another plan or plans. Since past and current law generally prohibit using the assets of one plan to pay benefits required under another plan, such netting would generally not be permitted. Thus, where one plan is overfunded and another is underfunded, the amount by which the latter plan is underfunded should be disclosed. Similarly, where a company discloses unfunded past or prior service cost for more than one plan, the amount by which one plan is overfunded should not be used to reduce the amount of the unfunded liability to be disclosed.

The Opinion does not call for any disclosure where the total of the pension fund and balance sheet accruals, less any pension prepayments or deferred charges, exceeds the value of vested benefits (overfunding), although it is not considered inappropriate for a company to include this information in the notes to financial statements.

Comparison With SEC Requirements

Disclosure requirements of the Securities and Exchange Commission are shown in the right column of Figure 6–2. Although disclosure of the amount of unfunded past or prior service cost is not required (in published financial statements) under APB Opin-

FIGURE 6–2

Pension Plan Disclosure Requirements Under APB Opinion No. 8 and Under Rules and Regulations of the Securities and Exchange Commission

APB OPINION NO. 8— Paragraph 46

1. A statement that such plans exist, identifying or describing the employee groups covered.
2. A statement of the company's accounting and funding policies.
3. The provision for pension cost for the period.

4. The excess, if any, of the actuarially computed value of vested benefits over the total of the pension fund and any balance sheet pension accruals, less any pension prepayments or deferred charges.

5. Nature and effect of significant matters affecting comparability for all periods presented, such as changes in acounting methods (actuarial cost method, amortization of past and prior service cost, treatment of actuarial gains and losses, etc.), changes in circumstances (actuarial assumptions, etc.), or adoption or amendment of a plan.

SEC—Rule 3–16 (g) of Regulation S–X

1. A brief description of the essential provisions of any employee pension or retirement plan and of the accounting and funding policies related thereto.
2. The estimated cost of the plan for each period for which an income statement is presented.

3. The excess, if any, of the actuarially computed value of vested benefits over the total of the pension fund and any balance sheet pension accruals, less any pension prepayments or deferred charges.
4. If a plan has not been fully funded or otherwise provided for, the estimated amount that would be necessary to fund or otherwise provide for the past service cost of the plan as of the date most recently determined.
5. A statement of the nature and effect of significant matters affecting comparability of pension costs for any periods for which income statements are presented.

ion No. 8, unfunded past service cost is required to be disclosed in financial statements filed with the SEC pursuant to Rule 3-16 (g) of Regulation S-X (item 4 in the right column of Figure 6–2). (The SEC generally does not consider nondisclosure of unfunded past service cost in published financial statements to result in a material inconsistency between those statements and statements filed with the SEC.)

It can be seen that, other than item 4, the disclosures required by the SEC are similar to those required under APB Opinion No. 8. Questions have been raised with respect to item 4 (right column) as to whether the SEC intended to call for unfunded, unprovided-for prior (rather than past) service cost, and whether all actuarial cost methods are considered appropriate in its calculation. Some accountants believe the same actuarial cost method used for determining the cost provision should be used to determine the amount of such unfunded, unprovided-for past service cost, or else the fact that a different method was used should be disclosed in the SEC filing. The SEC may be addressing these and other issues in the near future.*

SPECIAL SITUATIONS

Special consideration is needed for regulated companies, non-profit organizations, deferred compensation contracts, and death and disability benefits.

Regulated Companies

The applicability of APB Opinion No. 8 to financial statements of regulated companies is subject to the provisions of the Addendum to APB Opinion No. 2. The Addendum identifies regulated companies as "public utilities, common carriers, insurance companies, financial institutions, and the like that are subject to regulation by government, usually through commissions or other similar agencies." Paragraph 2 of the Addendum states that where the regulated company is allowed to defer an expense which "in a nonregulated business would be written off currently," the deferment is appropriate "only when it is clear that the cost will be recoverable out of future

---

* See "Funding" in Chapter 4 for discussion of forthcoming regulations to ERISA which may require use of one set of actuarial assumptions, and possibly of one actuarial cost method and one asset valuation method, for all purposes.

revenues, and . . . not appropriate when there is doubt, because of economic conditions or for other reasons, that the cost will be so recoverable." Such deferment of pension expense would generally be indicated by appropriate accounting or rate orders having been obtained, or by substantially equivalent evidence, and a reasonable expectation that costs will be recoverable from future revenues.

Nonprofit Organizations

Generally, statements of the Accounting Principles Board (or its predecessor, the Committee on Accounting Procedure) do not apply to nonprofit organizations (see Accounting Research Bulletin No. 43, Introduction, paragraph 5). There is no reason, in principle, however, why the provisions of the Opinion should not apply to nonprofit organizations, particularly if their accounts are maintained on the accrual basis.

Deferred Compensation Contracts

Accounting for deferred compensation contracts is generally governed by the provisions of paragraphs 6, 7, and 8 of APB Opinion No. 12, which specifically relate to these contracts. APB Opinion No. 8, however, also refers to these contracts, indicating that its provisions are applicable thereto if the contracts taken together are equivalent to a pension plan, but does not specify the circumstances indicative of such equivalence. This equivalence might be most likely when a company's policy is to enter into deferred compensation contracts with an entire group or class of employees (such as officers of a certain level), instead of with only certain individuals in that group or class. The principal difference in the accounting methods called for under the two Opinions is that APB Opinion No. 12 requires accrual of deferred compensation generally over the remaining service lives of individual employees, whereas APB Opinion No. 8 permits accrual of pension costs over varying time periods due to the alternative treatments allowed for providing for prior service cost.

Death and Disability Benefits

APB Opinion No. 8 states that the benefits to be considered in calculating the annual cost of a pension plan are ordinarily the retirement benefit payments but that in many instances they may also include death and disability payments unless provided under separate arrangements. Generally, death and disability benefits should be considered as part of pension cost only if they are an integral part of the benefits provided by the pension plan.

ACCOUNTING EFFECTS OF ERISA

There has been much publicity, discussion, and uncertainty regarding the accounting impact of ERISA on employers. The Financial Accounting Standards Board (FASB) has placed the overall subject of pension accounting on its technical agenda and issued, pending completion of that project, Interpretation No. 3, "Accounting for the Cost of Pension Plans Subject to the Employee Retirement Income Security Act of 1974, an interpretation of APB Opinion No. 8." The following discussion covers issues in that Interpretation and other issues related to the impact of ERISA on accounting for pension costs.

Liability for Unfunded Prior Service Cost

APB Opinion No. 8, in paragraph 18, states: "If the company has a legal obligation for pension cost in excess of amounts paid or accrued, the excess should be shown in the balance sheet as both a liability and a deferred charge." An argument has been presented that since companies are now obligated by law to fund unfunded prior service cost (generally over a period of not more than 30 or 40 years), they have a legal obligation for pension cost, and thus should record a liability in the amount of unfunded prior service cost not already recorded.

The FASB Interpretation states that, based on an analysis of information presently available, the Board does not believe that ERISA creates a legal obligation for unfunded pension costs that warrants accounting recognition as a liability pursuant to paragraph 18 of APB Opinion No. 8. The Interpretation points out, however, that unless a waiver from the minimum funding requirements is obtained from the Secretary of the Treasury, the amount currently required to be funded should be recognized as a liability.

This accords with the view of some lawyers that although ERISA's funding requirements in one sense impose a legal obligation upon the company, the amount of the legal obligation *at any point in time* is only that portion of unfunded prior service cost required to be funded to date under the law.

Liability for Unfunded Vested Benefits

As indicated in Chapter 4 under "Plan Termination Insurance," if a plan is terminated with unfunded vested benefits, the Pension Benefit Guaranty Corporation (PBGC) will provide the beneficiaries with the prescribed benefits, up to the limits specified in ERISA, and will be able to place a priority lien on the employer's assets to the extent of 30% of the employer's net worth. The question has been raised as to whether a company's unfunded vested benefits (up to the amount that potentially could become payable to the PBGC) should be recorded on the balance sheet as a liability, assuming the company does not purchase insurance coverage to protect against such a liability.

The FASB Interpretation indicates that a liability for unfunded vested benefits need not be recorded unless a plan is to be terminated. Without a plan termination, no benefits will be paid by the PBGC on behalf of the company and no liability to the PBGC will be created.

The Interpretation states that when there is convincing evidence that a pension plan will be terminated (perhaps a formal commitment by management to terminate a plan) and the liability on termination will exceed fund assets and related prior accruals, the excess liability shall be accrued. The Interpretation states further that if the amount of the excess liability cannot be reasonably determined, disclosure of the circumstances shall be made in the notes to the financial statements, including an estimate of the possible range of the liability.

In some instances, circumstances may indicate that a plan termination is more than a remote possibility and yet the aforementioned "convincing evidence" is absent. Such circumstances would include a tentative decision on the part of management to terminate a plan, or the possibility that the company may not be in a financial position to continue a plan. (The latter instance may be indicated when the auditor deems it necessary to express an opinion containing what is commonly referred to as a "going concern" qualification.)

Although this type of situation is not discussed in the Interpretation, it would appear that recording a liability in such a situation is not necessary, but appropriate disclosure of the amount of the contingent liability should be made.

Pension Expense

Although APB Opinion No. 8 requires that the minimum provision for pension cost to be recorded in the financial statements include interest on unfunded prior service cost (and in certain instances a provision for unfunded vested benefits), amortizing prior service cost as part of the provision is not required. The question has been raised as to whether the minimum provision should be changed in light of ERISA's requirement that prior service cost be funded.

The FASB Interpretation states that a fundamental concept of APB Opinion No. 8 is that the annual pension cost to be charged to expense for financial accounting purposes is not necessarily determined by the plan's funding. Accordingly, the FASB stated that no change in the Opinion's minimum and maximum limits is required as a result of ERISA. (The Interpretation points out, however, that the amount of pension cost to be charged to expense periodically for financial accounting purposes may change, even though no change in accounting methods is made, because of the need to comply with ERISA's participation, vesting, or funding requirements.)

The authors' view on this matter differs somewhat from that set forth in the FASB Interpretation. Although the annual pension cost to be charged to expense is not *necessarily* determined by a pension plan's funding, ERISA's funding requirements impact upon the rationale on which the Opinion's minimum limit for the annual provision for pension cost is apparently based. The rationale for not requiring amortization of prior service cost appears to be based on the concept (described in paragraph 13 of APB Opinion No. 8) that in many cases a provision for normal cost plus an amount equivalent to interest on unfunded prior service cost will be adequate to meet, on a continuing basis, all benefit payments under the plan. The APB decided that so long as the provision is sufficient to amortize unfunded vested benefits over a reasonable period, no specific provision for unfunded prior service cost is required. The implication is that since unfunded prior service cost might never be paid, there is no necessity to charge such cost to expense.

It would appear, however, that since prior service cost must now be funded, it is more difficult to argue that such cost need not be provided by charges to income. We believe that, when ERISA's funding requirements become effective, it would be appropriate for the provision for pension cost to include, in addition to normal cost and interest on unfunded prior service cost, an amount sufficient to amortize unfunded prior service cost (not already provided for) over a reasonable period (e.g., the funding period).* We anticipate that many companies which are presently not amortizing unfunded prior service cost as part of the provision will be doing so in the future. By expensing unfunded prior service cost a company will not only avoid building up an asset on its books that may never be recovered, but will also be more likely to enter such cost into its product cost system and will thus be more likely to recover that cost through reflection in the company's pricing structure.

Despite the arguments set forth above, we believe that auditors should respect the view of the FASB and should not take exception where pension cost is accounted for in accordance with the principles set forth in the Interpretation. The auditor may, however, encourage his clients to include as part of their annual provision for pension cost an amount sufficient to amortize unfunded prior service cost not already provided for over a reasonable time period.

The Interpretation also states that any change in pension cost resulting from compliance with ERISA shall enter into the determination of periodic provisions for pension expense *subsequent* to the date a plan becomes subject to ERISA's participation, vesting, and funding requirements, i.e., either the effective dates prescribed by ERISA or earlier if the company so elects. It appears that companies are *prohibited* from including in the determination of the

---

* We believe that it would be appropriate for the provision for pension cost to include amortization of unfunded prior service cost even when the full funding limitation applies (see "Full Funding Limitation" in Chapter 4). If, for example, fund assets appreciate sufficiently in value so that no contribution is required in a particular year, an actuarial gain will likely result which, in determining the provision for pension cost, should be spread or averaged over time as described under "Actuarial Gains and Losses" earlier in this chapter. Thus, the benefit of the appreciation will be reflected in the provision in a consistent manner as anticipated by APB Opinion No. 8.

provision for pension expense a change in pension cost resulting from compliance with ERISA *prior* to the date a plan becomes, or elects to become, subject to ERISA's requirements. Although we do not believe that this prohibition is warranted, the Interpretation seems reasonably clear.

A change in expense recognition from the minimum level under APB Opinion No. 8 (where a provision for prior service cost is not included) to a provision which includes amortization of prior service cost can be made at any time. Such a change is considered a change in accounting method which should be accounted for prospectively (see paragraph 47 of APB Opinion No. 8) and which would require a consistency exception in the auditor's report if the effect of the change is material.

Disclosures

Paragraph 46 of APB Opinion No. 8 calls for disclosure of, among other items, the excess of the actuarially computed value of vested benefits over the total of the pension fund and any balance sheet accruals, less any pension prepayments or deferred charges. There has been no requirement to disclose the amount of unfunded prior service cost not already provided for (except to the extent that disclosure of past service cost is required in connection with financial statements filed in accordance with SEC Regulation S-X, as described under "Disclosures" earlier in this chapter), and the FASB Interpretation does not call for such disclosure.

It would appear, however, that the new requirement that prior service cost be funded makes disclosure of unfunded prior service cost of greater importance to readers of financial statements than in the past. Some accountants believe that since unfunded prior service cost now represents an amount that will be funded through future cash outlays, that amount, along with the funding period, should preferably be disclosed. Other accountants believe that such disclosures are not necessary because financial statements already reflect amounts funded in charges either to income or to a deferred asset account. In any event, unless called for by the FASB, such disclosures are not required.

The FASB states that certain other disclosures may be required. The Interpretation indicates that if, prior to the date a plan becomes subject to ERISA's participation, vesting, and funding requirements, it appears likely that compliance will have a significant future effect on the amount of an enterprise's (1) periodic provision for pension expense, (2) periodic funding of pension cost, or (3) unfunded vested benefits, this fact and an estimate of the effect shall be disclosed in the notes to the financial statements.

Complying with these disclosure requirements may present practical problems. For example, although companies may know what plan modifications must be made in order to comply with ERISA's requirements, they may not have made final decisions regarding other plan modifications that may increase or decrease the cost of required modifications. Another potential problem is that the demand that will be placed upon actuarial and benefits consultants may preclude a company from obtaining data needed for including these disclosures in the financial statements.

The Interpretation deals with these practical problems by stating that the Board recognizes that actuarial computations or other information may not be available in time to permit disclosure of an estimate of the effect in notes to financial statements for fiscal periods ending in 1974 or early in 1975; * if an estimate cannot be furnished, an explanation shall be provided. Minimum disclosure in these circumstances should include an indication, where appropriate, that ERISA will necessitate plan amendments or other action which will (or may) increase the provision for pension expense, initiate or accelerate the funding of unfunded prior service cost, and/or increase unfunded vested benefits.

Other disclosures growing from ERISA would include the amount or range of any liability or contingent liability arising in the event of a potential or possible plan termination as discussed under "Liability for Unfunded Vested Benefits" earlier in this chapter. As noted in that section, such disclosure would be necessary only under the circumstances described therein.

Liability to Acquiring Company

Questions have been raised as to whether ERISA impacts upon APB Opinion No. 16 requirements for reporting the results of business combinations. The Opinion states (in a footnote to paragraph 88h) that, in a business combination accounted for under the purchase method, a liability should be recorded in the amount of

---

* Although the FASB Interpretation refers to fiscal periods ending in 1974 or early in 1975, recent discussions with actuarial and benefits consultants indicate that similar considerations may be involved in 1976.

the greater of (1) accrued pension cost computed in conformity with the accounting policies of the acquiring company for one or more of its pension plans or (2) the excess, if any, of the actuarially computed value of vested benefits over the amount of the pension fund.

One argument favoring changed requirements is that since (1) APB Opinion No. 16 indicates that the acquiring company should record as a liability all liabilities, including pension cost, related to the acquired company, whether or not shown in the financial statements of the acquired company, at the present value of amounts to be paid and (2) ERISA indicates that unfunded prior service cost must now be funded, then unfunded prior service cost (rather than the greater of accrued cost computed in conformity with the policies of the acquiring company or unfunded vested benefits) is the amount that now represents the present value of amounts to be paid. APB Opinion No. 16 should therefore be revised to require the recording of unfunded prior service cost as a liability in a purchase situation.

A counter-argument states that since a liability for unfunded prior service cost is not normally required to be recorded, even in light of ERISA, such an amount should not be recorded in a purchase transaction. Some proponents of this argument believe that APB Opinion No. 16 should remain unchanged, while others believe that the requirement for recording unfunded vested benefits should be eliminated (because no such liability need be recorded where an acquisition is not involved).

Still another argument relates to the fact that ERISA requires an acquiring company to assume responsibility for unfunded vested benefits, as limited by ERISA, in the event of a plan termination. Because of this provision, it is argued, the term "vested benefits" referred to in APB Opinion No. 16 should be modified to read "vested benefits as limited by the termination insurance provisions of ERISA."

The FASB will most likely be considering the current appropriateness of the APB Opinion No. 16 requirements with respect to the amount of pension liability to be recorded in a combination accounted for under the purchase method. Until the FASB addresses this matter, however, one should proceed on the basis that ERISA has no direct impact upon the present use or interpretation of the principles set forth in APB Opinion No. 16.

7

AUDITING EMPLOYER'S PENSION COSTS

The attention given to the auditing of pension costs increased greatly with the issuance of Opinion No. 8 of the Accounting Principles Board; the enactment of ERISA will undoubtedly cause auditors to give still greater attention to the auditing of pension costs.

While the broad applicability of APB Opinion No. 8 is basically unchanged, ERISA impacts upon the auditing of the employer company in two general ways: first, the effect of the law on the accounting for pension costs and related reporting, as set forth in FASB Interpretation No. 3 and discussed in Chapter 6, should be reflected in auditing procedures, and, second, the potentially significant impact on a company's financial statements of noncompliance with ERISA requires that additional audit procedures be considered.

This chapter summarizes the principles of basic audit procedures and adaptations needed therein to allow for the effects of ERISA. Detailed auditing procedures related to pension costs are set forth in a specimen audit program shown in Appendix A.

BASIC OBJECTIVES AND AUDIT PROCEDURES

The audit of pension costs entails obtaining pertinent information regarding a company's pension plan as a basis for reaching a conclusion that the pension expense reported, when considered in relation to the financial statements taken as a whole, is stated in conformity with generally accepted accounting principles consistently applied, and that the appropriate related disclosures are made.

The materiality of pension costs, and the materiality of any possible understatement or overstatement of such costs upon the fairness of presentation of the financial statements, should influence the selection of audit procedures and the extent and depth of the examination, just as materiality is considered in any other audit procedure.

Some of the information needed by the auditor can be obtained from the actuary's report, some is in the company's records, and some may be obtained by direct correspondence with (or through a supplementary report from) the actuary. Items of information related to pension plans which may be needed by the auditor are summarized in Figure 7–1. This listing is furnished only for guidance and its inclusion herein should not be construed as a conclusion that all the items listed are needed in every case or, conversely, that in some cases additional information should not be sought.

Audit procedures employed to substantiate pension costs must be selected to meet the requirements of particular circumstances. The selection of appropriate audit procedures is a matter of judgment to be applied to the facts of a particular situation. Procedures would normally include the following:

- Inquiry into the existence of pension plans or a practice of paying pensions which may constitute a plan under Opinion No. 8 and ERISA (applies to all subsidiaries and divisions—foreign and domestic).
- Comparison of data relating to pension costs and information disclosed in the financial statements to prior year's data for comparability.
- Review of the actuary's report and related information, and audit-

FIGURE 7-1

Information That May Be Needed for the Audit of Pension Costs of Employer Companies

I. GENERAL

1. Name of the plan.
2. Whether the plan is voluntary or negotiated.
3. Whether the plan is contributory.
4. Eligibility requirements.
5. Basis for determining benefit payments under the plan.
6. When employees are entitled to receive benefits, i.e., normal retirement age, early retirement provisions, etc.
7. Vesting rights provided under the plan.
8. Custodian or trustee of the plan assets.
9. Tax qualification status of the plan.
10. Qualifications of the actuary.

II. ACCOUNTING AND FUNDING POLICIES

1. Actuarial cost method used.
2. Basis of providing for prior service cost.
3. Actuarial assumptions.
4. Basis for recognizing unrealized appreciation and depreciation.
5. Method of dealing with actuarial gains and losses.

III. ACTUARIAL VALUATIONS

1. Date as of which valuations are made.
2. Frequency of valuations.
3. Basis on which plan assets are stated.

4. Employee data on which the actuarial determinations are based.

IV. CURRENT YEAR'S TRANSACTIONS

1. Amount of the charge to expense, broken down by normal cost, amortization of prior service cost, provision for actuarial gains and losses, and interest equivalents.
2. Funding contribution, broken down by normal cost, amortization of prior service cost, amortization of actuarial gains and losses, interest equivalents, and other details of the funding standard account and alternative minimum funding standard account.
3. Changes during the year in actuarial cost methods or actuarial assumptions for accounting and funding purposes.
4. Amount of employees' contributions.
5. Value of unfunded prior service cost at beginning and end of the year.
6. Value of unfunded vested benefits at beginning and end of the year.
7. Amount of actuarial gains and losses arising during the year.

ing of data used by the actuary in his calculations, as described in the following section.

Determination that the provision for pension costs is within the limits established by APB Opinion No. 8.

Each pension plan that has a separate accountability under APB Opinion No. 8 should be considered independently in the audit of pension costs.

Auditing Actuarial Information

The Role of the Actuary.   The actuary's role, which expanded with the issuance of APB Opinion No. 8, has now been further expanded by the enactment of ERISA. In making the calculations needed to determine the amounts required for financial statement purposes, he needs to work closely with his client's accountant; he may be called upon to make determinations in addition to those which have customarily been included in actuarial reports, such as those called for in FASB Interpretation No. 3.

Suggested Audit Procedures.   In considering the determinations made by the actuary in relation to the financial statements, the auditor needs to obtain and review sufficient competent evidential matter, normally by reviewing the actuary's report. (If the auditor believes that he does not have sufficient technical competence to do so, he should obtain the services of a qualified professional, such as an actuary, to assist with the review.)

Before reviewing the actuary's report, most auditors will seek to satisfy themselves as to the actuary's qualifications, which can usually be done by determining that the actuary is a member of a recognized professional actuarial society (e.g., a Fellow of the Society of Actuaries or a member of the American Academy of Actuaries) or by obtaining competent professional advice on the actuary's qualifications from an actuary known by the auditor to be qualified.

The auditor will need to work closely with the actuary and consult with him when report items require clarification or explanation. The necessity for such consultation may be substantially reduced by making advance arrangements with the actuary to ascertain that the actuary's report will contain all the information required by the auditor. It might also be helpful, and appropriate, for the auditor to advise the actuary of changes in conditions about which he knows and which he believes would affect the actuary's determinations.

In considering the reasonableness of the actuarially determined information, the auditor may find the procedures summarized in Figure 7–2 to be appropriate. In following those procedures, the auditor should not expect to rely upon an actuary's conclusion as to the conformity of actuarially computed amounts with generally accepted accounting principles. Such a conclusion requires a skilled and experience-based knowledge of accounting principles, including the concept of materiality. Conversely, the auditor should refrain from making actuarial judgments.

FIGURE 7–2

Suggested Audit Procedures for Examining Actuarially Determined Information

(a) Determine that the actuary is familiar with the current terms of the pension plan and that he has accorded such terms proper recognition in his calculations. This may be accomplished by reviewing the actuary's report or by contacting the actuary directly.

(b) Review and test the employee data given to the actuary, on which the actuarial calculations are based. [Procedures outlined in (k) through (o) of Figure 9–1 should be used as a guide.]

(c) Determine that the actuarial cost method used by the actuary is appropriate and whether it is the same method as was used in the prior period.

(d) Determine that the actuarial assumptions used give due consideration to all pertinent factors and appear reasonable on an overall basis, including determi-

nation that the basis for the investment return and other assumptions appears reasonable in relation to actual experience.

(e) Determine that the value of pension fund assets used in actuarial calculations appears reasonable.

(f) Determine that the effect of any changes in actuarial methods and assumptions has been disclosed.

(g) Review the period from the date of the actuarial valuation to the fiscal year end (and beyond, to the extent known) to see whether any significant events have occurred which would materially affect amounts reflected in the financial statements (e.g., plant closings, changes in plan, changes in market value of equity securities). If such events have occurred, consult with the actuary and obtain an estimate of the dollar effect on such amounts.

Confirmation from Actuaries. The authors do not consider it generally necessary to obtain from actuaries direct confirmation of information already in reports they have prepared and which have been submitted to the client. It may, however, be desirable under certain circumstances for the auditor to request the actuary to confirm the date of the most recent actuarial valuation made by him. And, as indicated in procedure (b) of Figure 7–2, where employee data used by the actuary in his calculations are not summarized in the actuary's report, such data should be confirmed directly with him.

Insured Plans

In the examination of insured pension plans (other than deposit administration type contracts, which are similar to uninsured pension plans), the auditor should obtain the applicable information listed in Figure 7–1. The audit procedures will vary substantially, however, from those discussed earlier in this chapter.

Normally the insurance company's procedures in calculating premium charges will meet the requirements of APB Opinion No. 8 for determining normal cost. Similarly, the insurance company's procedures for arriving at dividends are normally satisfactory to meet the requirements of the Opinion for accounting for investment gains. However, consideration should be given to spreading or averaging termination credits in accounting for gains related to turnover. In addition, consideration should be given to providing for the cost related to employees expected to become covered under the pension plan where a mandatory waiting period has excluded employees from participation.

Auditing procedures normally involve examination of insurance company premium statements, review of amounts of dividends and termination credits in relation to those of prior years, and determination as to whether any provision is needed for employees expected to become covered under the plan. Although such procedures would appear to give an auditor reasonable satisfaction that the provision for pension costs complies with paragraph 41 of Opinion No. 8, the enactment of ERISA and the time lapse since Opinion No. 8 was issued may give auditors reason to re-evaluate such procedures and determine whether they are still sufficient. Auditors might now give consideration as to whether it would also be appropriate, for example, to review the method used by the insurance company in making its premium, dividend, and related calculations.

AUDIT PROCEDURES DIRECTLY RELATED TO ERISA

While basic audit procedures will continue to follow past practice, some aspects of ERISA introduce requirements which will normally necessitate additional procedures, depending generally upon materiality of items affected by the law. As in other areas, however, materiality is not the sole consideration. For example, while the materiality of penalties is an important factor in ascertaining that the client is in compliance with ERISA, the auditor should nevertheless be alert to instances of noncompliance so as to be in a position to advise clients of a need to consider taking corrective action.

The auditor is concerned principally with the accounting-related impact of ERISA and various aspects of compliance with ERISA.

Accounting-Related Impact

Recorded Liability. As indicated in Chapter 6 (pages 101–2), a company should record as a liability the pension cost amount required to be funded to date under the law. The auditor should verify, by reference to the actuary's report, that the appropriate liability has been recorded.

Potential Plan Termination. Because of liabilities that may be involved in a plan termination, the auditor should be alert, in reading minutes of meetings of the company's board of directors and pertinent committees and in performing other audit procedures, to any evidence of a potential pension plan termination. In addition, the auditor may wish to inquire of management as to the possibility of a plan termination. Where a plan termination is more than a remote possibility, the auditor should ensure that the financial statements contain appropriate entries or disclosures as described in Chapter 6 (pages 102–3).

Minimum Provision. While the authors believe it would be appropriate for the minimum provision for pension cost to parallel the minimum amount to be funded under the law (see Chapter 6, pages 103–5), a provision consistent with the minimum amount set forth in APB Opinion No. 8 is considered to be in accordance with generally accepted accounting principles. The auditor should determine, as he has in the past, whether the provision is in accordance with the principles set forth in APB Opinion No. 8. Where the provision is based on the minimum required under APB Opinion No. 8, the auditor may recommend that the client make appropriate modification so that the provision is consistent with the minimum amount required to be funded under ERISA, but the auditor should take no further action if the recommendation is rejected.

Disclosure. As indicated under "Disclosures" in Chapter 6 (pages 105–6), additional financial statement disclosures with regard to pension costs may be required under FASB Interpretation No. 3, such as the future effect (estimated where practicable) that compliance with ERISA will (or may) have on the provision for pension expense, on the funding of pension cost, and on unfunded vested benefits.

Because some or all of such amounts may be difficult to determine, the auditor should work closely with the client and the client's actuary to attempt to resolve difficulties on a timely basis. The auditor should ascertain whether the client has arrived at decisions on plan amendments, and whether the actuary will be in a position to determine the financial impact of those planned amendments in time for inclusion in the footnotes to the financial statements. Where required disclosures are not made, the auditor should be guided by the discussion under "Departures from the Opinion and Interpretation," later in this chapter.

Compliance With ERISA

Audit considerations related to determining whether a client is in compliance with ERISA fall into five main categories: (1) compliance of individual plan provisions with ERISA, (2) funding, (3) reporting and disclosure, (4) fiduciary responsibilities, and (5) record keeping. The following discussion includes for each category a description of the requirements and the penalties involved, including cross-references for further details, and suggested audit procedures to test compliance. Audit procedures of course need not be performed with respect to a particular ERISA requirement until the plan becomes subject to that requirement. The effective dates are outlined in Chapters 4 and 5.

It is suggested that, in addition to the procedures described herein, the auditor obtain a representation from the client (in the letter of representation) that the client is in compliance with ERISA.

Compliance of Individual Plan Provisions With ERISA. In order to conform to ERISA, plans may have to be amended in one or more areas, including participation, vesting, limits on benefits and contributions, back-loaded benefits, and joint and survivor annuities. (Requirements for each are described under the same captions in Chapter 4.)

The auditor's concern with whether individual plan provisions comply with ERISA is based generally on the potential impact that noncompliance may have on the financial statements of the employer. This impact may be in the form of (1) an understatement of the provision for pension cost and of related actuarial disclosures (e.g., unfunded, unprovided-for vested benefits); if, for example, the plan did not cover all employees required by ERISA to participate in the plan, the provision for pension cost and other actuarially calculated amounts would likely be understated; and (2) penalties (as discussed in Chapter 4) which may need to be reflected in the financial statements.

Where a plan's noncompliance with ERISA could have a material effect on the financial statements, as described in (1) and/or (2) above, the auditor should take appropriate steps to determine whether the plan is in compliance. The auditor might give consideration to checking for plan compliance with ERISA as a service to his client where noncompliance would be immaterial for financial statement purposes but nevertheless significant from his client's viewpoint.

The auditor can normally satisfy himself that the provisions of the pension plan comply with ERISA in one of two ways. First, the auditor can determine that the plan is a qualified plan under provisions of the Internal Revenue Code. Because the Internal Revenue Code has been modified by ERISA to be virtually identical to the participation, vesting, and other provisions of ERISA described above, by establishing that the plan is qualified under the Code the auditor is able to conclude that the plan complies with the provisions of ERISA. The auditor may normally gain reasonable satisfaction that a plan is qualified by examining a tax qualification letter, where such a letter has been issued by the Internal Revenue Service covering the current plan provisions. It should be noted in this connection that the Service may not be able (or willing) to issue a tax qualification letter for many plans for one or more years after ERISA's provisions become effective and, even if a letter is issued, it may contain comments and caveats with respect to a determination that the plan is qualified. Accordingly, the auditor may, in the early years of ERISA's effectiveness, be unable to examine a tax qualification letter and, where he is able to, he must read it carefully.

The second way in which the auditor can satisfy himself that the provisions of the pension plan comply with ERISA is to obtain a letter from the client's lawyer stating that the plan complies with ERISA.

The procedures discussed in the preceding paragraphs would be appropriate for the first year in which a plan is subject to ERISA. If there are no plan amendments thereafter, theoretically little or no additional work related to plan compliance would be required in subsequent years. In practice, however, a tax qualification letter or other evidence of plan compliance normally carries less weight with the passage of time, inasmuch as the Internal Revenue Service is concerned not only with the plan provisions themselves but also with the manner in which the plan operates in accordance with those provisions. Therefore, the auditor, in subsequent years, should be alert to changes in the manner in which plan provisions are applied.

Any findings relating to potential penalties which may need to be reflected in the financial statements, pursuant to the audit procedures described in this or the following sections of this chapter, should preferably be discussed with the client's legal counsel.

Funding. The funding requirements of ERISA and penalties which may be imposed for failure to comply therewith are summarized under "Funding" in Chapter 4. The auditor should satisfy himself that the funding provisions of ERISA have been complied with. This would likely include reviewing the entries in the funding standard account and the alternative minimum funding standard account, if applicable, agreeing entries to the actuary's report, cash disbursements records, etc. Where the alternative minimum funding standard is used, the auditor should satisfy himself that its use is permitted.

Reporting and Disclosure. The reporting and disclosure requirements of ERISA and penalties which may be imposed for failure to comply therewith are described in Chapter 5.

The auditor should ascertain that a plan description and summary plan description (and amendments thereto) have been properly filed with the Secretary of Labor and furnished to participants and beneficiaries as required.

The auditor should also ascertain that the required pension fund financial statements (containing the appropriate disclosures), schedules, opinion of the qualified accountant, and actuary's report (where appropriate) have been filed with the Secretary of Labor, and that the summary of the annual report and required schedules have been furnished to participants and beneficiaries. Because of the fact that during the first plan year covered by ERISA's requirements the auditor will likely express an opinion on the employer company's financial statements well before the date on which the fund's financial statements are to be filed, the auditor will probably not be in a position, when auditing the employer's financial statements, to ascertain that the appropriate pension fund financial statements are filed. In the following years, however, the auditor will be able to determine whether the prior year's financial statements were filed.

Unless the auditor is engaged to express an opinion on the fund's financial statements and supporting information (in which case he should refer to Chapters 8–10), he should generally confine his review of fund information to a reading of the financial statements, schedules, accountant's opinion, and actuary's report.

The auditor should determine from the client the volume of requests by plan participants or beneficiaries for plan information. Where large numbers of requests have been received, the auditor should consider reviewing the client's procedures for controlling and processing such requests and review open files or logs for long outstanding items.

Fiduciary Responsibilities. The auditor should determine whether the employer company is, as will often be the case, considered to be a fiduciary (as well as a party in interest) under the law, in which case he will need to apply audit procedures related to fiduciary responsibilities established by ERISA. Where the employer company is considered to be only a party in interest, the auditor may confine his review to transactions prohibited with a party in interest. Fiduciary responsibilities and related penalties which may be imposed for failure to comply are summarized in Chapter 4.

While the auditor should inquire as to the occurrence of any prohibited transactions, and should be alert for them during the course of the audit, few additional audit procedures for prohibited transactions should be needed because the auditor's normal audit work should familiarize him with significant transactions which might be prohibited under the law.

Record Keeping. ERISA requires employers to maintain such records as are sufficient to determine the benefits which are due, or may become due, to each employee (see Chapter 4). In most cases, such records must include data such as age, length of service, hours worked, salary, employee contributions, vesting percentage, etc. In multi-employer plans the necessary information is to be furnished by the employers to the plan administrator who is to maintain such records.

The auditor should ascertain that the record-keeping requirements of ERISA are met (noncompliance penalties are also described in Chapter 4). The auditor's regular audit work, particularly his review and testing of the client's payroll system, should normally enable him to make such a determination.

REPORTING CONSIDERATIONS

In expressing an opinion on a company's financial statements, the auditor needs to be concerned about comparability and consistency and about conformity with APB Opinion No. 8 and FASB Interpretation No. 3.

Comparability and Consistency

The comparability of financial statements is affected by material changes in charges to pension expense which do not result from changes in volume of operations. Such material changes may result from either changes in accounting principles or methods which thus require a comment as to consistency in the auditor's report, or changes in conditions which, while requiring disclosure, would not need to be commented upon in the auditor's report [other than in reports accompanying financial statements to be filed with the Securities and Exchange Commission—see note to section 420.12 of the AICPA's Statement on Auditing Standards (SAS) No. 1].

Examples of material changes in pension expense which call for a comment as to consistency because they stem from a choice by management from among two or more accounting methods include:

- Adoption of a different actuarial cost method for pension costs, e.g., changing from the accrued benefit to a level cost method.
- A change in period of amortization of prior service cost.
- A change in the method of accounting for actuarial gains or losses and unrealized appreciation or depreciation, e.g., from spreading to averaging or vice versa.
- A change in the method of valuing the pension fund, as for example, changing from a valuation equal to 90% of market value to 75% of market value or vice versa, without a change in circumstances.

Examples of changes which do not involve consistency of accounting since they stem from altered conditions include:

- Changes in actuarial assumptions based on historical experience under a plan or current or prospective changes in employment conditions.
- Adoption of a new plan or an amendment to an existing pension plan.

Material changes in charges to pension expense from such causes should be disclosed. If such a change has not materially affected the year's pension expense but will materially affect future years' expense, the nature of the change should be disclosed, with some indication of the effect, if determinable.

Although a company may adopt either a "minimum" or a "maximum" basis of determining pension expense under APB Opinion No. 8 (as discussed in Chapter 6), any changes in the basis or method selected involves a change in accounting. All changes in methods of accounting for pension costs, whether to comply with the provisions of APB Opinion No. 8 or for other reasons, should be dealt with prospectively (see paragraphs 47 and 49 of the Opinion).

Departures from the Opinion and Interpretation

Departures from APB Opinion No. 8 in determining pension expense constitute departures from generally accepted accounting principles and, if they have a material effect upon the financial statements, should be dealt with as called for in paragraphs 15 through 18 of the AICPA's Statement on Auditing Standards (SAS) No. 2.

Examples of departures, other than as to disclosure requirements, from APB Opinion No. 8 which, if material, may require qualification in the auditor's report are:

- Use of terminal funding or pay-as-you-go basis of accounting.
- Failure to recognize appropriately actuarial gains or losses and unrealized appreciation or depreciation.
- Use of a method which results in a provision for pension cost which does not fall within the specified minimum and maximum limits.

Failure to observe the disclosure requirements of APB Opinion No. 8 and of FASB Interpretation No. 3 also constitutes a departure from generally accepted accounting principles where pension costs or the related information are significant. If a client is unwilling to observe the aforementioned disclosure requirements and the amount of pension costs, properly computed, is material in relation to income before extraordinary items or to net income, the auditor should consider whether a qualified opinion is necessary. Qualification of the auditor's opinion with regard to nondisclosure of required pension information should be dealt with as recommended in section 545 of the AICPA's Statement on Auditing Standards (SAS) No. 1.

As stated in Chapter 6, APB Opinion No. 8 regards as acceptable the determination of pension accruals within relatively broad limits, and allows for the choice of a number of actuarial cost methods, each of which, in turn, involves a number of actuarial assumptions. Thus, careful consideration and experienced judgment are required to determine whether a particular factor which appears to be at variance with the provisions of APB Opinion No. 8 results (when considered in relation to the overall effect of all pertinent factors) in pension expense being stated at an amount which materially departs from that which is acceptable under the Opinion.

PART III

Pension Fund Accounting, Auditing, and Financial Reporting

8

APPLICATION OF GENERALLY ACCEPTED ACCOUNTING PRINCIPLES

Accounting principles and financial reporting presentations applicable to other entities can generally be applied to pension funds, subject to adjustments and adaptations for characteristics peculiar to their nature and purpose. But because pension fund financial statements have heretofore not commonly been issued to the public, the nature of such adjustments and adaptations may be subject to some initial uncertainties and differences of opinion, and perhaps to a somewhat wider range of options than may ultimately evolve.

This chapter describes how generally accepted accounting principles and financial reporting apply to pension funds, and describes alternatives where options exist.

METHODS OF ACCOUNTING

Although many pension funds maintain their accounts on a cash basis or modified cash basis, and some funds have issued cash basis financial statements, generally accepted accounting principles call for financial reporting under the accrual method of accounting. The omission of significant assets and liabilities under cash basis reporting could have a material effect on the fund's financial position and on changes in net assets available for plan benefits.

Accordingly, where such omission would have a material effect on their financial statements, funds will need either to change to the accrual method of accounting or to develop procedures for adapting cash basis accounts to the accrual method so that users of their financial statements will be able to determine the fund's financial position and changes in net assets.

Accounting Changes

Some accountants believe that changing from the cash basis to the accrual method of accounting for financial reporting constitutes a change in accounting principle as discussed in paragraphs 7 to 9 of APB Opinion No. 20, while others believe that a change from the cash basis to the accrual method constitutes a correction of an error as discussed in paragraph 13 of APB Opinion No. 20. Under either premise, it appears that, in order for annual financial statements to be most meaningful and useful, such a change having a material effect thereon should be accounted for by restating prior-period financial statements.

Under the premise that a change from the cash basis to the accrual method of accounting is a change in accounting principle, it might appear that restatement of prior-period financial statements is prohibited under APB Opinion No. 20, paragraph 19. Paragraph 4 of the Opinion, however, allows an exception to its general prohibition, as follows: "An industry audit guide prepared by a committee of the AICPA may also prescribe the manner of reporting a change in accounting principles. Accordingly, the provisions of this Opinion do not apply to changes made in conformity with such pronouncements issued in the past or in the future." Under this provision, retroactively applying the accrual method of accounting and restating a pension fund's financial statements of prior periods which are presented (as described in paragraphs 27 and 28 of APB Opinion No. 20) seem appropriate because of similar requirements included in AICPA Industry Audit Guides, "Audits of Employee Health and Welfare Benefit Funds," issued February 1972 and "Audits of Pension Funds," exposure draft issued March 1973, both of which cover similar situations.

Under the premise that changing from the cash basis to the accrual method constitutes a correction of an error, treatment of the change as a prior-period restatement is in accordance with paragraph 36 of APB Opinion No. 20, which states that correction of an error should be reported as a prior-period adjustment in the manner described in paragraph 18 of APB Opinion No. 9.

Difficulties may arise in determining the appropriate value of assets and liabilities on an accrual basis where accounts were previously maintained on the cash basis. The lack of precision, however, should not normally be a problem because reasonable estimates can usually be made. It must be recognized, of course, that in some situations the fund's records may not be adequate for forming reasonable estimates of accrued assets and liabilities, in which case the independent auditor may be precluded from expressing an unqualified opinion.

When the sponsoring employer company changes its actuarial cost method or actuarial assumptions, a corresponding change will normally be made on the part of the fund. In accordance with APB Opinion No. 8, the employer company will account for the effect of such changes prospectively, and it would seem to be appropriate for the fund to adopt the same method of accounting for the change. Footnotes to the fund's financial statements should disclose the effects of such changes on contributions, present value of vested benefits, and actuarially determined prior service cost.

FUND ASSETS

Principal pension fund assets are contributions receivable and investments (held directly or through a bank or an insurance company); the following sections discuss their treatment under generally accepted accounting principles.

Contributions Receivable

Contributions receivable from employers (and employees, where applicable) should be included in the Statement of Net Assets Available for Plan Benefits in the total amount which may reasonably be expected to be contributed to the fund with respect to the year being reported upon. Due consideration should be given to collectibility.

Multi-Employer Funds. Since each employer in a multi-employer plan is ordinarily obligated to contribute monthly for work performed by all of its participant employees in the preceding month, the fund normally receives contributions the month after they accrue. In funds with a large number of contributing employers, the determination of contributions receivable at any month end may have to depend upon estimates.

At the statement date, an estimate may be based primarily on contributions received by the fund during the year and in the subsequent month or months, adjusted to allow for contributions known to be delinquent, for any related penalties (if collectible), and for amounts deemed to be uncollectible.

In addition, for defined benefit plans, the receivable reported should be consistent with information in the actuary's report and it normally should be not less than the minimum amounts required to be funded under the provisions of ERISA.

Single-Employer Funds. Determining the amount of contributions receivable to be included in the Statement of Net Assets Available for Plan Benefits of a single-employer pension fund for a given fiscal year requires consideration of the following:

- Contributions authorized for the year by the employer's management and/or board of directors;
- Contributions actually received by the fund during the year;
- Amount of the employer's legal obligation to the fund for the year, which is generally not less than the minimum amount required to be funded under the provisions of ERISA, and which will usually be reflected in the memorandum funding standard account(s); and
- Information in the actuary's report relating to the above items.

Investments

Since investments are in virtually all instances a pension fund's largest asset, their valuation is particularly important. Present practice indicates that pension funds currently use any one of the following methods, each of which is considered to be in conformity with generally accepted accounting principles: (1) cost,* (2) equity securities at fair value ** and bonds at cost, (3) fair value, and (4) methods which include a portion of the appreciation or depreciation in the carrying amount of the investments under formulas which avoid giving undue weight to short-term market fluctuations.†

In theory, the differences among acceptable valuation methods could result in substantial differences in asset value, e.g., between cost and fair value in a fund with substantial unrealized appreciation or depreciation. In practice, however, parenthetic or footnote disclosure of cost where fair value has been used—and of fair value where cost or a method which recognizes appreciation or depreciation over a period of time has been used—usually gives the financial statement user additional information with which to assess the fund's status and performance.

Where investments are valued at cost, and fair value is substantially lower than cost, consideration should be given to whether the securities should be written down to their fair values. In making such determination, the fund's management can be guided by the considerations outlined in the AICPA's Auditing Interpretation on "Evidential matter for the carrying amount of marketable securities" issued in early 1975.

Differences of viewpoint on valuation methods within the ac-

---

* The term "cost" when applied to bonds generally means original cost plus or minus amortized discount or premium.

** The terms "market value," "fair market value," "current market value," and "fair value" are often used interchangeably, as can be seen by the terminology used in quoted material contained herein. Some accountants restrict use of the terms market value, fair market value, and current market value to the value of investments regularly traded on a securities market (where market quotations are readily available), and the term fair value to investments not regularly traded on a securities market and thus valued in good faith by the fund's board of trustees or administrative committee. For convenience, however, the term fair value is used in this chapter as an all-inclusive term covering both of the above.

† Some accountants would apply this method to equity investments, valuing bonds to be held to maturity at cost.

counting profession are reflected in positions taken in AICPA Industry Audit Guides:

- "Audits of Employee Health and Welfare Benefit Funds," issued February 1972, requires that investments be carried at cost, but then states: "The accounting for marketable securities not having a fixed maturity date is currently under study by the Accounting Principles Board. Any future APB announcements on this subject may be applicable to investments of employee health and welfare benefit funds."
- "Audits of Colleges and Universities," issued May 1973, states that investments purchased are usually reported in the financial statements at cost, but that, as a permissible alternative, they ". . . may be reported . . . at current market value or fair value, provided this basis is used for all investments of all funds."
- "Audits of Voluntary Health and Welfare Organizations," issued September 1973, states: "Although presently the prevalent basis of valuation is cost, the carrying of investments at market value is also deemed acceptable . . . pending further study and the issuance of an authoritative pronouncement by the Financial Accounting Standards Board."

The AICPA has been studying the problems of pension fund accounting for many years, and in draft position papers issued in December 1973 and November 1974, The Institute's Health, Welfare and Pension Fund Task Force and its predecessor committee favored the use of fair value as the standard for valuing fund investments. In its November 1974 position paper, the Task Force observed:

> While the presentation of investments at their market value is not without limitations, it is the Committee's view that this method is the most meaningful and is preferable to other methods.
> Cost is irrelevant to the presentation of financial position of a pension fund. Investment cost has no bearing upon the fund's ability to provide for the payment of pension benefits either at the balance sheet date or in the future.

The phrase "the fund's ability to provide for the payment of pension benefits" is the key to the Task Force position. Noting that the financial statements of pension funds differ fundamentally from those of a business enterprise, the position paper defines the purpose of pension funds as, not to make profits, but rather "to provide the resources from which retirement and other benefits can be paid." Accordingly, the primary concern for the users of a fund's financial statements is "the relationship of the net assets of the fund to the present value of vested benefits and the actuarially determined prior service cost."

In proposing that investments be carried at fair value, the position paper observes: "Most of this committee favors a recommendation of the use of fair value in the financial statements. Nevertheless, some of the members of the committee believe that the matter cannot be so simply dealt with and further study of an alternative valuation method is especially warranted in this case, particularly in view of the long-term nature of pension funds." A minority report expresses preference for use of a method in which (1) fixed income investments are valued at cost and realized gains and losses are averaged or spread and (2) equity investments are valued at cost adjusted by a systematic recognition of unrealized gains and losses.

The use of a method which recognizes appreciation or depreciation over a period of time seems to be particularly well suited to defined benefit pension plans, in that such a method of investment valuation (1) fosters consistency with the valuation method used in the determination of the employer company's pension contribution, and (2) reflects the economic substance of events from the viewpoint of participants and beneficiaries. This latter point is illustrated by a situation where a fund has experienced significant appreciation. In such a case it might be misleading to carry investments at the appreciated value because, assuming a "going concern," the gains accrue not to the benefit of plan participants and beneficiaries but rather to the employer company through a reduced level of future contributions.

On the other hand, following this line of reasoning, it would be more appropriate to value investments of a defined contribution plan at fair value since the gains or losses would not affect future contributions but would affect the level of future benefit payments.

Determining Fair Value. The fair value of investments normally must be determined, either to establish the carrying amount of investments or for disclosure purposes. The relative difficulty in determining fair value depends upon the nature of investments held. For traded securities, published market price can be used as the basis for the determination. The closing price on the statement date will usually be the fair value unless the security was not traded that day, in which case the price will be either the appropriate closing bid or the average of bid and asked prices. Where a fund's investments include restricted securities which cannot be offered to the public without first being registered, the board of trustees or the administrative committee must give appropriate consideration to the effect of the restriction in determining the fair value of the restricted securities. In the case of other investments without a readily determinable value, such as real estate or securities of closely held corporations, various special procedures may be required to determine fair value, including, where the circumstances warrant, obtaining the opinion of independent experts qualified to make such valuations.

For considering fair value determinations, the AICPA's Industry Audit Guide, "Audits of Investment Companies," excerpted in Figure 8–1, may be found useful.

Effective Date of Transactions. In order to prepare financial statements on the accrual basis, purchases and sales of securities should be reflected on a trade-date basis. Thus, where the fund's books are maintained on a settlement-date basis, the accounts should be adjusted to a trade-date basis to reflect year-end transactions unless the effect of such adjustment would not be material to the financial statements taken as a whole.

Similarly, dividend income should be recorded on the ex-dividend date, rather than on the record or payment date. Income from other investments, such as interest and rent, should be recorded as earned and appropriate accruals made. Income from investments should be disclosed under a separate caption (such as "Interest and Dividend Income") in the Statement of Changes in Net Assets Available for Plan Benefits.

Disposition of Securities. For determining cost of securities sold, any consistent method should be acceptable, such as the following: (1) average, (2) identified (e.g., specific blocks of stocks at their actual cost), (3) first-in, first-out, or (4) last-in, first-out. Where the cost is determined on other than the average cost basis, however, the fund should preferably disclose in a note, if practicable, what gain or loss would have resulted if average cost had been used.

Statement Presentation. Because investments are normally the largest and most important asset, it is suggested that investments

FIGURE 8-1

Recommendations for Valuing Securities, as Stated in AICPA Industry Audit Guide "Audits of Investment Companies"

Securities Traded on a National Securities Exchange. Ordinarily, little difficulty should be experienced in valuing securities listed or traded on one or more security exchanges, since quotations of completed transactions are published daily. If a security was traded on the valuation date, the last quoted sales price generally is used. In the case of securities listed on more than one national securities exchange, the last quoted sales price up to the time of valuation on the exchange on which the security is principally traded should be used or, if there were no sales on that exchange on the valuation date, the last quoted sale price up to the time of valuation on the other exchanges should be substituted. Registered companies value their portfolio at the time of the close of trading on the New York Stock Exchange.*

If there were no sales on the valuation date but published closing bid and asked prices are available, the valuation in such circumstances should be within the range of these quoted prices. Some companies, as a matter of general policy, use the bid price, others use the mean of the bid and asked prices, and still others use a valuation within the range considered best to represent

value in the circumstances. Each of these policies is considered to be acceptable if consistently applied. Normally, it is not considered to be acceptable to use the asked price alone. Where, on the valuation date, only a bid price or an asked price is quoted or the spread between bid and asked price is substantial, quotations for several days should be reviewed. If sales have been infrequent or there is a thin market in the security, further consideration should be given to whether "market quotations are readily available" as a practical matter. If it is decided that they are not readily available, the alternative method of valuation, i.e., "fair value as determined in good faith by the board of directors" should be used.

Over-the-Counter Securities. Quotations are available from various sources for most unlisted securities traded regularly in the over-the-counter market. These sources include tabulations in the financial press, various quotation publications and financial reporting services, and individual broker/dealers. A company may adopt a policy of using a mean of the bid prices, or of the bid and asked prices, or of the prices of a representative selection of broker/dealers quoting on a particular security; or it

* Rule 22c-1(b) of the 1940 Act.

FIGURE 8–1

Continued

may use a valuation within the range of bid and asked prices considered best to represent value in the circumstances. Any one of these policies is considered to be acceptable if consistently applied. Normally, the use of the asked prices alone is not acceptable.

Ordinarily, quotations for an over-the-counter security should be obtained from more than one broker/dealer unless available from an established market-maker for that security, and quotations for several days should be reviewed. In all cases, the quotations should be from unaffiliated persons. NASDAQ may be the most convenient source of such quotations. Where quotations appear questionable, consideration should be given to valuing the security at "fair value as determined in good faith by the board of directors."

United States Treasury bonds and notes usually bear longer term maturities than those classified under "Short-Term Investments" below and are often purchased, at least partially, for their capital appreciation potential. Such securities are valued at quoted market.

Securities Valued "In Good Faith." It is incumbent upon the board of directors to satisfy themselves that all appropriate factors relevant to the value of securities for which market quotations are not readily available have been considered and to determine the method of arriving at the fair value of each such security. To the extent considered necessary, the board may appoint persons to assist it in the determination of such value, and to make the actual calculations pursuant to the board's direction. Consistent with this responsibility, the board also must review continuously the appropriateness of the method used in valuing each issue of securities in the company's portfolio. The directors must recognize their responsibilities in this matter and whenever technical assistance is requested from individuals who are not directors, the findings of such individuals must be carefully reviewed by the directors in order to satisfy themselves that the resulting valuations are fair.

As Accounting Series Release No. 118 states, no single standard for determining fair value in good faith can be laid down, since fair value depends upon the circumstances of each individual case. As a general principle, the current "fair value" of an issue of securities being valued by the board of directors would appear to be the amount which the owner might reasonably expect to receive from them upon their current sale, although there usually is no intention to make a current sale. Current sale should be interpreted to mean realization in an orderly disposition over a reasonable period of time. Methods which

FIGURE 8–1

Continued

are in accord with this principle may, for example, be based on a multiple of earnings, or a discount (or less frequently a premium) from market of a similar, freely traded security, or a yield to maturity with respect to debt issues, or a combination of these and other methods. Some of the general factors which the directors should consider in determining a valuation method for an individual issue of securities include (1) the fundamental analytical data relating to the investment; (2) the nature and duration of restrictions on disposition of the securities; and (3) an evaluation of the forces which influence the market in which these securities are purchased and sold. In the case of investments made in several securities of the same issuer, such as those made by many SBICs and venture capital companies, the valuation of the "package" as a whole may be appropriate. Among the more specific factors which must be considered are the type of security (debt or equity), financial standing of the issuer, availability of current financial statements, cost at date of purchase, size and period of holding, discount from market value of un-

restricted securities of the same class at the time of purchase, special reports prepared by analysts, information as to any transactions or offers with respect to the security, existence of merger proposals or tender offers affecting the securities, reported prices and extent of public trading in similar securities of the issuer or comparable companies, maintenance of investee's business and financial plan, use of new funds to achieve planned results, changes in economic conditions including those in the company or industry, and other relevant matters.* This guide does not purport to delineate all factors which may be considered. The directors should take into consideration all indications of value available to them in determining the "fair value" assigned to a particular security. The information so considered and, insofar as practicable, the basis for the board's decision, should be documented in the minutes of the directors' meeting and the supporting data retained for the inspection of the company's independent auditor.

* Accounting Series Release Nos. 113 and 118.

be the first asset presented in the Statement of Net Assets Available for Plan Benefits. Practice indicates, however, that investments may instead be presented after cash and receivables.

Other Financial Statement Disclosures. Other investment-related disclosures normally needed by financial statement users include the following:

- Fair value (and methods used by the fund's administrative committee or board of trustees to determine fair value) and cost of any restricted securities and other investments without a readily determinable market value.
- The carrying value, and cost or fair value, as appropriate, of major classes of fund investments, such as U. S. Government securities, commercial paper, common stocks, mortgages, real estate, plus the aggregate principal amount (face amount) of long-term investments with fixed maturities.
- Where investments are carried at a value determined under a method which recognizes appreciation or depreciation over a period of time, a description of the manner in which gains and losses are being recognized; where investments of a defined benefit plan are carried at a value determined under another method, i.e., cost or fair value, an explanation that appreciation serves to reduce future contributions that would otherwise be required to provide for the defined level of benefits.
- Other pertinent matters, such as amounts of investments in employer securities or real estate leased to the employer or other related groups when material in relation to the fund's assets. ("Employer" as used here includes parents, subsidiaries, and other entities under common control.)

Assets Held by Insurance Companies

Where a plan's benefits are funded through insurance companies, the related assets should be excluded from the pension fund's financial statements where plan benefits are fully guaranteed upon payment of a specified premium to the insurance company. This is usually the case under individual retirement income or annuity contracts, deferred group annuity contracts (allocated), group life insurance or group disability contracts, and others.

In the case of insurance company deposit administration accounts, immediate participation guarantee accounts, and similar contracts, the assets should be included in the fund's financial statements at the same valuation basis as that used for other investments because such contracts do not result in a guarantee of benefits by the insurance company.

Property and Equipment

Although ERISA indicates that a pension fund's financial statements and supplemental schedules should be prepared in conformity with generally accepted accounting principles, an apparent conflict arises in connection with the valuation of property and equipment. In stipulating that assets and liabilities included in the supplemental statement of assets and liabilities be valued at their current value * (see Table 5–1, first item under "Supplemental Schedules"), ERISA implies that all assets must be so valued, thus apparently violating the accounting principle that assets used in normal operations (i.e., not held for investment purposes) should be valued at cost.

In fact there may be no conflict since generally accepted accounting principles would not preclude the disclosure, in a supplemental schedule, of the fair market value of assets so long as they were carried at cost (less accumulated depreciation) in the basic financial statements. A practical problem might arise, however, in attempting to disclose the fair value of property and equipment used in the fund's operations, in that an independent appraiser may be needed to value the assets. In most instances such assets would not be material to the financial statements and it would therefore seem that buildings, equipment, furniture and fixtures, and leasehold improvements used in the operations of a pension fund may be shown in the supplemental schedule at cost if an appropriate explanation is provided.

ACCRUED BENEFITS

Heretofore, pension fund balance sheets (i.e., Statements of Net Assets Available for Plan Benefits) have generally not included accrued benefits as a liability, and ERISA does not appear to require such inclusion. Accordingly, it would appear that pension funds should generally not include accrued benefits in the balance sheet

---

* Defined in ERISA as ". . . fair market value where available and otherwise the fair value as determined in good faith by a trustee or named fiduciary. . . ."

but rather should disclose appropriate related actuarial information.

REPORTING ACTUARIAL INFORMATION

Before passage of ERISA, the financial statements of pension funds reported almost exclusively upon the custodianship and protection of assets rather than upon the fund's ability to provide for the payment of pension benefits. Accordingly, their statements disclosed little, if any, information about the plan or related actuarial information.

Whether pension funds will now be required to include actuarially calculated amounts and related information in their financial statements is a subject of disagreement. ERISA indicates that the financial statements on which the accountant is to express an opinion should be in conformity with generally accepted accounting principles, and it is the authors' view that pension fund statements based on actuarially determined information * would not be in conformity with generally accepted accounting principles unless they include appropriate disclosure of pertinent actuarial information. In the absence of actuarial data relative to future benefits, the fund's financial position cannot be properly evaluated or understood.

Whether funds are required by law to make such disclosures in their financial statements is unclear because of ambiguities in ERISA. ERISA provides that the annual report required to be filed with the Secretary of Labor must include certain actuarial information [see Figure 5–1, items (e) and (j)], but it does not specify whether that information is to be included in the financial statements (or the supporting schedules). On the one hand, the only actuarial information ERISA specifically calls for is that contained in the statement to be supplied by the actuary, thus implying that such information need not be included in the financial statements. On the other hand, ERISA calls for certain financial statement footnote disclosures, including "any other matters necessary to fully and fairly present the financial statements of such pension plan," thus implying that actuarial information may be required therein.

Accordingly, management of some funds may decide not to

---

* Such statements would include those related to defined benefit plans and certain defined contribution plans (i.e., certain money-purchase plans) but generally not to most other defined contribution plans, e.g., profit-sharing, savings, and similar types of plans.

disclose actuarial information in their financial statements. In such instances, they would omit the disclosures suggested herein and also those disclosures indicated by an asterisk in the following section on "Other Financial Statement Requirements and Disclosures" (see page 141). However, independent auditors may decide that it would be inappropriate to render an unqualified opinion on financial statements that omit such actuarial information.

Disclosures

The authors' views described above are consistent with those of the AICPA's Health, Welfare and Pension Fund Task Force and its predecessor committee which recommended in their 1973 and 1974 draft position papers that pension fund financial statements include appropriate disclosures of actuarial information. The Task Force concluded that pension fund financial statements should generally disclose the following with respect to all benefits provided by the plan: *

1. The present value of vested benefits (i.e., the actuarially computed value) and
2. The actuarially determined prior service cost on a going concern basis.

Present Value of Vested Benefits. The Task Force suggested that the present value of vested benefits (based upon the most recent actuarial valuation) should be broken down into the following two classifications:

1. Present value of vested benefits expected to be provided to retired plan participants and/or plan participants who terminated before retirement but are currently receiving benefits based on prior vesting.
2. Present value of vested benefits expected to be provided to employees in active service and/or to plan participants who termi-

---

* It would appear that such disclosures should be made only to the extent that assets related to the liabilities are included in the financial statements; thus, in the case of plans where benefits are fully guaranteed by the insurance company and the related assets are not reflected in the fund's financial statements, the amount of vested benefits and prior service cost should not reflect such fully insured benefits.

In the case of defined contribution plans, the amounts of vested benefits and prior service cost would still be required (except in the case of benefits fully insured by the insurance company as discussed above) but such amounts would not involve actuarial determinations (except for noninsured money-purchase plans which would involve actuarial determinations), and the description of the disclosed amounts should be appropriately modified.

nated before retirement with vested rights to benefits payable later.

Prior Service Cost. For separately disclosing the actuarially determined prior service cost, the Task Force suggested that the prior service cost may be determined either:

1. On the basis of the accrued benefit cost method (unit credit method), reflecting benefits for service to the valuation date, or
2. On the basis of one of the projected benefit cost methods.

The Task Force concluded, however, that the prior service cost reported should be not less than the prior service cost as determined under the accrued benefit cost method (unit credit method).

The Task Force decision is apparently the result of a compromise. Some accountants believe that the accrued benefit cost method is most appropriate and its use should be mandatory. Others believe that use of projected benefit cost methods should be allowed, particularly where such a method is used for other actuarial calculations related to the plan. Use of a projected benefit cost method, however, could produce a prior service cost significantly greater or less * than that computed under the accrued benefit cost method. The compromise position appears reasonable in that no one method is mandated, yet prior service cost disclosed is not less than the present value of benefits credited to date.**

Because of the importance of the present value of vested benefits and prior service cost, the authors believe they should be shown on the same page as the Statement of Net Assets Available for Plan Benefits (below, not within, the statement). If this is impracticable, however, this information and the caption "Net Assets Available for Plan Benefits" should be clearly cross-referenced.

OTHER FINANCIAL STATEMENT REQUIREMENTS AND DISCLOSURES

The AICPA's Health, Welfare and Pension Fund Task Force indicated that pension funds should issue both a Statement of Net

---

* Under certain projected benefit cost methods, past service cost is not separately determined and would thus be zero.

** See "Funding" in Chapter 4 for discussion of forthcoming regulations to ERISA which may require use of one set of actuarial assumptions, and possibly of one actuarial cost method and one asset valuation method, for all purposes.

Assets Available for Plan Benefits and a Statement of Changes in Net Assets Available for Plan Benefits to disclose and adequately describe all significant changes. Examples of the suggested statements may be seen in the illustrative financial statements provided at the end of Chapter 10.

The notes to the financial statements should disclose any matters necessary to present the fund's financial position fairly, such as the following:

1. Description of the plan, including any significant changes in the plan and the impact of such changes on benefits.
2. Whether a plan is contributory or noncontributory.
3. Funding or contribution policy (including policy with respect to prior service cost), and any changes in such policy.
*4. Most recent actuarial valuation date used to compute the present value of vested benefits and prior service cost.
*5. Actuarial assumptions used to determine the present value of vested benefits.
*6. Actuarial cost method and assumptions used to determine prior service cost.
*7. Description of the effect, if material, of any change in the actuarial assumptions or cost method.
*8. Explanation of the terms "prior service cost" and "vested benefits."
*9. Description of the impact of any changes in plan benefits on the present value of vested benefits and on prior service cost.
10. Description of material lease commitments, other commitments, and contingent liabilities.
11. Agreements and transactions which may involve parties in interest.
12. Information concerning whether a tax ruling or determination letter has been obtained.

In addition, consideration should be given to disclosing material changes in the fair value of investments subsequent to the date of the Statement of Net Assets Available for Plan Benefits and also a general description of priorities upon termination of the plan. While the latter disclosure is suggested by ERISA and by the AICPA Task Force, many accountants believe it is not required since the financial statements are prepared on a "going concern" basis.

* Not required where the fund has decided to omit disclosure of actuarial information (see discussion in preceding section on "Reporting Actuarial Information").

Because a pension plan may maintain its investments in more than one fund, financial statements of all funds relating to such a plan may have to be set forth on a combined basis in order to present fairly financial information relative to the plan.

INTERNAL CONTROL

Internal control for pension funds has some special characteristics. Although detailed discussion is not feasible in the scope of this chapter, those special features of internal control methods and procedures for pension funds which the AICPA's Health, Welfare and Pension Fund Task Force identified in its November 1974 draft position paper are summarized below. (The language, with certain modifications, is that of the position paper.)

Contributions to Multi-Employer Funds

Contributions from employers, on a self-assessed basis, will represent the majority of the fund receipts. Contributions are generally determined by the number of hours or days worked or gross earnings of the participant at a standard contribution rate.

Employers commonly report contributions on standard pre-printed forms that are supplied by the fund. These forms generally show the employer's name, participant's name, social security number, and bases upon which the contributions are made. The fund should have a procedure for establishing initial accountability over the reporting forms immediately upon receipt (e.g., by document number or dollar or other control total), and the forms should be controlled throughout the processing operations, from the time of receipt of contributions to final postings to the participants' eligibility records and employers' contribution records.

The fund's internal control procedures should be adequate for disclosing and following up missing or delinquent employer reports and contributions as well as for detecting and following up employer overpayments or underpayments. Such internal control procedures may include the auditing of employers' records on a systematic or exception basis, the mailing of periodic statements requesting participants to report any discrepancies in hours worked and/or contributions reported on their behalf by employers, or a reconciliation of employee status reports furnished by the union to employer contribution reports.

Contributions are generally mailed directly to a bank for credit to the fund's account or received at the fund's office, in which latter case prenumbered receipt forms should be used. The numerical sequence of the forms and subsequent depositing of the cash in the bank should be subjected to internal review and checking. Contributions received should be ·deposited intact on a timely basis, and not be used for payment of fund expenses.

A method which generally provides for good internal control over the receipt and deposit of contributions is the adoption of a "lock box" system, under which employers mail the remittances and contribution reports to a bank. The bank deposits all receipts, prepares a record of the deposit, and forwards the deposit record and related contribution reports to the fund for further processing.

When an office has been established to serve more than one fund, proper controls are necessary to insure that remittances are deposited to the proper accounts. The controls established should include an audit trail which can be traced through to the general ledger postings.

The fund should maintain a cumulative record of employers' contributions, because the fund is required to report annually on contributions made by employers. The totals of contributions recorded in the cumulative record should be periodically reconciled with records of participants' eligibility and with the cash receipts book.

Investments

The fund's investment policy and the responsibility for custody of its securities should be established by the board of trustees. The trustees should abide by any restrictions that may be imposed by the trust agreement or by governmental regulations.

Where the plan administrator is directly responsible for making the investment decisions, significant transactions should be approved by the board of trustees or by an appropriate committee. Where the investment decisions are made by a custodian who also acts as trustee, the fund's agreement with the custodian/trustee should be approved by such board or committee. The board or committee should also monitor investment performance.

Benefits

Applications for the commencement of benefit payments should be carefully processed. An individual not involved in the original processing procedures should review the applicant's eligibility and determine that the retirement benefits have been properly determined in conformity with the participant's payroll and personnel records and with the plan documents. The board of trustees (multi-employer fund) or the administrative committee or its designee (single-employer fund) should approve all applications for benefits.

Controls should be established to ensure that individuals receiving benefits are eligible for the continuation of such benefits. Procedures might include periodic comparison, by an individual not involved in processing benefit applications, of endorsements on paid checks with signatures in personnel records or on benefit applications; sending of greeting cards to pensioners, returnable to the fund in the event of nondelivery; reviewing obituary notices; and visiting pensioners.

Bonding Requirements

The Welfare and Pension Plans Disclosure Act specifies minimum amounts of fidelity bond coverage for trustees, administrators, and other fund employees. ERISA continues these requirements, specifying that (with certain exceptions) every fiduciary of a pension plan (fund) and every person who handles funds or other property of such a plan shall be bonded.

Multi-employer pension funds may require employers to provide, at their own expense, a performance bond or other security to cover the payment of contributions in the event of insolvency. Performance bonds or other security should be periodically reviewed for adequacy.

Administrative Expenses of Multi-Employer Funds

Although the trustees are responsible for the approval of all administrative expenses, responsibility for approving routine expenses is usually delegated to the administrator or other responsible employees of the fund. Because of their fiduciary responsibility, the trustees should make certain that the internal control procedures for administrative expenses are adequate. The board of trustees will generally also retain the authority to approve any such expenditures over a stated amount.

Contract or professional administrators are paid according to various criteria, e.g., the number of participants covered by the fund, employer's reports processed, and so forth. Therefore, it is important that the fund's records provide the information necessary to determine the reasonableness of such payments.

9

AUDITING FINANCIAL STATEMENTS OF PENSION FUNDS

As independent auditors begin the first examinations of the financial statements of pension funds under the requirements of ERISA, they will find that, while generally accepted auditing standards apply, such examinations will present certain unique problems.

This chapter reviews principal audit areas in the light of generally accepted auditing standards—as explained and interpreted in the

Statements on Auditing Standards issued by the AICPA's Auditing Standards Executive Committee—and indicates how those standards apply to pension fund audits.

The suggested auditing procedures are not intended to be complete but rather to serve as a guide to the unusual features likely to be encountered in examining the financial statements of pension funds. For more detail on audit procedures, the reader may refer to Appendix B, which is a specimen audit program. Many of the audit procedures outlined in this chapter and in Appendix B (e.g., ascertaining that the terms of the plan comply with the requirements of ERISA, reviewing the actuary's report and employer payroll and other pertinent records, etc.) will already have been performed in those instances where the auditor also serves as auditor of the employer company, in which case such steps need not be repeated.

The applicability of procedures discussed herein to specific situations will vary with the circumstances, and thus audit procedures to be performed on a particular audit engagement must necessarily be designed to meet the circumstances of that engagement. The results of the auditor's review, testing, and evaluation of the fund's system of internal control will largely determine the nature, extent, and timing of the validation (substantive) audit procedures to be performed.

Before accepting an engagement, the auditor should carefully consider any relationship he may have with the fund, or parties in interest to the fund, to satisfy himself that he is in compliance with the AICPA's second general standard, which states that: "In all matters relating to the assignment, an independence in mental attitude is to be maintained by the auditor or auditors." It is not likely to be considered an infringement upon independence if the auditor is also the auditor for the union whose members are participants in the pension fund, or is the auditor for one or more of the contributing employers. If, however, an auditor acted in the capacity of fund trustee or administrator, he would not be considered independent for purposes of auditing that fund.

CONTRIBUTIONS

Audit procedures needed for considering the correctness of the information the fund uses in determining contributions received and receivable for the year depend upon whether the fund is based upon a single-employer plan or a multi-employer plan.

Multi-Employer Funds

Determining contribution amounts in multi-employer funds has a complexity and uncertainty not present in single-employer funds, and thus the auditor needs special procedures to obtain the needed degree of confidence in the amount of contributions the fund reports for the year. In testing the reported amount, the auditor should determine that the fund is maintaining adequate records of the contributions of the various employers and of the cumulative benefit credits of the individual plan participants of those employers.

This normally requires a review of employers' contribution reports which usually accompany each periodic payment under the terms of the plan, for the purpose of checking the total hours worked, dollars earned, or whatever basis is used for determining contributions, and for allocating benefit credits to individual plan participants. The auditing procedures to be used might include, but are not necessarily limited to, those shown in Figure 9–1 * (note that these procedures are directed at noncontributory plans; where a multi-employer fund is based on a contributory plan, the auditor should consider, in addition to the procedures shown therein, certain of the procedures provided in the section on single-employer funds, e.g., confirming contributions directly with participants). Whether to include all these and other procedures, and the extent to which individual procedures are to be performed, will depend upon judgments formed in the evaluation of internal control. (In some cases, internal control may be found so substantially deficient as to preclude the expression of an unqualified opinion. An illustrative auditor's opinion and further discussion are included in Chapter 10.)

Single-Employer Funds

Audit procedures suggested for single-employer funds include, but are not necessarily limited to, those shown in Figure 9–2.

---

* The figures in this chapter are generally based on procedures set forth in the November 1974 draft position paper of the AICPA's Health, Welfare and Pension Fund Task Force.

FIGURE 9–1

Suggested Audit Procedures for Examining Contributions Received and Receivable in Financial Statements of Multi-Employer Pension Funds

CONTRIBUTION RECORDS

(a) Reconciliation of total cash receipts shown by cash receipts book for a selected period to (1) the total amount credited to the general ledger contribution accounts, (2) the total amount posted to the employers' contribution record, and (3) deposits shown by the bank statements.

(b) Testing of amounts transferred to bank accounts of related benefit funds when employer contributions are deposited in a central bank account.

(c) Comparison of selected individual employer contribution payments as shown by the cash receipts book to (1) the amount shown on the employer's contribution reports and (2) the amount posted to the individual employer contribution record, accompanied by the tracing of selected postings from the employer contribution record to the cash receipts book and to the employer's contribution report.

(d) Testing the arithmetical accuracy of a selected number of contribution reports and ascertaining whether the correct contribution rate was used.

(e) Review of employers' contribution reports to test the accuracy of the postings to participants' records, and tracing entries on the participants' records to the contribution reports on a test basis.

(f) Reconciliation of total participants' credits posted to the records for a selected period to the total credits shown by employers' contribution reports.

(g) Determination of the reasonableness of contributions receivable at the statement date by comparing to collections received subsequent to the statement date, with an accompanying test review of the related employer contribution reports to ascertain that such receipts apply to the year under examination; if the fund's books are held open after the year end, ascertain that amounts received in the new year that pertain to the year under examination have been properly recorded as accounts receivable.

(h) Employing such tests as may be deemed appropriate in the circumstances to ascertain the nature and amount of any delinquent or unreported contributions.

(i) Review of the adequacy of the allowance for doubtful accounts.

CONFIRMATIONS

(j) Confirmation of contributions recorded as received and receivable during the period under examination on a test basis by

FIGURE 9-1

Continued

direct correspondence with selected employers. The extent of confirmation procedures and the type of request (positive or negative) to be used are a matter of judgment. The auditor should select the accounts to be confirmed and control the preparation and mailing of the requests. All exceptions reported in the confirmation replies should be investigated. When positive confirmations have been used and no reply received (to either a first or second request), the auditor should use alternate auditing procedures to provide evidence as to the validity of significant nonresponding accounts.

EMPLOYER RECORDS *

(k) Reconciliation of total gross earnings shown by the employees' earnings records with total wages shown by the general ledger and the payroll tax reports.

(l) Comparison of employer's contribution report data for a selected number of participants with the data shown on the employees' earnings records, and tracing of a selected group of employees' earnings records to the employer's contribution reports to ascertain that they have been properly included in or excluded from the reports.

* Note: For alternative procedures to use when the auditor is unable to examine employer records, see "Alternative Procedures for Employer Records," pages 152–53.

(m) Comparison of payroll journal data for a selected group of employees to the employee earnings records and time records.

(n) Determination of whether the employer has complied with the applicable provisions of the plan instrument and collective bargaining agreement, where applicable.

(o) Testing to ascertain the reliability of the basic data used by the actuary in his calculations (e.g., work force size, age distribution, sex, and so forth), including tracing key data to the actuary's report if shown therein, or confirming such data with the actuary. If contributions are not based on actuarial determinations, as with most defined contribution plans, test the data (e.g., hours worked) used in the calculation of contributions.

ACTUARY'S REPORT

(p) For defined benefit plans, review of the actuary's report to determine that the amount of contributions is consistent therewith.

COMPLIANCE

(q) For defined benefit plans (other than certain tax-qualified or insured plans), money-purchase plans and target benefit plans, determination that the fund is maintaining the (memorandum) funding standard account(s) and that the contributions required to be made are in accordance with the provisions of ERISA.

FIGURE 9–2

Suggested Audit Procedures for Examining Contributions Received and Receivable in Financial Statements of Single-Employer Pension Funds

CONTRIBUTION RECORDS

(a) Tracing of contributions recorded in the fund's general ledger to the cash receipts book and to deposits shown by bank statements.

(b) Review of amounts received subsequent to the statement date to ascertain whether reported contributions receivable are consistent therewith.

CONFIRMATIONS

(c) Confirmation of contributions received and receivable by direct correspondence with the employer company or by comparison to employer company records.

(d) In contributory plans, confirmation of employee contributions directly with participants, where deemed appropriate, on a sample basis.

EMPLOYER RECORDS

(e) Such audit procedures from (k) through (o) in Figure 9–1 as may be deemed appropriate, or the suggested alternative procedures referred to therein where employer records are inaccessible.

ACTUARY'S REPORT

(f) For defined benefit plans, review of the actuary's report to determine that the year's reported amount of contributions is consistent therewith.

COMPLIANCE

(g) Review of the criteria used by the fund in accruing employer company contributions to determine that such criteria have been consistently applied and that contribution amounts comply with the provisions of ERISA.

Employer Records

The examination of employer records is necessary to enable the auditor to gain reasonable satisfaction as to the correctness of contributions reported. This is because, in the case of a defined contribution plan, the employer records are the source of hours worked, pay rates, or other data which form the basis of contribution amounts. Similarly, in a defined benefit plan, the source of pertinent data used by the actuary in determining contribution amounts is also the employer records. In both cases, the reliability of the information used in the determination of contributions is an audit responsibility.

Thus, the auditor should examine employer records even when a limitation exists on the scope of the audit with respect to actuarial information (see "Scope Limitations" later in this chapter). The examination of employer records remains necessary even under these circumstances, because the auditor is taking exception only with respect to adjustments which might arise from reviewing actuarial matters—which does not change his basic responsibility to review data used by the actuary in his calculations.

Alternative Procedures for Employer Records

It is important to note that, in some circumstances, the auditor may be unable to examine employer records, in which case he should attempt to perform appropriate alternative auditing procedures to satisfy himself that the information on which contributions and other actuarially determined amounts are based is reasonable. In the case of a single-employer fund, the auditor should attempt to obtain a report from the employer's auditor stating that the appropriate auditing procedures have been performed.

In the case of a multi-employer fund, the auditor may likewise attempt to obtain reports from the auditors of selected employers stating that appropriate auditing procedures have been performed. Alternatively, if the fund or related union maintains a complete record of participants available for work, the auditor may deem it appropriate to test the data on which contributions and other actuarially determined amounts are based by corresponding directly with participants. Such correspondence, which should call for confirmation by the participant of employer, hours, pay rates, etc., may be administered by the auditor or by the fund or union under the auditor's control.

There may be other alternative procedures which might be appropriate for the auditor to perform, depending on the particular circumstances. For example, if the fund, as part of its normal procedures, periodically visits employers to verify data submitted to the fund, the auditor may deem it appropriate to review and test the fund's procedures.

When reports are obtained from the employer's auditor or from the auditors of selected employers, the auditor should, in addition to reviewing such reports, satisfy himself as to the independence and professional reputation of the other auditors and perform such other procedures as he considers appropriate in the circumstances, as described in section 543.04 of the AICPA's Statement on Auditing Standards (SAS) No. 1.

The auditor may sometimes be unable to satisfy himself using the alternative procedures. (See "Scope Limitations" for further discussion of employer records.)

INVESTMENTS

While the audit procedures related to investments will parallel those used for other entities whose principal assets are investments, various adaptations are necessary because of the nature of pension fund operations and the requirements of ERISA.

Internal Control

As in many other audit areas, evaluation of the system of internal control will enable the auditor to determine the reliability of records on which financial reporting is based so as to facilitate his determination of the nature and extent of validation audit procedures. Such procedures will include those relating to physical accountability, cost, and valuation of investments.

Physical Accountability

The auditor should perform procedures to satisfy himself that securities reported as held at the statement date actually exist and are the property of the fund. The auditor can verify the existence of securities either by inspecting and counting them or by obtaining a confirmation from the custodian. In order to rely on a confirmation, the auditor must be satisfied with the custodian's reputation and financial resources. (See "Custodial Relationships" later in this chapter for further discussion.)

The auditor should inspect deeds, title policies, and leases covering real property. Loan and mortgage instruments should be examined, and the balances and terms should be confirmed, with appropriate consideration of collectibility.

Cost

The auditor should substantiate the cost of investments and the amount of realized gains and losses by comparing reported cost as reflected in investment records (tested in prior or current year's examination) to cash records and by examining brokers' advices and other relevant documents, such as notes, mortgages, and closing statements.

Where marketable securities are carried at cost and market value is substantially lower than cost, the auditor should consider the implications of the AICPA's Auditing Interpretation on "Evidential matter for the carrying amount of marketable securities" issued in January 1975, in determining whether such securities should be written down to their market values and/or other disclosures made in the financial statements and as to the type of opinion to be expressed.

Fair Value

Determining the fair value of publicly traded securities as of the statement date presents little difficulty, because trading prices are usually published. Substantiating the reported fair value of investments without a readily determinable value, however, can present some difficulties. The most common such investments are real estate, securities of closely held corporations and securities with restricted marketability (e.g., unregistered securities).

The fair value of securities for which market quotations cannot be readily obtained should be determined by the fund's administrative committee or board of trustees. The auditor must remember that he does not function as an appraiser and is not expected to substitute his judgment for that of management, but rather should ascertain whether the procedures followed and results obtained by management appear to be reasonable and adequate. He is justified in expecting that the fund's administrative committee or board of trustees will have developed a body of information and documentation as the basis for their judgment of fair value and that that information and documentation will be available for his consideration.

For considering securities valuations, see Figure 8–1 (pages 133–35). The auditor may also find it useful to refer to Accounting Series Releases Nos. 113 and 118 of the Securities and Exchange Commission.

The auditor should review the various reports, analyses, computations, appraisals, and other material used in determining the fair value as of the statement date. Written representations from independent experts qualified in the area of the particular assets under consideration may be used as the basis for considering the reasonableness of values reported by the fund.

When the auditor is unable to satisfy himself as to the reasonableness of the amounts at which a significant amount of investments without a readily determinable value are stated, appropriate qualification of the auditor's opinion should normally be made. In such instances, the "subject to" * form of qualified opinion would be appropriate when the auditor is satisfied that the procedures followed and the information obtained by the fund with respect to the valuation of such investments are adequate to enable the fund to value the securities.**

If the auditor determines that the fund's valuation procedures are inadequate or unreasonable, or if the underlying documentation does not appear to support the valuation, then the auditor should appropriately qualify his opinion, with an "except for" introduction, with respect to the securities carried at "fair value." The exception should relate to lack of conformity with generally accepted accounting principles.

Perhaps a useful rule of thumb for taking exception would be that when the auditor cannot make the positive representations found in the explanatory middle paragraph of the recommended "subject to" opinion, then an "except for" opinion is appropriate as to all or a significant portion of the securities being valued.†

Where circumstances warrant, an adverse opinion, or possibly a disclaimer of opinion, may be appropriate; see AICPA Statement on Auditing Standards (SAS) No. 2 for further discussion.

Other Valuation Method

If investments are valued according to a method whereby gains and losses are recognized over a number of years, the auditor should, in addition to verifying the cost and fair value of securities, verify the manner in which the resulting gains and losses are recognized. The verification of the manner in which gains and losses are recognized should normally involve reviewing the arithmetic computa-

---

* An example of the "subject to" form of opinion is provided under "Departures from the Standard Report" in Chapter 10.

** Where the range of possible values of such securities would not have a significant effect on the fairness of presentation of the financial statements, the auditor should normally express an unqualified opinion.

† See "Departures from the Standard Report" in Chapter 10 for further discussion.

tions and ascertaining that the method is reasonable and consistent with that applied in the prior year.

Other Considerations

Investment Restrictions and Limitations. The auditor should assure himself that fund investments do not violate any restrictions and limitations on types of investments imposed by plan documents, plan policy, or law [such as those mentioned in Figure 4–1, items (c) and (d)].

Where approval of investment transactions by the board of trustees or administrative committee is required, the auditor should examine evidence of approvals.

Income. The auditor should test amounts of interest and dividend income received and receivable by computation, reference to appropriate published sources, or reviewing cash receipts and related documentation. Such procedures should include tests for unrecorded amounts.

Custodial Relationships

If the fund maintains its own set of books and records, with supporting evidential matter (such as brokers' advices), the auditor may perform his normal auditing procedures. There are instances, however, in which investment-related transactions are initiated by a custodian/trustee (such as a bank) which issues periodic reports to the fund but retains the brokers' advices supporting those transactions. Although the fund may perform internal procedures to control the accuracy of such reports and/or maintain its own records of the transactions, the fund's lack of brokers' advices may require the auditor to alter his normal procedures.

Some auditors believe an acceptable procedure is to obtain a report from the independent auditor of the bank stating he has performed a review of pertinent internal controls of the bank's accounting system. Other auditors believe that a report on internal control might not provide the fund auditor with sufficient assurance that the periodic reports of the fund's transactions prepared by the bank can be relied upon. They maintain that reports of the bank's independent auditor should state that validation (substantive) tests, including examination of brokers' advices, were performed with respect to the fund's transactions. Those auditors believe it would be appropriate for the fund auditor either to:

- Obtain a report from the independent auditor of the bank stating he has performed appropriate validation tests of the transactions and balances relating to the fund, or
- Make appropriate examination of pertinent books and records at the bank,

where such procedures would be performed in addition to obtaining a confirmation from the custodian, as discussed under "Physical Accountability" above. We understand that a task force of the Auditing Standards Division of the AICPA is studying this situation and will likely prescribe acceptable auditing procedures.

In a number of situations, securities are held by a third-party depository for the account of a fund's custodian. A procedure which has sometimes been followed in such cases is for the fund's auditor to:

- Obtain a report issued by the depository's independent auditor indicating that he has counted the securities held by the depository and has confirmed such counts with the depository's clients, e.g., the custodian, and
- Obtain a report from the custodian's independent auditor indicating that he has confirmed with the depository security holdings as shown on the custodian's records and performed appropriate tests of the custodian's records, and that such records indicate the securities listed in an attached schedule are being held at the depository for the account of the fund. When the securities listing is as of a date different from that of the fund's fiscal year end, the report of the custodian's auditor would indicate that he has reviewed the system of internal control and/or performed the stated audit procedures at various times throughout the year; this would normally be necessary to enable the fund auditor to rely on such report in reconciling to the fund's year-end balances.

Alternatively, in such situations, the fund's auditor might attempt to obtain, directly from the custodian, a confirmation which lists the securities and specifically states that although they are in the physical possession of a depository, the custodian is nevertheless financially and legally responsible for such securities. To rely on such a confirmation, the auditor would have to be satisfied with the reputation and financial resources of the custodian.

Where some or all of the fund's investments are held in pooled or commingled funds or trusts (common trusts), the auditor normally should:

- Review the financial statements of the common trust examined and reported upon by the trust's independent auditor, and
- Verify, by physical examination or confirmation with the trust, the number of units of the trust held by the client.

In order to rely on the reports of other auditors as discussed in this section, the fund's auditor has to satisfy himself as to their independence and professional reputation and should proceed in accordance with the guidelines established in section 543 of SAS No. 1, "Part of Examination Made by Other Independent Auditors" with respect to this and other matters.

ASSETS HELD BY AN INSURANCE COMPANY

Where pension fund assets are held by an insurance company, many of the procedures described for investments in general may apply, but additional procedures may sometimes be necessary to allow for the circumstances under which the assets are held.

Procedures are needed to establish the existence of the assets, to substantiate the asset cost and fair value and compliance with the contract with the insurance company, and to ascertain that the changes in such assets during the period are fairly presented. Accordingly, the auditor should review the contract between the fund (or plan sponsor) and the insurance company, review the insurance company's experience reports, and correspond directly with either the insurance company or its independent auditor to obtain information such as that summarized in Figure 9–3. Additional procedures may be needed in some cases, such as the following:

- Testing of the interest calculation and, where applicable, compliance with the minimum guaranteed interest rate in the insurance contract.
- Testing of annuity purchases.
- Testing of benefit payments in accordance with the audit procedures for benefit payments summarized in Figure 9–4.

FIGURE 9–3

Summary of Information Needed from Insurance Companies Which Hold Pension Fund Assets

(a) Type of contract or contracts.

(b) Information on how assets are held, i.e., whether in pooled "separate accounts," in individual employer "separate accounts," or in the insurance company's general funds.

*(c) Assets in other funds or funding media, but requiring consideration for comparison with the actuarially determined present value of vested benefits, and the plan's prior service cost.

(d) Contributions (premium payments) made during the year, including the dates received by the insurance company.

(e) Reconciliation of contributions (premiums) paid to the insurance company with amounts

* Not required when a scope limitation exists because of the client's instructions to the auditor not to perform audit procedures with respect to actuarial information. See the discussion in the "Scope Limitations" section in this chapter.

the pension fund received from employees and employers.

(f) Interest and dividends, and realized and unrealized gains, earned or credited during the year, plus the basis for crediting investment earnings.

(g) Refunds and credits paid or payable by insurance company during year due to termination of plan members.

(h) Dividend or rate credit given by insurance company.

(i) Annuities purchased and/or benefits paid or payable during the year.

(j) Amount of asset management fees, commissions, sales fees, premium taxes, and other expenses (sometimes collectively referred to as "retention") charged or chargeable by insurance company during the year.

*(k) The actuarially determined present value of vested benefits and prior service cost.

(l) Special conditions applicable upon termination of contract.

BENEFIT PAYMENTS

Audit procedures related to benefit payments are aimed at determining that recipients of payments were eligible beneficiaries, that payments were made in the correct amounts, and that persons no longer eligible for benefit payments are being removed from the benefit rolls. The auditor's evaluation of internal control normally determines the nature and extent of the tests of benefit pay-

FIGURE 9-4

**Some Representative Procedures for Auditing
Benefit Payments**

(a) Review, on a test basis, the approved applications for benefits and ascertain that the current benefit amounts have been properly approved.

(b) Check, on a test basis, employees' eligibility for the payment of benefits and the continuation of benefits.

(c) Check, on a test basis, the benefit payment calculation, and ascertain whether a responsible individual has reviewed the calculation independently.

(d) Compare data (including endorsements) on paid benefit checks with payment records, and ascertain that long outstanding checks are investigated.

(e) Confirm, on a test basis, payments recorded as paid during the period under review by direct correspondence with selected participants or beneficiaries.

(f) Ascertain that payments made to participants or beneficiaries over an unusually long number of years are still appropriate.

(g) Ascertain that benefit payments to retirees (and benefits for participants with vested benefits separated from the employer's service prior to retirement) have not been decreased due to increases in social security benefits after September 2, 1974 (or, if later, the earlier of a participant's first receipt of plan benefits or separation from service), in accordance with provisions of ERISA.

(h) Ascertain that the fund maintains a claims procedure for advising participants or beneficiaries whose claims for benefits are denied of their right to have a review made of the decision denying their claim, as required by ERISA.

ments. Some representative procedures the auditor may wish to use are shown in Figure 9-4.

ADMINISTRATIVE EXPENSES

In reviewing a pension fund's administrative expenses, the auditor should ascertain whether they were authorized and supported by appropriate documentation and whether amounts were recorded in the proper accounts. For this purpose the auditor may review the terms of the plan agreement and minutes of the meetings of the board of trustees or administrative committee to determine whether administrative expenses were properly authorized, and examine contracts, invoices, and other supporting documentation.

Where the fund uses a contract administrator, the propriety and reasonableness of the payments should be evaluated by testing the basis of the contract payment.

Where one office functions as a service organization for several funds, the auditor should review how the organization allocates administrative expenses not directly associated with a specific fund, in order to ascertain that the allocation is based on an equitable method. He should also determine that the method selected was approved by the board of trustees.

SUBSEQUENT EVENTS

Since investments normally represent the major portion of a pension fund's assets, the auditor should consider whether there have been any material changes in the market value of securities subsequent to the statement date, particularly where his opinion is dated near the end of the filing period permitted by ERISA.

Where such changes, if any, have been material, the auditor should consider whether there is adequate disclosure in the financial statements (see sections 560.05 and 560.07 of SAS No. 1). Such disclosure, if deemed appropriate, should normally refer to the portfolio as a whole. There may be exceptions, however, as in the case of a material change in the market value in a substantial holding of the employer company's stock, where disclosure relating only to that stock might be made. Such disclosure might be as follows:

> The market value of the Able Corporation common stock has declined from $11.25 per share at June 30, 1976 to $7.875 per share at January 16, 1977. Based upon the 31,128 shares held at June 30, 1976, this represents an aggregate decrease in market value from $350,190 to $245,133. The market value at January 16, 1977 of the other common stocks held at June 30, 1976 was approximately the same as the market value at June 30, 1976.

AUDITING ACTUARIAL INFORMATION

As observed in Chapter 8, the issue of whether pension fund financial statements should include specified actuarial disclosures is the subject of disagreement. Furthermore, because ERISA provides that the auditor may rely on the actuary's report, some people have suggested that such reliance eliminates the need for the auditor to review actuarial information disclosed in financial statements filed in accordance with ERISA. Others cite prior pension fund financial statements issued without actuarial disclosures, or with an auditor's statement of reliance upon the actuary, as justification for omitting actuarial disclosures and not reviewing actuarial information.

Nonetheless, the authors believe that financial statements not containing disclosures of appropriate actuarial information are not prepared in conformity with generally accepted accounting principles and, under this view, the auditor should not express an unqualified opinion on the financial statements unless such disclosures are made and unless the auditor is permitted to perform related audit procedures.

Management of some funds may, for economic reasons or otherwise, request the auditor not to perform audit procedures with respect to actuarial information. This would, in the authors' opinion, constitute a scope limitation, the effect of which is discussed in the following section on "Scope Limitations."

Suggested Audit Procedures

In considering the reasonableness of the actuarially determined information, the auditor should follow the procedures discussed under "Suggested Audit Procedures" in Chapter 7.

SCOPE LIMITATIONS

As noted in the preceding section, there is disagreement about whether actuarial information must be disclosed in financial statements. Since ERISA is unclear on the requirements,* management of some funds may omit such disclosures and request their auditors not to perform audit procedures with respect to actuarial information. Management of other funds which make such disclosures may request their auditors not to perform audit procedures with respect

---

* See "Reporting Actuarial Information" in Chapter 8.

to actuarial information. In the authors' view, such cases constitute scope limitations and thus preclude the auditors from expressing unqualified opinions on the financial statements.

A scope limitation will also exist when the auditor is unable either to examine employer records on which the financial statements are based or to apply satisfactory alternative procedures.

Actuarial Information

The auditor's inability to express an unqualified opinion on financial statements where an actuarial scope limitation exists in either of the two forms described above does not mean that the auditor should not accept such an engagement. Indeed, there is considerable support for the view that Congress, in drafting ERISA, intended that the independent auditor should concern himself with only non-actuarial matters in order to avoid placing an unreasonable economic burden upon pension funds.

Before accepting an engagement based upon the above-mentioned scope limitation, however, the auditor should advise the prospective client that although such action is not anticipated, the Secretary of Labor has the right, under ERISA, to reject any annual report containing a qualified opinion.

The audit procedures suggested in this chapter should generally be performed whether or not a scope limitation as described above exists, except that when such a scope limitation exists, procedures should normally be modified as follows:

1. The auditor need not review actuarially determined information. He should, however, trace any actuarially related information contained in the financial statements to the actuary's report and, as indicated elsewhere in this chapter, examine employer records.
2. The auditor would not need the information with respect to assets held by insurance companies described in (c) and (k) of Figure 9–3.
3. The auditor should note that some financial statement disclosures (items 4–9 under "Other Financial Statement Requirements and Disclosures" in Chapter 8) would not be made.

The nature of the auditor's opinion to be expressed where a scope limitation exists is described under "Departures from the Standard Report" in Chapter 10.

Employer Records

If a scope limitation exists because the auditor is unable to examine employer records or to perform appropriate alternative audit procedures, he should be guided by SAS No. 2. Where the examination of employer records is an important aspect of the audit procedures to be performed, as is usually the case when auditing a pension fund, the auditor facing such a scope limitation generally should disclaim an opinion. There may be certain situations, however, where the auditor concludes that a qualified opinion would be appropriate.

ADDITIONAL AUDIT REQUIREMENTS DUE TO ERISA

Some features of ERISA require the modification of audit procedures, or the development of additional procedures, to allow for matters which could have significant effects on the financial statements.

Principal areas where this will be required, other than those discussed earlier in this chapter, are plan compliance with ERISA, transactions prohibited by ERISA, and reporting and disclosure requirements of ERISA.

Plan Compliance With ERISA

Although penalties for failure to comply with requirements of ERISA are generally not likely to impact directly on the pension fund (as discussed in Chapter 4), the auditor should normally determine that the participation, vesting, joint and survivorship coverage, and certain other plan provisions comply with ERISA's requirements for two reasons:

1. With respect to a qualified pension plan, failure to comply with ERISA's requirements could result in disqualification of the plan and loss of tax-exempt status of the fund. In such an event it would be necessary to provide for income taxes with respect to investment income (including net realized gains) of the fund.
2. With respect to either a qualified or nonqualified plan, failure to meet ERISA's requirements could result in misstatement of contributions receivable and, where applicable (generally, defined benefit plans), misstatement of prior service cost and vested benefit amounts.

The procedures to be followed by the auditor to determine that the terms of the plan comply with pertinent requirements of ERISA should normally parallel those discussed under "Compliance of Individual Plan Provisions with ERISA" in Chapter 7. As indicated earlier, where the auditor of the fund also audits the financial statements of the employer, he need not duplicate his efforts. Where the fund's auditor does not audit the employer, an alternative procedure to those mentioned in Chapter 7 would be to obtain a report from the employer's independent auditor indicating the procedures he followed and his findings with respect to plan compliance with ERISA. Such a report can be relied upon only where the fund's auditor satisfies himself as to the independence and professional reputation of the employer's auditor and performs such procedures as he considers appropriate, as described in section 543.04 of SAS No. 1.

Transactions Prohibited by ERISA

Transactions prohibited by ERISA could give rise to significant receivables because a plan fiduciary is liable to make good any losses to the plan resulting from a breach of fiduciary duties and to restore to the plan any profits which he made through the use of the plan's assets. Accordingly, the auditor should apply procedures to ascertain whether there has been a breach of fiduciary duties as listed in Figure 4–1 or whether prohibited transactions such as those listed in Figure 4–2 have occurred, and if so, whether a receivable and/or other disclosure should be reflected in the financial statements.

Such procedures might include:

1. Inquiring whether any activities or transactions which might be considered prohibited have occurred;
2. Obtaining from the plan administrator a list of all parties in interest (to use as a reference point during the course of the auditor's examination), reviewing the administrator's procedures for identifying parties in interest, and examining related documentation to determine whether the list appears to be complete;
3. Ascertaining whether any prohibited transactions have been disclosed as a result of past Internal Revenue Service or other governmental examinations.

Because the auditor should, as a result of his regular audit work, be familiar with significant transactions which might be prohibited, it is anticipated that few, if any, additional procedures will be deemed necessary in most instances.

Reporting and Disclosure Requirements of ERISA

As part of his examination, the auditor should determine whether the financial statements, schedules, and summary of the annual report have been prepared in conformity with ERISA (see "Material Covered by Accountant's Opinion" in Chapter 5). He normally need not be unduly concerned, however, as to whether the other reporting and disclosure requirements of ERISA [see items (a)–(c), (e)–(m), (o), and (p) in Figure 5–1] * have been complied with, because any penalties imposed for noncompliance are not likely to have an impact on the fund (see the discussion under "Enforcement" in Chapter 4). The auditor should nonetheless be alert to instances of noncompliance with respect to such items so as to be in a position to advise his client of a need to consider taking corrective action.

Supplemental Schedules. The auditor's normal audit procedures should be sufficient to permit him to report on most of the information included in the supplemental schedules. To satisfy himself as to the completeness and correctness of the information in certain of the schedules, however, the auditor may have to perform additional procedures, e.g., schedules dealing with transactions with parties in interest.

Even with such additional procedures, however, the auditor may decide they yield no more than negative assurance with respect to parties-in-interest information and thus that an unqualified opinion would be inappropriate. For further discussion and an example of the type of opinion the auditor might express in such circumstances, see "Departures from the Standard Report" in Chapter 10.

Another schedule which might require additional audit consideration is that relating to fund assets held by banks, insurance carriers, etc., which are not regulated, supervised, and subject to periodic examination by a state or federal agency (see Note 2 to Table 5–1). Since virtually all banks and insurance carriers are regulated, supervised, and subject to periodic examination by a state or federal

---

* Reviewing the actuarial statement [item (e) in Figure 5–1] is of course important for audit purposes, as discussed in other sections, but determining the statement's compliance with ERISA is not a matter of specific concern because any penalties arising from noncompliance are not likely to have an impact on the fund.

agency, however, the need for additional audit procedures with respect to fund assets held by such organizations should be rare.

Summary of the Annual Report. Whether the auditor will need to perform additional audit procedures in order to report on the plan's annual report summary for participants and beneficiaries cannot be determined until the Secretary of Labor has prescribed its format and content. Depending upon the information required by the prescribed format and content, the auditor may decide that he is able to report on some or all of the information contained therein.

OTHER AUDIT CONSIDERATIONS

Bonding

The auditor should determine whether the fund maintains at least the required minimum amount of fidelity insurance in accordance with provisions of ERISA (see pages 62 and 144).

Taxes and Other Reports

The auditor should review tax returns and other reports filed pursuant to government regulations, and should ascertain whether a tax ruling or determination letter has been obtained and that appropriate information is reflected in the financial statements.

Transaction Approval

The auditor should acquaint himself with the collective bargaining agreement, the declaration of trust, the insurance contract, and other plan documents, and be alert to any transactions that require the approval of the board of trustees or administrative committee.

Potential Plan Termination

The auditor should be alert to any evidence of a potential pension plan termination, in reading minutes of meetings of the board of trustees and administrative committee, and in performing other audit procedures. In addition, the auditor may wish to inquire of the employer's management as to the possibility of a plan termination. Where a plan termination is more than a remote possibility, the auditor should ensure that the situation is appropriately reflected or disclosed in the financial statements.

Letter of Representation

Immediately prior to the completion of the field work, it is desirable that the auditor obtain a letter of representation, signed by the appropriate official(s) and worded to fit the individual circumstances of the engagement. The letter should normally include representations related to compliance with ERISA, any potential plan termination, changes in plan provisions, party-in-interest transactions, value of securities including those stated at fair value as determined by the board of trustees or administrative committee, assets pledged or assigned, unrecorded or contingent assets, unrecorded or contingent liabilities, and other pertinent matters.

10

AUDITOR'S REPORTS ON PENSION FUND FINANCIAL STATEMENTS

The auditor's report on his examination of the financial statements of a pension fund will be included as part of the annual report the fund is required to file with the Secretary of Labor. This chapter discusses the appropriateness of the standard report, departures that may be required from the standard report (with examples of language for use when departures occur), special reports, and illustrative financial statements.

ERISA requires the auditor's report to cover one year only, with the exception of the supplemental schedule of assets and liabilities which is required to be presented in comparative form, and the illustrative basic financial statements contained herein are thus presented for one year only. Where the fund engages the auditor to report on two-year basic financial statements, appropriate modifications should be made.*

STANDARD REPORT

When the auditor has examined a pension fund's financial statements in accordance with generally accepted auditing standards and finds that they have been prepared in conformity with generally accepted accounting principles and that such principles have been applied on a basis consistent with the preceding period, a standard report is appropriate. Illustrative financial statements following ERISA requirements and the auditor's standard report thereon are provided on pages 182–95.

Reference to Actuaries in Auditor's Report

A question arises as to whether the auditor, in expressing an opinion on the fairness of presentation of pension fund financial statements, should refer in his report to the role of the actuary. The majority view of the AICPA's Health, Welfare and Pension Fund Task Force, as stated in its November 1974 draft position paper, is that the auditor should not make such reference (unless the auditor intends to disclaim an opinion). The following discussion is taken from the Task Force paper:

> In the past it has been the practice for some independent auditors to refer, in the opinion paragraph of their reports, to the role of the actuaries in various ways. In many instances, it has not been clear whether the independent auditor intended such reference as an indication of a division of responsibility (for example, as if between two auditors) or as an explanation of how the independent auditor had satisfied himself with respect to gathering of sufficient competent evidential matter related to actuarially-determined amounts.
>
> In arriving at his opinion on financial statements of any entity the independent auditor takes into consideration the advice and opinions of various types of experts such as geologists, appraisers, engineers, etc., and in his audit of financial statements of a pension fund the independent auditor will, as a general rule, avail himself of the advice and opinion of an actuary as he would use the expertise of other professionals. How-

---

* A two-year basic financial statement of assets and liabilities may be required if the Department of Labor's annual report form in effect combines the supplemental schedule of assets and liabilities with the basic financial statement and calls for a comparative basic financial statement (see "Material Covered by Accountant's Opinion" in Chapter 5 for discussion). But, as indicated therein, it appears unlikely that such a comparative basic financial statement will be required.

ever, just as is the case with respect to other professionals, so it is regarding actuaries, that the independent auditor cannot diminish his responsibility to satisfy himself as to actuarially determined amounts by referring in his opinion to actuaries.

. . .

The use of actuarial expertise is a fulfillment of the independent auditor's responsibility for obtaining sufficient evidential matter in accordance with generally accepted auditing standards. The independent auditor must be satisfied with actuarially-determined amounts, but there is no requirement to explain how he was satisfied or to elaborate upon the steps he followed, including use of varying forms of expertise, in performing such tests of the accounting records and such other auditing procedures as he considered necessary in the circumstances. Reference to the assistance furnished by actuarial expertise in the opinion paragraph of the independent auditor's report should not be made unless it is the independent auditor's intention to disclaim an opinion.

Accordingly, so that there may be no misunderstanding as to the significance of the actuaries [sic] participation insofar as it relates to the degree of responsibility being assumed by the independent auditor expressing an opinion on overall financial position and results of operation, it is considered preferable not to refer to the utilization of actuarial expertise in the scope paragraph. Such disclosure may be interpreted as an indication that the independent auditor making such reference had performed a more thorough audit than an independent auditor not making such reference, thereby implying an additional degree of assurance.

Since the foregoing defines or establishes procedures which go beyond current practice, it is not intended to be retroactive with respect to opinions which have been issued previously. Accordingly, where comparative financial statements are presented, it may be necessary for independent auditors to continue to make reference to actuaries in reports on earlier periods, but to omit such reference in subsequent reports. However, in those cases where reference in prior reports was not required because the independent auditor had satisfied himself as to actuarially determined amounts, it is suggested that such reference be omitted for all years.

This majority view is supported by the August 15, 1975 exposure draft of a proposed Statement on Auditing Standards on "Using the Work of a Specialist" which indicates that the auditor should not refer to an actuary in his report when reporting under ERISA (unless he expresses other than an unqualified opinion).

A minority report included in the Task Force draft position paper, however, expressed the view that the auditor should be permitted to express reliance in his opinion on the actuary's report. This view is based on the belief that many auditors do not have and should not be expected to have the expertise needed to satisfy themselves as to the actuarially determined amounts. The minority report indicated that the auditor's primary responsibility with respect to actuarially determined amounts is to satisfy himself that the employee data used by the actuary were correct and that the actuarial method and significant assumptions used by the actuary are reported; to require the auditor to assume full responsibility is placing an unwarranted burden upon the profession.

The minority view influenced the Task Force as a whole sufficiently to cause it, in submitting its paper to senior committees of the Institute, to indicate that members of the Task Force reconsidered their position and that the matter requires further study.

It is anticipated that any further deliberations on this matter will be based in part on what legal protection, if any, will be afforded an auditor who expresses reliance on an actuary as a result of the ERISA provision enabling an auditor to rely on matters certified to by an enrolled actuary if the auditor so states his reliance.

Reference to Other Auditors in Auditor's Report

As indicated under "Custodial Relationships" in Chapter 9, there may be instances in which the auditor of a pension fund will obtain a report from another independent auditor. In the authors' view, in such cases, particularly where such report covers transactions and balances relating to the fund, the auditor normally should make reference in his report to the examination of the other auditor [see section 543.06 of the AICPA's Statement on Auditing Standards (SAS) No. 1].

Section 543.09 of SAS No. 1 illustrates the manner in which an auditor utilizing the work and report of another independent auditor who has examined the financial statements of a subsidiary would make reference to the examination of the other auditor. It would appear that that illustration may generally serve as a guide for the auditor of a pension fund. But reference to percentages (such as the illustration's reference to the percentages of assets and revenues of the subsidiary examined by the other auditor to the assets and revenues of the consolidated totals) might not be appropriate. For example, when investment-related transactions are initiated by a custodian/trustee which maintains the documentation supporting those transactions and the fund auditor obtains a report from the independent auditor of the custodian/trustee (as discussed in Chapter 9), the authors believe that reference to percentages similar to those described in the section 543.09 illustration might be misleading. This is because the fund auditor may have himself performed auditing procedures (e.g., confirming securities owned at year end, checking interest income and receivable calculations, tracing dividends and market prices to published sources, checking investment gain and loss calculations) that complement procedures performed by the other auditor.

Whether or not reference to the work of other independent auditors will be made will no doubt be influenced by the fact that some auditors have indicated that they may prohibit fund auditors from expressing reliance on their reports. This entire matter is being studied by a task force of the Auditing Standards Division of the AICPA, which will likely be prescribing auditing and reporting standards.

DEPARTURES FROM THE STANDARD REPORT

Under some circumstances, the standard report will be inappropriate and the auditor will have to express other than an unqualified opinion. Some of the situations likely to lead to a departure from an unqualified opinion involve scope limitations and problems related to investment valuation, parties-in-interest information, and internal control.

Scope Limitation—Actuarial Information

As discussed in Chapter 9, management of a pension fund may exclude actuarial matters from the scope of the auditor's examination—regardless of whether financial statements include disclosures of actuarial information. In the authors' view, such cases constitute a scope limitation which would normally call for a qualification of the auditor's opinion. Language suggested for the auditor's report is provided in Figures 10–1 and 10–2,* and pertains generally to funds based upon defined benefit pension plans. [In the case of certain defined contribution pension plans (i.e., noninsured money-purchase plans) where the employer contributions are not based

---

* The italicized words in the figures in this chapter represent modifications of the illustrative opinions set forth on pages 184 and 191.

FIGURE 10–1

Language Suggested for Qualifying the Auditor's Report Where Pension Fund Financial Statements Disclose Appropriate Actuarial Matters But the Fund Restricts the Scope of the Auditor's Examination to Non-Actuarial Matters Only

We have examined the financial statements and supplemental schedules and material of [name of fund] as listed in the accompanying index on [page number]. *Except as explained in the following paragraph,* our examination was made in accordance with generally accepted auditing standards, and accordingly included such tests of the accounting records and such other auditing procedures as we considered necessary in the circumstances. Securities owned at December 31, 1975 were [confirmed to us by the custodian and brokers] [counted by us].

In accordance with the terms of our engagement, we did not review the Fund's actuarial statements as of December 31, 1975 and December 31, 1974. The information in such statements was used by the Fund in determining the amounts of contributions receivable— employer and net assets available for plan benefits as of December 31, 1975 and December 31, 1974 and contributions—employer and net additions for the year ended December 31, 1975, and determining the other actuarial disclosures shown below the statement of net assets available for plan benefits and those contained in [note number] to the financial statements.

In our opinion, *except for the effects of such adjustments, if any, as might have been determined to be necessary had we reviewed the actuarial statements,* the financial statements listed on [page number] present fairly the financial position of [name of fund] at December 31, 1975, and the changes in net assets available for plan benefits for the year then ended, in conformity with generally accepted accounting principles applied on a basis consistent with that of the preceding year; and, *except for the effects of such adjustments, if any, to the supplemental schedules of assets and liabilities as might have been determined to be necessary had we reviewed the actuarial statements,* the supplemental schedules and material listed on [page number] present fairly in all material respects the information contained therein when considered in conjunction with the financial statements taken as a whole.

FIGURE 10-2

Language Suggested for Qualifying the Auditor's Report Where Pension Fund Financial Statements Do Not Disclose Appropriate Actuarial Matters and the Fund Restricts the Scope of the Auditor's Examination to Non-Actuarial Matters Only

We have examined the financial statements and supplemental schedules and material of [name of fund] as listed in the accompanying index on [page number]. *Except as explained in the following paragraph,* our examination was made in accordance with generally accepted auditing standards, and accordingly included such tests of the accounting records and such other auditing procedures as we considered necessary in the circumstances. Securities owned at December 31, 1975 were [confirmed to us by the custodian and brokers] [counted by us].

In accordance with the terms of our engagement, we did not review the Fund's actuarial statements as of December 31, 1975 and December 31, 1974. The information in such statements was used by the Fund in determining the amounts of contributions receivable—employer and net assets available for plan benefits as of December 31, 1975 and December 31, 1974 and contributions—employer and net additions for the year ended December 31, 1975.

The financial statements do not disclose the actuarially determined present value of vested benefits, prior service cost, actuarial cost method and assumptions used in the calculation of such amounts, and certain other information which is included in the actuarial statement as of December 31, 1975 filed as a part of the Annual Report to the Secretary of Labor.

In our opinion, *except for the effects of such adjustments, if any, as might have been determined to be necessary had we reviewed the actuarial statements, and except for the omission of the information mentioned in the preceding paragraph,* the financial statements listed on [page number] present fairly the financial position of [name of fund] at December 31, 1975, and the changes in net assets available for plan benefits for the year then ended, in conformity with generally accepted accounting principles applied on a basis consistent with that of the preceding year; and, *except for the effects of such adjustments, if any, to the supplemental schedules of assets and liabilities as might have been determined to be necessary had we reviewed the actuarial statements,* the supplemental schedules and material listed on [page number] present fairly in all material respects the information contained therein when considered in conjunction with the financial statements taken as a whole.

upon actuarial calculations but other information is based upon actuarial calculations, the suggested language should be modified to omit reference to contributions receivable—employer, net assets available for plan benefits, contributions—employer, and net additions.] The language is also based on the assumption that the summary of the annual report does not contain any actuarially related information which would cause a need to vary the suggested language.

Scope Limitation—Employer Records

Where a scope limitation exists because the auditor is unable to examine employer records or to perform appropriate alternative audit procedures (as discussed under those captions in Chapter 9), the auditor should be guided by the considerations outlined in paragraphs 10 to 12 of the AICPA's Statement on Auditing Standards (SAS) No. 2. For a discussion of the type of opinion to be expressed, see page 164.

Investment Valuation

Where investments which a fund values "in good faith" involve a significant amount of securities without a readily determinable fair value (as discussed in Chapter 9), the auditor may find it inappropriate to express an unqualified opinion. Figure 10–3 presents language suggested for the auditor's report where the auditor is unable to satisfy himself as to the reasonableness of the amounts at which such investment are stated, but is satisfied that the procedures followed and the information obtained by the fund are adequate to enable the fund to value the securities.

In cases where the auditor is unable to satisfy himself as to the reasonableness of such amounts and determines that the fund's valuation procedures are inadequate or unreasonable or that the underlying documentation does not appear to support the valuation, the auditor must qualify his opinion in a different way. In such instances, the auditor's opinion should include an "except for" introduction (relating to lack of conformity with generally accepted accounting principles) with respect to the securities carried at "fair value," and he should include appropriate disclosures in an explanatory middle paragraph of his report as required by paragraph 33 of SAS No. 2. Where circumstances warrant, an adverse opinion or a disclaimer of opinion may be appropriate, in which instances

FIGURE 10–3

Language Suggested for Qualifying the Auditor's Report Where Pension Fund Financial Statements Contain a Significant Amount of Securities Without a Readily Determinable Fair Value and the Auditor Is Satisfied With the Procedures Used by the Fund Management But Is Unable to Satisfy Himself as to the Reasonableness of the Values Determined "In Good Faith" by the Management of the Fund

We have examined the financial statements and supplemental schedules and material of [name of fund] as listed in the accompanying index on [page number]. Our examination was made in accordance with generally accepted auditing standards, and accordingly included such tests of the accounting records and such other auditing procedures as we considered necessary in the circumstances. Securities owned at December 31, 1975 were [confirmed to us by the custodian and brokers] [counted by us].

As discussed more fully in [note number] to the financial statements, securities amounting to $_____ (__% of the net assets available for plan benefits) have been valued at fair value as determined by the board of trustees. We have reviewed the procedures applied by the trustees in valuing such securities and have inspected underlying documentation; while in the circumstances the procedures appear to be reasonable and the documentation appropriate, determination of fair values involves subjective judgment which is not susceptible to substantiation by auditing procedures.

In our opinion, *subject to the effects, if any, on the financial statements of the valuation of securities determined by the board of trustees as described in the preceding paragraph,* the financial statements listed on [page number] present fairly the financial position of [name of fund] at December 31, 1975, and the changes in net assets available for plan benefits for the year then ended, in conformity with generally accepted accounting principles applied on a basis consistent with that of the preceding year; and, *subject to the effects, if any, on the supplemental schedules and material as of December 31, 1975 and for the year then ended of the valuation of securities as described above,* the supplemental schedules and material listed on [page number] present fairly in all material respects the information contained therein when considered in conjunction with the financial statements taken as a whole.

the auditor should be guided by the considerations outlined in paragraphs 41 to 47 of SAS No. 2.

Where marketable securities are carried at cost and market value is substantially lower than cost, the auditor should be guided by the considerations outlined in the AICPA's Auditing Interpretation on "Evidential matter for the carrying amount of marketable securities" issued in January 1975, in determining the type of opinion to be expressed.

Parties-in-Interest Information

Some auditors may be hesitant to express an unqualified opinion with respect to information relating to parties in interest required to be included in the supplemental schedules. Since the auditor might find it extremely difficult to obtain assurance that he is aware of the identity of all persons considered to be parties in interest under the law, he might be unable to gain reasonable satisfaction that all transactions and related information required to be reported in the schedules is complete. In certain cases, therefore, it may be deemed desirable for the auditor to give only negative assurance in his opinion with respect to such matters, in which case language shown in Figure 10–4 might be used.

Since an opinion giving only negative assurance is in accordance with section 518.03 of SAS No. 1, it is believed likely that such an opinion will be acceptable to the Secretary of Labor.

Internal Control Deficiency

As discussed under "Contributions to Multi-Employer Funds" in Chapter 8, in a typical multi-employer fund employers generally determine their liability to the fund and submit reports and contributions to the fund on a self-assessment basis. It is the responsibility of the board of trustees to ascertain whether the employers' contributions are being determined and made in accordance with the provisions of the applicable agreement.

Since employer contributions are normally the fund's principal source of revenue, an important aspect of the fund's system of internal control involves the establishment of effective procedures (e.g., examination of employer payroll records, confirmation with participants, etc.) to determine the correctness of employer contributions. The inadequacy or absence of such procedures may prevent the auditor from satisfying himself that contributions re-

FIGURE 10–4

Language Suggested for the Auditor's Report Where the Auditor Decides He Can Give Only Negative Assurance With Respect to Parties-in-Interest Information Required To Be Reported

We have examined the financial statements and supplemental schedules and material of [name of fund] as listed in the accompanying index on [page number]. *Except as explained in the following paragraph,* our examination was made in accordance with generally accepted auditing standards, and accordingly included such tests of the accounting records and such other auditing procedures as we considered necessary in the circumstances. Securities owned at December 31, 1975 were [confirmed to us by the custodian and brokers] [counted by us].

With respect to the information relating to parties in interest contained in the aforementioned supplemental schedules and material, it was not practicable for us to determine whether such information is complete. However, we have made inquiries of certain management officials of the Fund who have responsibility for financial and accounting matters as to whether said schedules and material contain all appropriate disclosures of information relating to parties in interest as required by the Employee Retirement Income Security Act of 1974, and we have otherwise subjected such information to the audit procedures applied in the examination of the basic financial statements. The procedures outlined in this paragraph do not constitute an examination made in accordance with generally accepted auditing standards nor would they necessarily reveal the identity of all parties in interest. Nothing came to our attention as a result of the foregoing procedures, however, that caused us to believe that the information relating to parties in interest required to be included in the aforementioned supplemental schedules and material is not fairly stated in all material respects in relation to the basic financial statements taken as a whole.

In our opinion, the financial statements listed on [page number] present fairly the financial position of [name of fund] at December 31, 1975, and the changes in net assets available for plan benefits for the year then ended, in conformity with generally accepted accounting principles applied on a basis consistent with that of the preceding year; and, *except with respect to the information relating to parties in interest as described in the preceding paragraph,* the supplemental schedules and material listed on [page number] present fairly in all material respects the information contained therein when considered in conjunction with the financial statements taken as a whole.

FIGURE 10-5

Language Suggested for Disclaiming an Opinion Where the Auditor Finds Internal Control Procedures To Be Inadequate or Absent and Alternative Audit Procedures Are Impractical

We have examined the financial statements and supplemental schedules and material of [name of fund] as listed in the accompanying index on [page number]. *Except as set forth in the following paragraph,* our examination was made in accordance with generally accepted auditing standards, and accordingly included such tests of the accounting records and such other auditing procedures as we considered necessary in the circumstances. Securities owned at December 31, 1975 were [confirmed to us by the custodian and brokers] [counted by us].

The internal control procedures adopted by the Fund are not adequate to assure the completeness of employer contributions to the Fund and the Fund's records do not permit the application of adequate alternative procedures regarding employer contributions.

Since the internal control procedures adopted by the Fund are not adequate to assure the completeness of employer contributions to the Fund and we were unable to apply adequate alternative procedures regarding employer contributions, as noted in the preceding paragraph, the scope of our work was not sufficient to enable us to express, and we do not express, an opinion on the financial statements listed on [page number], on the supplemental schedules of assets and liabilities and of cash receipts and disbursements, and on the summary of annual report; however, in our opinion, the *other* supplemental schedules listed on [page number] present fairly in all material respects the information contained therein.

ceivable and contribution revenue are fairly presented in the financial statements. In instances where there is an inadequacy or absence of such internal procedures, and where alternative audit procedures either do not result in the necessary assurances, are impractical, or have been limited by the client, the auditor should generally disclaim an opinion on the financial statements. An illustration of the wording of a disclaimer of opinion in one such instance is shown in Figure 10-5.

SPECIAL REPORTS

It has not been uncommon for auditors to be asked to report on pension fund financial statements prepared on a cash or other incomplete basis for special purposes, in which case the standard opinion is normally not appropriate.

While the incidence of such requests will likely decline because of ERISA's requirement that the accountant express an opinion as to whether the financial statements are presented fairly in conformity with generally accepted accounting principles, managements of some pension funds may still have occasion to ask the auditor to report on financial statements prepared on a cash or other incomplete basis, in which case the requirements of section 620 of SAS No. 1 relating to "Special Reports" would apply.

Information Furnished to Plan Participants and Beneficiaries

ERISA requires that certain supplemental schedules and a summary of the fund's annual report be furnished to participants and beneficiaries, and further provides that such material must be covered by the auditor's opinion as part of the annual report filed with the Secretary of Labor.

Managements of some funds may wish to include an auditor's opinion with the supplemental schedules and summary of the annual report furnished to participants and beneficiaries. Language suggested for the auditor's report in such instances is provided in Figure 10–6, and is based on the assumption that the summary of

FIGURE 10–6

Language Suggested for the Auditor's Report Accompanying the Supplemental Schedules and Summary of the Annual Report Furnished to Participants and Beneficiaries

We have examined the *statement of net assets available for plan benefits* of [name of fund] *as of December 31, 1975 and the related statement of changes in net assets available for plan benefits for the year then ended (which statements are not included in this report)* and *the* supplemental material listed in the accompanying index on [page number], *and have submitted our opinion thereon under date of [date of auditor's report covering basic financial statements].* Our examination was made in accordance with generally accepted auditing standards, and accordingly included such tests of the accounting records and such other auditing procedures as we considered necessary in the circumstances. Securities owned at December 31, 1975 were [confirmed to us by the custodian and brokers] [counted by us].

In our opinion, the supplemental material listed on [page number] presents fairly in all material respects the information contained therein when considered in conjunction with the financial statements taken as a whole.

the annual report is such that the auditor has decided that he can render an unqualified opinion thereon (see "Summary of the Annual Report" in Chapter 9 for further discussion).

Managements of other funds may wish to refer to the auditor's opinion included in the annual report filed with the Secretary of Labor, rather than include an opinion with the material furnished to participants and beneficiaries. In such instances, the following statement might be included with such material:

> The material contained herein is based upon the Annual Report to the Secretary of Labor, a copy of which is available in the Office of the Plan Administrator, which Annual Report contains financial statements and supplemental schedules of the Fund for the year 1975, together with the report of the independent certified public accountant. For a full understanding of the financial material contained herein, reference should be made to the complete financial statements.

If the auditor's opinion contains a qualification, the above statement should be modified to so indicate.

ERISA does not specifically require that either an opinion of the independent accountant or a reference thereto be included with the material furnished participants and beneficiaries.

ILLUSTRATIVE FINANCIAL STATEMENTS

Two sets of illustrative financial statements, including the auditor's reports thereon, are illustrated here:

- Single-employer fund (defined benefit plan), and
- Multi-employer fund (defined contribution plan).

These statements are based on the provisions of ERISA as interpreted by the authors. The statements and related auditor's reports are based on the premise that audited actuarially related information must be reflected in the statements (as discussed under "Scope Limitation—Actuarial Information" on pages 173 and 176). The auditor's reports are based on the premise that the auditor has gained satisfaction with respect to information relating to parties in interest required to be included in the supplemental schedules (see "Parties-in-Interest Information" on page 178). The statements and/or auditor's reports may have to be revised at such time as the Secretary of Labor prescribes the format and content of the financial statements (see Chapter 5) or prescribes the form for the Summary of the Annual Report (see Chapter 9).

ILLUSTRATIVE FINANCIAL STATEMENTS
SINGLE-EMPLOYER FUND (DEFINED BENEFIT PLAN)

Index of Financial Statements and Schedules

† Represents page number in the Annual Report to be filed with the Secretary of Labor, which material is incorporated herein by reference.

†† Represents material to be furnished to participants and beneficiaries, which material is not attached hereto but is incorporated herein by reference.

(1)

* Illustrative supplemental schedules and supplemental material are not presented here as they will most likely be required to be submitted on forms (Form 5500).

** If the schedule of assets and liabilities at December 31, 1974 was unaudited, that fact should be clearly disclosed. It is suggested that such disclosure be made on the index, on the schedule, and in the auditor's report.

Report of Independent Certified Public Accountants *

To the Pension Committee of
Able Company Pension Trust Fund:

We have examined the financial statements and supplemental schedules and material of Able Company Pension Trust Fund as listed in the accompanying index on page 1. Our examination was made in accordance with generally accepted auditing standards, and accordingly included such tests of the accounting records and such other auditing procedures as we considered necessary in the circumstances. Securities owned at December 31, 1975, except securities purchased but not received, were counted by us. As to securities purchased but not received, we requested confirmation from brokers, and, where replies were not received, we carried out other appropriate auditing procedures.

In our opinion, the financial statements listed on page 1 present fairly the financial position of Able Company Pension Trust Fund at December 31, 1975, and the changes in net assets available for plan benefits for the year then ended, in conformity with generally accepted accounting principles applied on a basis consistent with that of the preceding year; and the supplemental schedules and material listed on page 1 present fairly in all material respects the information contained therein when considered in conjunction with the financial statements taken as a whole.

[Signature]

[Street Address]
[City, State]
[Date]

(2)

---

* See "Reference to Other Auditors in Auditor's Report" earlier in this chapter for discussion relating to expression of reliance on other auditors.

ABLE COMPANY PENSION TRUST FUND

Statement of Net Assets Available for Plan Benefits

December 31, 1975

Assets		*Liabilities and Net Assets Available for Plan Benefits*	
Investments, at fair value		Accounts payable:	
(Note 3)	$42,300,000	Securities purchased	$ 500,000
Cash	100,000	Other	6,000
Receivables:			
Contributions:			
Employer	900,000		
Employee	100,000		
Securities sold	300,000		
Accrued interest and		Accrued expenses	9,000
dividends	100,000		
			515,000
Furniture and equipment,			
at cost, less accumu-			
lated depreciation of		Net assets available for	
$150,000	450,000	plan benefits	43,735,000
	$44,250,000		$44,250,000

Present value of vested benefits:	
For retired and terminated employees receiving benefits	$ 7,000,000
For active and terminated employees not presently receiving benefits	26,000,000
Total	$33,000,000
Estimated actuarially determined prior service cost	$45,000,000

The accompanying notes are an integral part of the financial statements.

(3)

ABLE COMPANY PENSION TRUST FUND

Statement of Changes in Net Assets Available for Plan Benefits

For the Year Ended December 31, 1975

Additions:
Contributions:

Employer	$7,800,000
Employee	1,200,000
Interest and dividend income	1,500,000
Rental income	10,000
Gains realized upon disposition of investments	1,000,000
Increase in unrealized appreciation of investments	2,000,000
	13,510,000

Deductions:
Benefits:

Retirement	700,000
Death	75,000
Termination	25,000
Administrative expenses	80,000
	880,000
Net additions	12,630,000
Net assets available for plan benefits, beginning of year	31,105,000
Net assets available for plan benefits, end of year	$43,735,000

The accompanying notes are an integral part of the financial statements.

ABLE COMPANY PENSION TRUST FUND

Notes to Financial Statements

1. Summary of Significant Accounting Policies

Investments Valuation

Investments in securities (U. S. Government and corporate bonds and common and preferred stocks) traded on a national securities exchange are valued at the last reported sales price on the last business day of the year; securities traded in the over-the-counter market and listed securities for which no sale was reported on that date are valued at the mean between the last reported bid and asked prices; investments in restricted securities and other security investments not having an established market are valued at fair value as determined by the administrative committee based upon the advice of its investment consultant; mortgages are carried at amortized cost; and real estate is carried at its fair value as determined by real estate appraisers.

Actuarial Method

The estimated actuarially determined prior service cost is calculated under the accrued benefit cost method—unit credit method.

Contributions

Contributions from employees are recorded in the period Able Company makes payroll deductions from plan participants.

Contributions from Able Company are accrued based upon amounts required to be funded under provisions of the Employee Retirement Income Security Act of 1974 (ERISA) or, if greater, amounts actually contributed for the year.

Other

Purchases and sales of securities are reflected on a trade-date basis. Gain or loss on sales of securities is based on average cost.

Dividend income is recorded on the ex-dividend date. Income from other investments is recorded as earned on an accrual basis.

In accordance with the policy of stating investments (other than mortgages) at fair value, net unrealized appreciation or depreciation for the year is reflected in the statement of changes in net assets available for plan benefits.

(5)

2. Benefits

The pension plan of Able Company Pension Trust Fund is a defined benefit plan to which member employees contribute 3% of their salaries on a monthly basis. The Able Company contributes such amounts as are necessary on an actuarial basis to provide the Fund with assets sufficient to meet the benefits to be paid to plan members. While Able Company has not expressed any intent to discontinue its contributions, it is free to do so at any time, subject to penalties set forth in ERISA. In the event such discontinuance results in the termination of the plan:

(a) The plan provides that the net assets of the Fund shall be allocated among the participants and beneficiaries of the plan in the order provided for in ERISA, and

(b) To the extent unfunded vested benefits exist, ERISA provides that such benefits are payable by the Pension Benefit Guaranty Corporation to participants, up to specified limitations, as described in ERISA.*

The contributions of Able Company are designed to fund the plan's current service costs on a current basis and to fund over twenty years the estimated accrued benefit cost arising from qualifying service before the establishment of the plan. The yield (interest, dividends, and net realized and unrealized gains and losses) on investments of the Fund serves to reduce future contributions that would otherwise be required to provide for the defined level of benefits under the plan.

The present value of vested benefits (benefits to which participants are entitled, regardless of future service with Able Company) under the plan and the actuarially determined prior service cost (cost assigned to periods prior to June 30, 1975) were calculated by consulting actuaries [name of actuaries], as of June 30, 1975. The actuaries have estimated that there would be no material change in such amounts as of December 31, 1975.

The more significant assumptions underlying the actuarial computations are as follows:

Assumed rate of return on investments	5%
Mortality basis	1951 Group Annuity Table, set back one year
Employee turnover	A moderate scale consistent with Able Company's experience

(6)

---

* Although ERISA suggests disclosure of general termination priorities, many accountants believe such disclosure is not required since the financial statements are prepared on a "going concern" basis.

| Salary increases | A 5% annual rate of salary increase |
| Retirement | Retirement at normal retirement age |

3. Investments

Investments held by the Fund at December 31, 1975 are summarized as follows:

Description	Fair Value	Cost
U. S. Government bonds	$ 850,000	$ 800,000
Corporate bonds	2,000,000	2,200,000
Preferred stocks	700,000	650,000
Common stocks:		
Able Company	3,070,000	3,000,000
Others	34,980,000	30,900,000
Mortgages	500,000	475,000
Real estate	200,000	150,000
	$42,300,000	$38,175,000

The aggregate fair value and cost of restricted securities and other security investments not having an established market were $1,225,000 and $1,200,000, respectively.

The Fund is authorized to invest up to 10% of the fair value of its total assets in the common stock of Able Company. Such investment aggregated 7% at December 31, 1975.

Investments in U. S. Government and corporate bonds having an aggregate principal amount of $3,075,000 have been stated at their fair value of $2,850,000.

The Fund's real estate investment is the ownership of land and building in which Able Company maintains its executive offices pursuant to a 25-year noncancellable lease expiring in 1996. The Fund has been advised by real estate appraisers that the rent of $10,000 annually is comparable to that which it could receive if the lease were with an unrelated third party. The building was purchased in 1971 for $150,000.

4. Tax Status

The United States Treasury Department advised on June 20, 1975 that the Fund constitutes a qualified trust under Section 401(a) of the Internal Revenue Code and is therefore exempt from federal income taxes under provisions of Section 501(a).

(7)

ILLUSTRATIVE FINANCIAL STATEMENTS
MULTI-EMPLOYER FUND (DEFINED CONTRIBUTION PLAN)

Index of Financial Statements and Schedules

Pages

† Represents page number in the Annnal Report to be filed with the Secretary of Labor, which material is incorporated herein by reference.

†† Represents material to be furnished to participants and beneficiaries, which material is not attached hereto but is incorporated herein by reference.

(1)

° See note, page 183.
°° See note, page 183.

Report of Independent Certified Public Accountants *

To the Pension Committee of
Industry Pension Trust Fund:

We have examined the financial statements and supplemental schedules and material of Industry Pension Trust Fund as listed in the accompanying index on page 1. Our examination was made in accordance with generally accepted auditing standards, and accordingly included such tests of the accounting records and such other auditing procedures as we considered necessary in the circumstances, including confirmation of securities owned at December 31, 1975, by correspondence with the custodian.

In our opinion, the financial statements listed on page 1 present fairly the financial position of Industry Pension Trust Fund at December 31, 1975, and the changes in net assets available for plan benefits for the year then ended, in conformity with generally accepted accounting principles applied on a basis consistent with that of the preceding year; and the supplemental schedules and material listed on page 1 present fairly in all material respects the information contained therein when considered in conjunction with the financial statements taken as a whole.

[Signature]

[Street Address]
[City, State]
[Date]

(2)

* See note, page 184.

INDUSTRY PENSION TRUST FUND

Statement of Net Assets Available for Plan Benefits

December 31, 1975

Assets		*Liabilities and Net Assets Available for Plan Benefits*	
Deposit with Roger Life Insurance Company, principally at fair value (Notes 2 and 3)	$407,650,000	Accounts payable	$ 750,000
Cash	3,000,000	Accrued expenses	535,000
			1,285,000
Contributions receivable (Note 4)	11,500,000		
Prepaid trustees' bond premium	1,200	Net assets available for plan benefits	420,866,200
	$422,151,200		$422,151,200

Present value of vested benefits for active employees
(Note 2) $200,000,000

The accompanying notes are an integral part of the financial statements.

(3)

INDUSTRY PENSION TRUST FUND

Statement of Changes in Net Assets Available for Plan Benefits

For the Year Ended December 31, 1975

Additions:	
Contributions from employers	$ 30,600,000
Interest and dividend income	11,400,000
Gains realized upon disposition of investments	2,000,000
Increase in unrealized appreciation of investments	10,000,000
Miscellaneous income	100,000
	54,100,000
Deductions:	
Benefits:	
Service retirement	4,700,000
Disability retirement	800,000
Death	120,000
Termination	2,100,000
	7,720,000
Insurance company charges	725,000
Administrator's fee	20,000
Professional fees	175,000
Conference expense	20,000
Trustees' bond and liability insurance expense	2,000
Printing and miscellaneous	50,000
	8,712,000
Net additions	45,388,000
Net assets available for plan benefits, beginning of year	375,478,200
Net assets available for plan benefits, end of year	$420,866,200

The accompanying notes are an integral part of the financial statements.

(4)

INDUSTRY PENSION TRUST FUND

Notes to Financial Statements

1. Summary of Significant Accounting Policies

Investments Valuation

Investments in common and preferred stocks traded on a national securities exchange are valued at the last reported sales price on the last business day of the year; securities traded in the over-the-counter market and listed securities for which no sale was reported on that date are valued at the mean between the last reported bid and asked prices; and U. S. Government and corporate bonds are stated at cost adjusted, as applicable, for unamortized discounts and premiums (discounts and premiums are amortized on a straight-line basis from date of purchase to maturity). It is generally the policy of the Fund not to dispose of bonds prior to their maturity date.

Contributions

Contributions from employers are accrued based upon hours worked during the year by covered employees.

Other

Purchases and sales of securities are reflected on a trade-date basis. Gain or loss on sales of securities is based on average cost.

Dividend income is recorded on the ex-dividend date. Interest income is recorded as earned on an accrual basis.

In accordance with the policy of stating common and preferred stocks at fair value, net unrealized appreciation or depreciation for the year is reflected in the statement of changes in net assets available for plan benefits.

2. Benefits

The Industry pension plan is a defined contribution plan to which employers contribute at the rate of 10¢ per hour worked by covered employees. Contributions received by the Fund are deposited with Roger Life Insurance Company, where they are accumulated in a separate account. Any benefits provided by the plan are paid by Roger Life Insurance Company from net assets available for plan benefits. The benefit to which a plan member is entitled is the benefit that can be provided by the contributions and income thereon (including net realized

(5)

and unrealized investment gains and losses) allocated to such member's account. Upon service or disability retirement, death, or termination, the participant or beneficiary may elect to receive either a lump sum amount equal to the value of the funds allocated to his account or an annuity contract with the insurance company of equivalent value.

The assets used to purchase annuity contracts or to provide lump-sum payments to retired and terminated participants (or their beneficiaries) are excluded from the deposit with Roger Life Insurance Company, and the present value of related vested benefits is accordingly not reflected herein.

The estimated prior service cost, as of December 31, 1975, approximates the net assets available for plan benefits.

*3. Deposit with Roger Life Insurance Company

The composition of the deposit with Roger Life Insurance Company at December 31, 1975 is summarized as follows:

Description	Fair Value	Cost
Cash	$ 500,000	$ 500,000
U. S. Government bonds	2,500,000	2,500,000
Corporate bonds	10,000,000	10,000,000
Common stocks	324,500,000	200,000,000
Preferred stocks	70,150,000	68,000,000
Total	$407,650,000	$281,000,000

All of the investments held by the insurance company represent marketable securities. U. S. Government and corporate bonds with an aggregate principal of $12,750,000 and a fair market value of $12,000,000 have been stated at their amortized cost of $12,500,000.

4. Contributions Receivable

Contributions receivable at December 31, 1975 principally represent amounts received in January 1976 from employers as contributions based on hours worked by covered employees in 1975.

5. Tax Status

The United States Treasury Department advised on July 27, 1975 that the Fund constitutes a qualified trust under Section 401(a) of the Internal Revenue Code and is therefore exempt from federal income taxes under provisions of Section 501(a).

(6)

---

* This information would usually not be available when the assets are not maintained by the insurance company in a separate account.

PART IV

Plan Management
Under ERISA

11

MANAGEMENT IMPLICATIONS OF ERISA

Pension costs have increased significantly in recent years due to the establishment of new plans and the improvement of existing ones. The need to comply with the provisions of ERISA will undoubtedly cause pension costs to increase further.

The extent to which modifications will be required to effect plan compliance will vary from plan to plan, but it is clear that every plan should be reviewed to determine what steps must be taken to effect compliance.

In addition to plan modifications required for compliance purposes, ERISA will likely have significant long-term effects on pension plan design and operation. For example:

- Vesting requirements could influence the rate at which employees terminate, and thus affect pension costs;
- The provision for withdrawal of employee contributions could create pressure upon employers to pay plan costs previously covered by employee contributions;

- The termination insurance and other provisions could discourage corporate acquisitions which would have previously been desirable;
- The increased overall cost of defined benefit plans could slow the rate at which new plans are established, and increase the incidence of defined contribution plans.

This chapter discusses these and certain other ways in which ERISA may affect plan design and operation.

DEFINED BENEFIT VERSUS DEFINED CONTRIBUTION PLANS

Because of the substantial additional requirements now applicable to defined benefit plans under ERISA, particularly the funding provisions and potential liability upon plan termination, a common reaction has been to consider shifting plans from a defined benefit basis to a defined contribution basis, where feasible. (In many cases, such as where a binding collective bargaining agreement or long-standing company policy applies, making such a shift may not be feasible.)

Another factor which may decrease the desirability of a defined benefit plan is inflation. Companies may be less inclined to guarantee payment of benefits many years in the future where those benefits will be based upon future wage or salary levels and inflation is expected to continue at a relatively rapid rate. The rate of inflation is of particular concern to companies sponsoring final pay plans, where benefits are based on participants' compensation in the final years of employment.

Any decision to shift from a defined benefit plan to a defined contribution plan should be made only after detailed study of the cost impact of ERISA on the plan, consideration of the various options available for minimizing that impact (e.g., modifying the benefit structure, changing actuarial cost methods), and determination of the potential adverse effect of changing to a defined contribution plan on employee/company relations. Although a defined benefit plan has the advantage of enabling a company to provide retirees with a predefined retirement income, management may find that the flexibility with respect to pension costs inherent in a defined contribution plan will better enable a company to fulfill its objectives under ERISA.

DEFINED BENEFIT PLANS

Managements of companies retaining their plans on a defined benefit basis will likely, as indicated earlier, be faced with the need to make plan modifications which will result in increased plan costs. Such managements will be focusing attention on two basic principles which have all too frequently been overlooked in recent practice.

First, an individual does not need as many spendable dollars after retirement as he does while he is working. Various work-associated expenses and certain other expenses, e.g., income and social security taxes, normally decline after retirement; a rule of thumb sometimes used by actuarial and benefits specialists is that a retiree requires approximately two-thirds of his preretirement income to maintain the same standard of living. This concept has been ignored in the design of some plans where participants may retire with benefits equaling or exceeding preretirement spendable income.

Second, there is a significant inverse relationship between pension fund investment income and pension costs. Managements of some companies have not devoted the attention to pension fund investments that is often devoted to other areas having less impact on company profits. To illustrate the significance of pension fund earnings, it is not unusual to find that an increase of one half of one per cent in the return on pension fund assets can decrease annual pension costs by 8 to 12 per cent.

In view of anticipated increases in pension costs due to requirements of ERISA, management will be looking more closely at these too often overlooked principles.

CONTRIBUTORY PLANS

Plans with benefits financed jointly by employer contributions and mandatory employee contributions that allow employees to withdraw their own contributions could be significantly affected by ERISA's provision that once 50% of an employee's accrued benefits are vested, the employee may withdraw his own contributions without—as was the case with most plans previously—incurring a reduction in benefits derived from employer contributions. It has been suggested that this provision may have the effect ultimately of eliminating mandatory employee contributions as a viable plan provision.

Under this view, it is assumed that if employees can withdraw money without losing any benefit from employer contributions, they are likely to do so and are further likely to apply pressure to induce the employer to reinstate the level of benefits that was once provided with both employer and employee contributions. Additional employer contributions would be needed to maintain that benefit level.

NONQUALIFIED PLANS

Because most ERISA provisions apply to nonqualified plans (other than unfunded excess benefit plans and certain other plans covering a select group of management or highly compensated employees) as well as to qualified plans, companies will be considering whether such nonqualified plans should retain their nonqualified status. Two of the most common reasons for establishing nonqualified plans have been to avoid the obligation for advance funding and to provide benefits only to particular classes of employees, and neither is possible for such nonqualified plans under ERISA. Because those advantages are no longer available, and because such nonqualified plans must comply with the funding, participation, and other requirements of ERISA, many companies will find it desirable to switch to qualified plans and thereby gain the tax advantages such plans offer both the company and the plan participants. Some companies may find it desirable to shift to a qualified plan that covers rank-and-file employees as well as the previously covered employee group and to add some form of excess benefit plan which is exempt from all or most provisions of ERISA for the latter group.

ERISA will also affect the manner in which the costs of certain nonqualified plans are funded. Many tax-exempt employer organizations such as hospitals and charitable organizations have commonly in the past merely recorded a liability for "contributions" to pension plans without making any payment to a funding agency; this will no longer be possible since pension plans must now be funded via a trust or insurance contract.

TURNOVER

Management will be considering whether historical turnover rates (i.e., the rate of employee termination before retirement) will change in view of the new vesting schedules required under

ERISA. On the one hand, increased turnover is encouraged by the fact that vesting (in many cases) will be earlier; since employees whose benefits are vested do not sacrifice accrued pension benefits by changing jobs, aggregate termination may be higher than before, creating higher financial obligations than anticipated by the historical turnover experience. On the other hand, vesting may begin to discourage turnover because employees for whom vesting has begun (or will shortly begin) may wait for partial or full vesting. After full vesting, employees may remain because all future accrued benefits will vest fully as earned.

Other factors which may affect the impact of ERISA's vesting provisions on turnover include wage or salary levels on the one hand and general economic conditions on the other. For instance, lower paid employees may be unwilling to sacrifice benefits to be partially or fully vested in the near future for the sake of only a marginal increment in wages, whereas higher paid employees may be willing to forego future vesting for the sake of a substantial salary increase and better advancement prospects. Similarly, when job conditions are tight, employees may not forfeit benefits which will be partially or fully vested in the near future, but in times of prosperity employees may be willing to change employment.

Another factor which may lead to an increased rate of turnover is the ERISA provision exempting from current federal income tax amounts of vested benefits transferred from one plan (through an Individual Retirement Account) to another.

While these opposing factors may tend to offset one another, the factors fostering increased turnover seem to be stronger, and thus a turnover assumption based on historical turnover rates may result in understated costs. Predicting whether historical turnover rates should be adjusted is, of course, difficult, and judgments as to the applicability of historical rates to future experience under new vesting provisions depend upon the characteristics of a particular plan. Management will nevertheless be attempting to determine the manner in which modification of a plan's vesting provisions will affect employee turnover rates and pension costs.

BUSINESS COMBINATIONS

Even before ERISA, the consideration of pension plan liabilities was a major concern in a prospective acquisition. There have been many situations in which an acquisition attempt has been stymied, if not terminated, by recognition that the pension plan liabilities make otherwise acceptable transaction terms economically unfeasible. In some cases it was learned that liabilities associated with the pension plan exceeded the recorded net worth of the company. Furthermore, in certain instances it was learned that a negotiated plan contained provisions whereby plan liabilities would double if an acquiring company materially changed the nature of operations, e.g., automated a production process.

ERISA highlights and aggravates the potential problems in an acquisition, particularly during 1975 and 1976 when many ERISA-related costs may not yet be known. In addition to potentially increased pension costs, an acquiring company is now less likely to benefit from terminating an acquired company's pension plan. Pursuant to the plan termination provisions of ERISA, termination of a plan with unfunded vested benefits could result in an obligation to the Pension Benefit Guaranty Corporation of up to 30% of the company's net worth. This is generally true even where a plan is terminated before a merger, since ERISA provides, in effect, that where a company ceases to exist by reason of liquidation into its parent, merger, or consolidation, the company's obligation upon termination becomes an obligation of the parent or successor.

ERISA will undoubtedly cause management to look more closely than ever at the pension plans of a potential acquiree.

RECORD-KEEPING SYSTEMS

Because of increased reporting and record-keeping requirements of ERISA, most employers will have to modify their present record-keeping systems.

Changes in record-keeping and information retrieval systems will likely be required in several areas. One such area relates to the ERISA requirement that a participant or beneficiary be provided with a statement showing his accrued benefits and vested benefits when the participant or beneficiary makes such a written request or when the participant terminates his employment or has a one-year break in service (as defined). Managements of many companies may find that it is less costly to prepare and issue such statements annually to all employees rather than only to employees requiring them.

Another area where information system changes will likely be necessary is related to ERISA's vesting requirements. The employer is required to maintain records of each employee's years of service and vesting percentage. Records may be needed of hours worked, to determine whether a participant has worked 1,000 hours in a 12-month period and is thus credited with a year of service, or whether he has worked 500 hours or less and thus incurs a break in service which may cause loss of previously credited service for vesting purposes. In addition, other data related to vesting must be maintained, such as service before age 22 (unless the Rule of 45 vesting method is used), service before January 1, 1971 (for employees having less than three years of service), and service during a period an employee failed to make mandatory contributions, which information may be needed in the determination of vested benefits.

As indicated in the preceding paragraph, record-keeping systems will likely have to be modified to record breaks in service for vesting requirements. Recording breaks in service is also important to enable companies to comply with other ERISA provisions. Under certain circumstances, pre-break and post-break service must be aggregated for determining accrued benefits or for other purposes. And, an employee who received a lump-sum distribution upon termination of employment can in certain instances, upon re-employment with the company, "buy back" into the plan, in which case he must be in the same position (with respect to accrued benefits, vested benefits, etc.) as he was when he terminated.

Management will undoubtedly be reviewing record-keeping and information retrieval systems to determine what changes are necessary to enable the company to comply with ERISA's provisions.

AUTOMATION

ERISA may give managements of labor-intensive companies and of companies with only marginally profitable product lines cause to reconsider whether it is desirable to make major changes in operations.

Company management which has been considering the installation of new labor-saving equipment may find that the requirements of ERISA make easier what had previously been a difficult decision. Similarly, management of a company with only a marginally profitable product line may find that the additional costs associated with complying with ERISA would cause that product line to operate at a loss in the foreseeable future.

Although management will not lightly make major changes in operations due to ERISA, there will undoubtedly be some situations where a company would be better off, in the long run, to shift to new operating processes and/or product lines. Such a shift may provide long-term benefits not only to the company, but to plan participants as well, since a struggling company might not be economically capable of preserving pension benefits at a level commensurate with participants' anticipations and needs.

PLAN MANAGEMENT

Pensions, being compensation-related, have in many companies been the primary responsibility of the personnel department. But now that pension plan financial implications, always significant, have become increasingly important, financial management is becoming more closely involved in plan design and operation, sometimes to the point where primary responsibility for the plan is transferred to the financial function.

Regardless of which functional area within a company has responsibility for the pension plan, it is becoming more and more evident to management that it must take a multidisciplinary approach to pension plan design and operation. While pensions have always required the use of various kinds of expertise, ERISA has heightened the need for coordinated professional judgment in the disciplines of actuarial science, law, taxation, accounting, auditing, and employee benefit design.

THE FUTURE

Pensions are inherently long-term in nature, and plan management will be considering observable factors which will ultimately influence plan operation and cost. Naturally, plan provisions requiring modification due to ERISA can be better revised where the future environment in which plans will operate is anticipated.

In enacting ERISA, Congress served notice that the practice of providing retirement income to employees is no longer a private affair between employer and employee. While not requiring employers to provide pensions, Congress has decreed that plans, once established, will meet prescribed design and operating requirements.

The impetus is clearly toward more regulation, and management can look at the record in other countries with similar legislation for an indication of the direction in which the U. S. private pension system may be heading. An example is Holland, which a few years ago operated with requirements similar to those established by ERISA. Today, employers in Holland are required to provide pensions which, with the equivalent of their social security system, will provide a level of benefits approximating 70% of an employee's final average pay.

While such legislation in the U. S. is not imminent, the prospect of ultimate enactment of legislation requiring minimum pension benefits and other requirements may be considered in formulating current plan amendments.

OPERATIONAL GUIDELINES FOR MANAGING PENSION FUND INVESTMENTS

The success of a pension fund depends significantly upon effective operational procedures and controls.* Such controls are important to the efficiency and effectiveness with which plan assets are managed.

In some instances, identifying control weaknesses and developing procedural or policy changes can result in improving the plan's investment performance. Such improvement is translated directly

---

* *Operational controls,* sometimes called *administrative* or *management controls,* relate to operational efficiency and effectiveness. They generally differ from *internal controls,* referred to in previous chapters, which relate to the accuracy of financial statements and safeguarding of assets. The latter term is technically called *internal accounting controls.*

into decreased employer contributions (in a defined benefit plan) or increased retirement benefits (in a defined contribution plan).

This chapter is designed as a guide to conducting an operational controls review and to instituting or modifying controls, where needed, to ensure that the system is operating effectively. Rather than provide a lengthy description of investment policies, systems, and procedures, this chapter is organized in the form of a checklist questionnaire to facilitate quick identification of areas which may require attention in a particular situation.

Where problems are identified (via "no" answers), remedial action should be considered. Such action may involve immediate implementation of needed controls or, where appropriate corrective action is not readily definable, obtaining professional assistance to study particular problem areas more fully. Certain checklist questions are referenced to related "Dollarization Steps" which may be helpful in quantifying, in dollars, the magnitude of potential improvement opportunities.

The checklist covers four categories:

- Organization and management policies
- Buying and selling
- Portfolio management
- Assessing portfolio performance.

ORGANIZATION AND MANAGEMENT POLICIES

The organization of the investment function and the policies prescribed by management normally have a direct effect on virtually all phases of a pension fund's operations. This section deals with basic (but frequently overlooked) organizational and policy considerations, including factors relating to the selection of and dealings with external money managers.

1. Does the investment function have:

    (a) An organization chart?
    (b) Job descriptions?
    (c) Clear-cut assignments of responsibility?

By providing job descriptions and defined responsibilities, people are directed so that their combined efforts are complementary rather than overlapping or inefficiently applied.

Lack of organization may have adverse results; for example, financial analysts may be researching too many industries or categories of securities, thus failing to become proficient in any one area.

2. Are there written policies covering the following areas:

   (a) Portfolio composition (e.g., concentrated, diversified, high risk, low risk, growth, income, etc.)?

   (b) Limitations or prohibitions as to investment type or technique (e.g., writing or investing in options, real estate, commodities, short sales of securities, unregistered securities, underwriting of securities of other issuers, or leverage techniques such as margin accounts or bank borrowings)?

   (c) Limitations as to funds available to each portfolio manager where there is more than one manager?

   (d) Conflicts of interest (to supplement applicable governmental regulations)?

   (e) Expected investment return (i.e., based on relative market indicators such as New York Stock Exchange Industrial Average or Standard & Poor's Stock Index or on absolute factors such as the per cent of expected investment return over a specified period of time)?

   (f) Formal portfolio review program (establishing the frequency of reviews, review team composition, techniques for following up deficiencies until they are corrected)?

   (g) Limitations upon portfolio turnover (providing a portfolio manager with guidelines to the amount of trading which is acceptable)?

   (h) Limitations upon the percentage of funds which may be invested in a particular security or group of securities?

Absence of objectives and policies can subject the organization to poor portfolio management decisions, and could subject officers to charges of failure to exercise fiduciary responsibilities effectively. It is important that the policies set forth cover all legal restrictions which apply, including restrictions prescribed in ERISA (see Chapter 4).

3. Are the investment activities of each portfolio manager treated as a separate profit center?

Establishing the activities of each portfolio manager as a separate profit center fixes accountability, responsibility, and authority for a manager's investments and allows for an objective evaluation of each manager's performance.

4. Has management evaluated the alternatives of managing the portfolio internally, compared to engaging one or more external money managers?

Factors that should be considered include availability of the necessary talent to manage the portfolio, relative costs involved, and willingness of management to assume direct responsibility for investment decisions and results.

Where it has been decided not to manage the portfolio internally, consideration should be given to engaging several external managers or management companies, rather than one. The purpose of splitting funds is to obtain a range of investment skills, in that certain money managers may excel in particular investment areas. For example, particular banks may be strong in general securities investing, insurance companies in real estate and private placements, investment counselors in aggressive growth stocks, and brokers in mutual funds and other investment vehicles. Other reasons for splitting funds are potential increased motivation on the part of the managers to perform well in order to obtain a larger share of the total portfolio, and the implicit safety that comes with diversification. These reasons for fund splitting must be weighed against counterarguments against it: the use of multiple managers may result in dilution of the quality of investment performance, overdiversification, increased expenses, and increased communication problems.

It should be noted that if no formal study of pertinent factors has been made and no conclusions have been reached, then officials have in effect made a "decision by default."

5. In selecting an outside investment manager, have the following criteria been considered:

(a) Whether he has a stated philosophy of operation and, if so, whether it is consistent with the fund's philosophy?

(b) Past performance in terms of a market indicator such as the New York Stock Exchange Industrial Average or Standard & Poor's Stock Index?

(c) Past performance in terms of ability to meet stated performance goals?

(d) History and approach toward investments?

(e) Recommendations of past and present clients regarding ability to perform basic research, ability to execute trades efficiently, and attentiveness to clients' needs?

(f) Dollar value, quality and types of accounts managed (e.g., growth, income, institutional)?

(g) Potential conflicts of interest?

(h) Fee schedule?

(i) Willingness to charge fees based, at least in part, on portfolio performance?

When officials do not consider the above points, they may select a manager whose investment philosophy, abilities, and experience are inconsistent with the needs of the fund, thereby inviting unacceptable portfolio performance.

6. Where an outside investment manager is engaged, are prescribed investment policies communicated to him?

It is important to communicate the fund's policies to the outside investment manager so that he will be aware of the fund's needs and its limitations upon holdings, investment vehicles, etc. Policies may be communicated to the advisor in a policy statement, in a trust agreement, or in a letter supplementing an agreement.

7. Are controls in effect by which appropriate officials are apprised of changes in the business associations and financial interests of directors, trustees, advisors, etc., of the fund which would place such persons in a position where conflicts of interest may exist?

An example of such a control is a requirement that all such persons periodically (e.g., annually) submit a signed statement indicating that no conflicts of interest exist. Absence of such a control could lead to conflicts of interest of which the fund is unaware.

8. Are controls in effect by which appropriate officials are apprised of persons or entities considered under ERISA to be fiduciaries and/or parties in interest?

It is important that fiduciaries and parties in interest be identified to enable prohibited transactions to be avoided (see Chapter 4 for details).

BUYING AND SELLING

In order for the decision-making process to be meaningful, buy–sell decisions must be carried out accurately and promptly. This section deals with the mechanics of executing securities transactions and related matters, including accuracy of brokerage charges, timing of payments, minimizing commissions, and controlling trading activity.

9. Are controls in effect to ensure that purchase and sale orders are executed accurately?

    Errors by stockbrokers, such as purchasing or selling the wrong stock or the wrong number of shares, can have a direct adverse effect. The fund should be in a position to detect errors promptly so that corrections can be made quickly. (See dollarization step 1, Error Control.)

10. Are controls in effect to verify that securities transactions are executed promptly?

    Significant differences should not normally exist between the market price at the time orders are placed and the price at which transactions are executed. Failure to control and analyze the effectiveness with which transactions are executed may lead to unfavorable changes in price. (See dollarization step 2, Prompt Execution.)

11. Where applicable, are controls in effect to verify that securities are traded within the day's high–low range?

    Typically, the fund should determine that securities are not sold below the day's low quote, nor purchased above the day's high quote. Management should also be alert to situations where purchases are *consistently* executed at or near the day's high price and sales are *consistently* executed at or near the day's low price; such a situation may point to the need for an evaluation of trading practices. (See dollarization step 3, Unfavorable Trade Prices.)

12. Are controls in effect to verify the correctness of commission cost, stock transfer tax, accrued interest, and any other items charged on securities transactions?

Commissions may be traced to memoranda regarding negotiated rates, stock transfer taxes may be checked to published tables, and interest accrued may be recalculated. Failure to verify the correctness of such charges could lead to overpayments. (See dollarization step 1, Error Control.)

13. Are payments for purchase transactions deferred until the settlement date in order to gain greater use of funds?

Failure to time payments to maximize the use of available funds could result in lost income. The settlement date is generally the fifth full business day following the transaction; stretching the settlement date to its maximum legal limits by using weekends and holidays is a useful technique to gain additional use of funds. (See dollarization step 4, Early Payments.)

14. Are brokerage commissions negotiated?

The failure to take advantage of negotiating may result in higher commission payments than would otherwise be necessary, as well as a possible breach of fiduciary responsibilities. (See dollarization step 5, Excess Commissions.)

15. Are controls in effect to avoid excessive trading with related excessive commissions?

While the portfolio manager may have discretion as to the frequency of trades, a situation where excessive commissions are generated without adequate related gains should be avoided. Controls should highlight situations where the same securities have been bought and sold within a limited time (e.g., one week, one month) so that the reasonableness of such transactions can be examined; and the portfolio turnover rate should be monitored in terms of prescribed policies and objectives.

16. Where the fund is purchasing or selling a large number of shares of a security in smaller lots, is the commission negotiated on the basis of the total transaction?

It is not unusual for trades involving large blocks of stock to be broken up into smaller lots to minimize the effect on the market price of executing a large transaction. When this is done, a lower commission cost can usually be negotiated with the broker, based on the total transaction. (See dollarization step 5, Excess Commissions.)

17. Where an outside investment manager is responsible for portfolio transactions, does he obtain the benefit for the fund of lower commission charges by combining transactions for the same security for several of his investment clients?

When an outside investment manager is purchasing the same security for several of his clients, he can sometimes negotiate a lower total commission, and the savings can be passed on to his clients. (This practice of combining transactions for more than one client is known as "bunching.")

18. Does the fund utilize "secondary" markets for very large transactions to effect the transaction at the most favorable price?

Where a very large transaction is contemplated, the fund should consider making the transaction in a secondary market (i.e., not through a securities exchange) so that the market price of the security is not adversely affected by an abrupt change in the available market demand for or supply of the security.

PORTFOLIO MANAGEMENT

This section deals with controls necessary for efficient and effective management of a fund's portfolio. It is divided into four subsections: "Management Information," which covers data normally required for making informed decisions; "Decision Control," which deals with controls over the portfolio decision-making process; "Revenue and Expense," which deals with means of controlling certain revenue and expense activities; and "Tax Considerations."

Management Information

19. Are cash requirements and cash flow projections prepared on a regular basis to enable portfolio managers to maximize the use of funds?

Failure to monitor and project cash requirements and flows may lead to the necessity to dispose hurriedly of securities to satisfy cash requirements, or to an unexpected inflow of funds creating an idle cash situation. (See dollarization step 6, Idle Funds, and step 7, Premature Sales.)

20. Do portfolio managers have the following information immediately accessible and current (i.e., daily):

   (a) Portfolio listing showing for each holding and each designated investment grouping the current market value in dollars and percentage to the total, and the range of prices for each stock during the preceding period (e.g., day, week, or month)?

   (b) Strategy grouping? (This involves grouping securities held, and those contemplated for purchase, by their expected reaction to certain events. The purposes of such grouping are to determine the risks involved in holding securities whose market prices are likely to be directly affected by a particular event, and to facilitate prompt action when such an event occurs.)

   (c) Funds available for investment?

Failure to maintain the above information places portfolio managers in a position where they must make investment decisions on incomplete or noncurrent information.

21. Do portfolio managers have available, on a timely and periodic basis (e.g., weekly), reports containing the following information required for short-term market strategy decisions:

   (a) Portfolio concentration by industry showing the dollar and percentage investment in particular industries?

   (b) Portfolio holdings experiencing higher than normal trading activity?

   (c) Portfolio performance reports (e.g., realized and unrealized gains and losses, investment income, rate of return, etc.)?

   (d) Tax basis of securities and holding periods, where necessary to determine whether a potential transaction will have tax implications (e.g., long-term vs. short-term, wash sales)? (Applicable only where the fund does not have tax-exempt status.)

Failure to make available the above information to portfolio managers on a timely basis places them in a position where they must make investment decisions on incomplete or noncurrent data.

22. Are reports that are issued to portfolio managers periodically reconciled with accounting records to ensure that managers are basing their decisions on accurate data?

The portfolio managers' effectiveness is dependent on the accuracy of information received.

23. Has management considered using computer capabilities to produce required information for portfolio managers on a timely basis?

Where large volumes of data are processed and reports must be generated quickly, the computer can be a useful tool. Where an in-house computer cannot be cost-justified, use of a service bureau might be considered. Considering the utilization of a computer may be particularly important where the answers to Questions 20 through 22 are negative.

24. Where there is more than one portfolio manager, is there adequate communication so that the managers do not work at cross-purposes?

There should be sufficient interaction between portfolio managers to avoid situations where: one manager is buying a security that another manager is selling, several managers are buying heavily in a particular security or industry without knowledge of the others' transactions, and the like. Failure to maintain adequate communication could lead to poor portfolio decisions, unnecessary commission expenses, and inadvertent concentration of risk within one security or industry.

Decision Control

25. Does the investment function have a formal long-range investment strategy?

A long-range investment strategy should be developed based upon economic data, forecasts, market research, potential legislation, etc. Absence of overall strategy may result in the making of one portfolio decision which negates the effect of another, and in failure to recognize pertinent events and to take appropriate action.

26. Does management provide guidelines, based on long-range strategy, with respect to investment vehicles, industries, or even specific securities for buying or selling during a specified period?

Providing direction to portfolio managers is necessary to ensure that long-range strategy is translated into specific investment decisions.

27. Are purchase selections of new portfolio managers either subject to approval by management or restricted to a prescribed list of approved securities?

The requisite approval or prescribed list serves to enforce investment policy, and to limit the potential risk associated with new portfolio managers who have yet to establish a successful "track record" within the fund organization.

28. Does management review and approve on a periodic basis (e.g., weekly, monthly) all trading activity and commitments from the previous period?

Failure to review previous activity may result in the prolongation of undesirable trading practices. By reviewing activity promptly exposure is limited.

29. Is the size of the portfolio, or of that portion of the portfolio assigned to a particular manager, maintained at a manageable level?

Unless very large pools of money are broken into smaller, more manageable funds, a situation may be created where the volume of a particular transaction, in order to have a desired effect, would be so large as to affect the market price of the security being traded; i.e., market supply and demand forces tend to push down the price of an unmatched sale order, and push up the price of an unmatched purchase order.

30. Do portfolio managers engage in arbitrage when the opportunity is available?

Arbitrage is the dealing in securities where an "automatic" profit can be earned through price differentials between: two or more markets over which a security is traded; realizable value of a security convertible into another security, and the market price of the latter security; etc. While profits can be generated through arbitrage, for arbitrage to be beneficial, such profits must exceed the related trading costs and the costs involved in monitoring price fluctuations of many securities.

Revenue and Expense

31. Are cash balances maintained at a level consistent with normal working requirements, whereby contingency and other "reserves" are invested?

    Portfolio managers sometimes tend to maintain cash balances to cover unexpected payments that may be required. Usually such "contingency reserves" should generate revenue by being invested, preferably in prime grade, highly liquid, short-term debt securities. On the other hand, cash balances should not be so low that securities must be sold prematurely to meet financial obligations. (See dollarization step 6, Idle Funds, and step 7, Premature Sales.)

32. Are controls in effect to ensure that proceeds from sales of securities, dividends, interest, and other cash receipts are:

    (a) Received when due?
    (b) Recorded in a manner whereby portfolio managers are informed promptly that such funds are available for investment?

    Failure to control receivables and related cash receipts properly may result in lost income on funds which should have been, but were not, available for investment. (See dollarization step 8, Late Receipts.)

33. Are brokers and advisors paid only for services which have been requested and received?

    Services by brokers and advisors may or may not be "bundled." Where additional services (e.g., research) are included within the basic fee structure, the fund should be sure that it, in fact, requires and receives such additional services and that it is willing to pay the price. Where such services are not required, an effort should be made to arrange for services on an "unbundled" basis. (See dollarization step 9, Investment Expenses.)

34. Where the fund utilizes the services of an outside organization (e.g., a bank) to handle cash receipts and disbursements, custodian functions, etc., is an analysis periodically performed to determine whether the fees paid are consistent with the services received?

The fund should establish that fees or other forms of remuneration (e.g., compensating balances) for the above-mentioned services are negotiated and are consistent with services received. The failure to be cognizant of the ability to negotiate proper remuneration could be costly. (See dollarization step 9, Investment Expenses.)

Tax Considerations

The questions in this section are pertinent only with respect to funds which do not have tax-exempt status.

35. Is adequate consideration given to such potential tax savings opportunities as:

 (a) Using the specific identification method of determining the cost of securities sold? (This enables a fund to gain maximum flexibility with respect to assigning costs to securities sold and thereby affecting taxable gain or loss.)
 (b) Timing sales of securities so as to maximize the excess of net long-term capital gains over net short-term capital losses?
 (c) Utilizing techniques such as acquiring a put option or selling short against the box to fix the economic gain or loss while postponing the tax impact?
 (d) Selling and repurchasing appreciated securities to offset capital losses or to obtain the benefit of a capital loss carryover which is about to expire? (The wash sale rules do not apply to gains.)
 (e) Investing in preferred stocks of domestic corporations rather than bonds, where advantage can be taken of the 85% dividends received deduction?
 (f) Expensing transfer taxes on securities transactions?

These are only a few examples of tax-planning opportunities that may be available. The intent of this question is to determine whether management is cognizant of such opportunities; the question is not designed to take the place of more comprehensive tax checklists or of analysis and planning of tax specialists.

36. Are controls in use to ensure that tax-planning decisions are effected?

It is important not only to arrive at appropriate tax-planning decisions (see Question 35) but also to ensure that such decisions are carried out. For example, when utilizing the specific identification method of costing securities sold, it is necessary that the appropriate block of stock be indicated; similarly, controls should be in effect to prevent wash sales which might negate the desired tax effect of an earlier transaction.

37. Has adequate consideration been given to state and local tax planning?

Although usually of relatively minor importance, there are situations in which state and local taxes (e.g., income, receipts, and use taxes) can be significant. In such cases, appropriate tax-planning techniques should be considered. For example, since most states tax obligations of other states but not their own obligations, purchase of the securities of the fund's own state should be considered. Similarly, if a state or municipality levies investment income taxes based on the issuer's operations allocated to its jurisdiction, consideration should be given to purchasing securities of issuers with low allocation percentages.

ASSESSING PORTFOLIO PERFORMANCE

Periodic review of performance in relation to investment philosophy and goals, by appropriate management personnel, enables management to take corrective action where necessary. This section deals with the nature of certain techniques for assessing portfolio performance.

38. Is portfolio performance evaluated in terms of:

   (a) An absolute measurement of performance (e.g., rate of return on investment)?
   (b) A measurement of performance relative to current market standards?

The rate of return on investment is the basis on which most other performance evaluators are founded. Also known as the "dollar weighted," "discounted," "average compounded," and "yield to maturity" rate of return, this and related techniques consider total return from investment income and realized and unrealized capital gains.

Selected market indicators have long been a standard for measuring relative investment performance. Such market indicators include Standard & Poor's Stock Index, Dow Jones Common Stock Averages, Dow Jones Bond Averages, and Moody's Common Stock Average. While there is disagreement as to the degree to which indicators are meaningful, these performance guides have long been present. The particular market indicator used as a yardstick against which performance is measured is not as important as the consistent use of the indicator. Frequent changes from one indicator to another might signify that an effort is being made to show the fund's performance in the most favorable light.

39. Are portfolio managers evaluated only with regard to items over which they have control, via the utilization of further appropriate techniques, as:

(a) Time-weighted rate of return?
(b) Unit-value method?

There are many different methods that can be used to evaluate portfolio managers' performance. The most popular and easiest to use, the rate of return and the market comparisons, are discussed in Question 38. These methods are suitable for evaluating total portfolio performance, but, because they do not allow for segregation of matters beyond a portfolio manager's control, they may not be sufficiently accurate to be used in evaluating a portfolio manager's performance.

A technical description of the time-weighted rate of return and the unit-value method is beyond the scope of this chapter. Of primary importance is the fact that they have the ability to desensitize the effect of cash flow. Although precise calculation using either of these two methods is time consuming and requires much data, both approaches are valid and should be considered.

DOLLARIZATION STEPS *

1. Error Control

(a) Select a sample of purchases and sales executed. (Consider segregating data by broker.)

---

* The applicability of extrapolation to any particular finding must be carefully weighed.

(b) For each selected transaction, verify the accuracy of:

Security
Number of shares or par value
Transaction price
Commission cost
Stock transfer tax
Accrued interest
Any other items
Computation of net amount of transaction

The name of the security, number of shares or par value, and (frequently) price may be traced to a record of the order placed by the portfolio manager. Commission costs may be traced to memoranda regarding negotiated rates; stock transfer taxes may be traced to published tables; and accrued interest and net amount may be recalculated.

(c) For any discrepancies noted in (b), complete the following schedule:

Security	Actual Amount	Correct Amount	Difference
_____	$ _____	$ _____	$ _____
_____	_____	_____	_____
_____	_____	_____	_____
_____	_____	_____	_____
_____	_____	_____	_____
_____	_____	_____	_____
_____	_____	_____	_____
	$ _____		$ _____

(d) Calculate the total excess charges by extrapolating the above calculation as follows:

$$\text{Total Sample Difference} \times \frac{\text{Total Dollar Value of All Transactions}}{\substack{\text{Total Dollar Value} \\ \text{(i.e., Actual Amount)} \\ \text{of Transactions in} \\ \text{Sample}}} = \text{Total Difference}$$

2. Prompt Execution

(a) Select a sample of transactions of varying dollar amounts. (Consider segregating data by broker.)

(b) Compare the time the order was placed with the time it was executed. For those trades with a time lag exceeding a specified period (e.g., one-half business day), compare the price at which the trade was executed with the market price at the time the order was placed (where such data are available). Complete the following schedule, offsetting the favorable effect of such price differentials against the unfavorable:

Security Traded	Trade Price	Market Price When Order Placed	Differ-ence	Number of Shares	Extended Differ-ence
	$	$	$		$
					$

(c) If a significant unfavorable difference exists, extrapolate the total extended difference computed in (b) to reflect the total potential difference between the actual value of transactions executed and the value of the transactions had they been executed at the market price when the order was placed.

$$\text{Total Extended Difference} \times \frac{\text{Total Dollar Value of All Transactions}}{\text{Total Dollar Value of Transactions in Sample}} = \text{Total Difference}$$

Caution: With respect to transactions of securities with limited market activity, a lengthy delay between the time an order is placed and the time it is executed may be justified. Furthermore, in many instances, the broker has little control over the final trade price, and he cannot be held responsible for rapid, sharp fluctuations in market prices. However, transactions should be placed within a reasonable period of time after the order is placed, and, on the average, the trade price should not vary significantly from the market price when the order is placed.

3. Unfavorable Trade Prices

(a) Select a sample of purchases and sales. (Consider segregating data by broker.)

(b) Compare the price at which the trade was executed to the average high/low trading price for the day, and multiply the difference by the number of shares. (Favorable differences should be shown as offsets.) Complete the following schedule:

Security	Actual Price	Day's Average High/ Low	Differ- ence	Number of Shares	Extended Differ- ence
	$	$	$		$
					$

(c) If the total extended difference is unfavorable, extrapolate the above results as follows:

$$\text{Total Extended Difference} \times \frac{\text{Total Dollar Value of All Purchases and Sales}}{\text{Total Dollar Value of Purchases and Sales in Sample}} = \text{Total Difference}$$

4. Early Payments

(a) Select a sample of cash disbursements, and obtain the related supporting documentation.

(b) Determine the number of days, if any, by which disbursements preceded the date required for payment. Take into account the method of payment (check, wire transfer, etc.), and appropriately identify weekends and holidays in making the determination. Complete the following schedule:

Payment Description	Amount	Date Paid	Date Payment Required	Days Lost	Lost Revenue
_____	$ _____	_____	_____	_____	$ _____
_____	_____	_____	_____	_____	_____
_____	_____	_____	_____	_____	_____
_____	_____	_____	_____	_____	_____
_____	_____	_____	_____	_____	_____
_____	_____	_____	_____	_____	_____
_____	_____	_____	_____	_____	_____
	$ _____				$ _____

$$\text{Lost Revenue} = \text{Amount} \times \text{Rate} \times \frac{\text{Days Lost}}{360}$$

The rate used in this formula should be based on the rate obtained by the fund on its short-term investments or, if such data are not readily available, on an appropriate standard such as the average Treasury bill rate in effect during the period.

(c) Extrapolate the total lost revenue computed in (b) above, as follows:

$$\text{Total Lost Revenue per Sample} \times \frac{\text{Total Cash Disbursements}}{\text{Cash Disbursements (i.e., Amount) in Sample}} = \text{Total Lost Revenue}$$

5. Excess Commissions

(a) Select a sample of transactions. All transactions for a particular security on a given day should be grouped together and treated as one transaction for the purpose of negotiating commissions.

(b) For each transaction selected in (a), compare actual commissions paid with an industry average for similar transactions. One such average that may be used is included in the "Analysis of Negotiated Rates," compiled and distributed quarterly by the Economist's Office of the New York Stock Exchange. The comparison may be made as follows, summarizing transactions by broker, and offsetting favorable differences against unfavorable ones:

Security Traded	Gross Dollar Value of Trade	Commission Paid	Commission per Industry Average	Difference
	$	$	$	$
	$			$

(c) Extrapolate the total difference computed in (b) to reflect the excess commissions paid:

$$\text{Total Difference per Sample} \times \frac{\text{Total Gross Dollar Value of All Trades}}{\text{Total Gross Dollar Value of Trades in Sample}} = \text{Total Excess Commissions due to Negotiation Practices}$$

Caution: The industry averages do not reflect differences in services (e.g., research) received from brokers, so caution must be exercised before concluding that commissions paid are excessive. These data may, however, indicate that a problem may exist with respect to commission costs.

6. Idle Funds

(a) Determine average cash balance during most recent fiscal period. Where cash does not fluctuate significantly, month-end or quarter-end balances may be used in calculation.

(b) Compute the excess average cash balance maintained:

Average cash balance per (a) above	$
Less: Normal working capital requirements	
Less: Compensating balances or other restricted cash balances	_____
Excess average cash balance	$ _____

(c) Compute the lost revenue by applying an appropriate estimated rate of return to the excess average cash balance. The rate used should be based on that obtained by the fund on its short-term investments or, if such data are not readily available, on an appropriate standard such as the average Treasury bill rate in effect during the period.

7. Premature Sales

(a) Ascertain whether any short-term debt investments (e.g., commercial paper, Treasury bills, etc.) were disposed of before maturity date during most recent fiscal period.

(b) For the items identified in (a), determine the revenue lost due to disposal of an investment before maturity. This determination should be made by comparing the revenue actually received with the revenue that would have been received had the fund purchased a shorter term investment that could have been held to maturity:

Investment	Actual Dollar Revenue	Potential Revenue of Shorter-Term Investment	Lost Revenue
	$	$	$
_____	_____	_____	_____
_____	_____	_____	_____
_____	_____	_____	_____
_____	_____	_____	_____
_____	_____	_____	_____
_____	_____	_____	_____
			$ _____

The potential revenue of the shorter term investment should be based on a like investment to that actually purchased.

Caution: This step should normally only be applied to certain short-term debt investments where an effective "penalty" is levied by the market if such an investment is sold rather than held to maturity. Such a "penalty" is relatively insignificant with respect to long-term debt investments, which may be sold at a substantial profit or loss when wide fluctuations in interest rates occur.

8. Late Receipts

(a) Select a sample of cash receipts and obtain the related supporting documentation.

(b) Determine the time lag, if any, between (1) when the receipt was due and when it was actually received, and (2) when it was actually received and when the portfolio manager received information indicating that such funds were available for investment. (Proceeds from the sale of securities are generally due on or before the fifth business day following the trade date. Dividend and interest payments are generally mailed by the distributing corporation before the payable date so as to be received by the investor on the payable date.) Complete the following schedule:

Payment Description	Amount	Time Lag per (b)(1) Above, in Days	Time Lag per (b)(2) Above, in Days	Lost Revenue per (b)(1) Above	Lost Revenue per (b)(2) Above
_____	$ _____	_____	_____	$ _____	$ _____
_____	_____	_____	_____	_____	_____
_____	_____	_____	_____	_____	_____
_____	_____	_____	_____	_____	_____
_____	_____	_____	_____	_____	_____
_____	_____	_____	_____	_____	_____
_____	$ _____			$ _____	$ _____

$$\text{Lost Revenue} = \text{Amount} \times \text{Rate} \times \frac{\text{Time Lag}}{360}$$

The rate used in this formula should be based on the rate obtained by the fund on its short-term investments or, if such data are not readily available, on an appropriate standard such as the average Treasury bill rate in effect during the period.

(c) Extrapolate the total lost revenue figures computed in (b) above, as follows:

Total Lost Revenue per(b)(1)	$\times$	$\dfrac{\text{Total Cash Receipts}}{\begin{array}{c}\text{Cash Receipts} \\ \text{(i.e., Amount)} \\ \text{per Sample}\end{array}}$	$=$	Total Lost Revenue due to Late Receipts
Total Lost Revenue per(b)(2)	$\times$	$\dfrac{\text{Total Cash Receipts}}{\begin{array}{c}\text{Cash Receipts} \\ \text{(i.e., Amount)} \\ \text{per Sample}\end{array}}$	$=$	Total Lost Revenue due to Late Reporting of Receipts

9. Investment Expenses

(a) Based upon examination of the fund's records, determine the dollar amount of investment expenses applicable to the investment program. Consider such items as management fees, advisory fees, custodian fees, commissions, etc.

(b) Ascertain whether an adverse trend is developing with respect to such expenses:

Expense	19— Dollar Amount	19— % to Total Average Investment	19— Dollar Amount	19— % to Total Average Investment	19— Dollar Amount	19— % to Total Average Investment
Management fees	$	%	$	%	$	%
Advisory fees						
Custodian fees						
Commissions						
Total	$	%	$	%	$	%

13

COMPLIANCE CHECKLIST

Introduction

This chapter has been designed in the form of a checklist to assist management in determining whether the pension plan and its operations comply with the requirements of the Employee Retirement Income Security Act of 1974 (ERISA). It is not intended to be all-inclusive, as it merely highlights the more significant points in each of five categories with which management may be particularly concerned. In those instances where a more complete explanation of the law is required, reference should be made to the referenced ERISA and/or IRC section numbers and to regulations promulgated by the Secretaries of Labor and Treasury, and, where necessary, the advice of legal counsel should be obtained.

The checklist has been structured in a questionnaire format so that a "yes" answer indicates compliance with an ERISA provision and a "no" answer signifies a potential or actual problem.

DEFINED BENEFIT PLANS

Part I—Plan Provisions

Effective Date: Except as otherwise noted below, first plan year beginning after 9/2/74 for plans not in existence on 1/1/74; first plan year beginning after 12/31/75 for plans in existence on 1/1/74. (ERISA: 211, 1017)

Participation

1. If the plan imposes age and/or service requirements on participation eligibility, are employees eligible to participate no later than the later of age 25 or completion of one year of service? (*Note:* If a plan provides for 100% vesting after three years of service, substitute a three-year service requirement for the one-year service requirement. In addition, for plans of certain tax-exempt educational institutions which provide 100% vesting after one year of service, substitute age 30 for age 25.) [ERISA: 202(a)(1), 1011; IRC: 410(a)(1)]

2. If the plan imposes age and/or service requirements on participation eligibility, does actual participation begin no later than the earlier of [ERISA: 202(a)(4), 1011; IRC: 410(a)(4)]:
   (a) The date six months following the date the age and/or service requirements are satisfied, or

(b) The first day of the first plan year beginning after the date the age and/or service requirements are satisfied?

3. Does the plan allow participation without imposing a maximum age limit prohibited by law? (*Note:* A plan may exclude from participation employees who are hired within five years of normal retirement age.) [ERISA: 202(a)(2), 1011; IRC: 410(a)(2)]

Vesting

4. Does plan vest employer-provided accrued benefits at a rate which meets or exceeds *at least one* of the following [ERISA: 203(a)(2), 1012(a); IRC: 411(a)(2)]:

(a) Twenty-five per cent vesting after five years of service, increasing 5% for each of the next five years (50% of vesting after 10 years) and at least 10% for each of the next five years (100% after 15 years of service),

(b) Full vesting after 10 years of service (no vesting required prior to completion of 10 years of service), or

(c) Fifty per cent vesting as of earlier of:

(1) Earliest date on which employee has completed at least five years of service and the total of his age and service equals at least 45, or

(2) Completion of 10 years of service,

with an additional 10% vesting for each year of service completed thereafter?

5. Is a participant 100% vested at normal retirement age? [ERISA: 203(a), 1012(a); IRC: 411(a)]

6. Are employee contributions 100% vested at all times? [ERISA: 203(a)(1), 1012(a); IRC: 411(a)(1)]

Service

7. Does the plan credit a full year of service for a 12-month period during which the employee or participant completed at least 1,000 hours? [ERISA: 202(a)(3)(A), 203 (b) (2) (A), 1011, 1012(a); IRC: 410 (a)(3)(A), 411(a)(5)(A)]

8. For participation purposes only, does the 12-month period used for crediting service commence on the employee's date of hire? [ERISA: 202(a)(3)(A), 1011; IRC: 410(a)(3)(A)]

9. Except for those years enumerated below, are all years of employment (whether or not continuous) taken into account in determining service under the plan? [ERISA: 202 (b)(1), 203(b)(1), 1011, 1012(a); IRC: 410(a)(5)(A), 411(a)(4)]

Note: The years of service which may be excluded from consideration are:

(a) Years of service prior to a "one-year break in service" (a specified 12-month period during which the participant or employee does not work more than 500 hours) unless the employee or participant returns to the employ of the employer and completes a year of service. [ERISA: 202(b)(3), 203(b)(3)(B), 1011, 1012(a); IRC: 410(a)(5)(C), 411 (a)(6)(B)]

(b) If the participant had no vested rights at the time of a "one-year break in service," all years prior to such break in service, but only if the number of consecutive "one-year breaks in service" equals or exceeds the number of years of service recognized under the plan immediately prior to the "one-year break in service." [ERISA: 202(b)(4), 203 (b)(3)(D), 1011, 1012(a); IRC: 410(a)(5)(D), 411 (a)(6)(D)]

(c) For participation purposes only, if the plan provides for 100% vesting after three years and requires three years of service for participation and if an employee has a one-year break in service before meeting the service requirement, all service prior to such break in service. [ERISA: 202(b)(2), 1011; IRC: 410(a)(5)(B)]

(d) For vesting purposes only [ERISA: 203(b)(1), 1012(a); IRC: 411(a)(4)]:

 (1) Years of service before age 22 (but if "rule of 45" is used for vesting, years of service during which the employee was a participant may not be disregarded);

 (2) If the plan requires employee contributions, years of service during a period for which the participant declined to make the required contribution;

 (3) Years of service prior to the date the plan was established (but if service for benefits is granted for any such period, such service cannot be excluded for vesting purposes just because it is prior to the date the plan was established);

 (4) Years of service prior to the date ERISA vesting rules become effective with respect to the plan (9/2/74 for plans not in existence on 1/1/74 and first plan year commencing after 12/31/75 for plans in existence on 1/1/74) which would have been disregarded under the rules of the plan with regard to breaks in service as in effect on the applicable date;

 (5) If the participant does not have at least three years of service after 12/31/70, all years of service before 1/1/71;

 (6) Years of service after a one-year break in service may be excluded from consideration in vesting benefits ac-

crued prior to such one-year break in service. [*Note:* Only applicable to certain insurance contract plans as defined in ERISA: 204(b)(1)(F), 1012(a); and IRC: 411(b)(1)(F).]

Retirement Benefits

10. Joint and Survivor Annuity [ERISA: 205, 1021(a); IRC: 401(a) (11); Effective Date: First plan year commencing after 12/31/75 —ERISA: 211(b)(1), 1021(a)(1)]:

    (a) If the plan provides for payment in the form of an annuity (which is the case with virtually all defined benefit plans), is the normal form of annuity payment for married participants a joint and survivor annuity which is the actuarial equivalent of a life annuity to the participant only, and which provides an annuity for the life of the participant and a survivor annuity for the life of the spouse which is not less than one-half of, nor greater than, the amount of annuity payable to the participant?

    (b) Does a married participant have a reasonable period before the date his benefits commence during which he may elect in writing not to take the joint and survivor annuity as the normal form?

    (c) Does the plan provide that a married participant be supplied with a written explanation of the terms and conditions of the joint and survivor annuity in order to make the election described in (b) above?

11. Is the normal retirement age under the plan no later than the later of age 65 or the 10th anniversary of the participant's commencement of participation in the plan? [ERISA: 2(24), 1012(a); IRC: 411(a)(8)]

12. Does the benefit formula under the plan provide for accrued benefits with respect to years of participation beginning with the first plan year to which this Part I applies which meet at least one of the following three tests designed to prevent backloading [ERISA: 204, 1012(a); IRC: 411(b); Effective Date: For certain collectively bargained plans in existence on 1/1/74, which provide certain supplementary or special plan provisions—see ERISA: 211(c)(2), 1017(c)(1)(D)—this question will not apply to these provisions until the first plan year beginning after the earlier of termination of the collective bargaining agreement or 12/31/80— ERISA: 211(c)(1), 1017(c)(1)]:

    (a) The accrued benefit as of any date is not less than 3% of the maximum benefit that would be payable to a participant who entered the plan at the earliest age and retired at normal retirement age, multiplied by actual years of service?

(b) The rate of accrual for any plan year is not more than 133⅓% of the rate of accrual for any prior plan year, unless such higher rate of accrual resulted from an amendment increasing the rate of accrual for future years?

(c) The accrued benefit as of any date is a fraction (actual years of service over years of service that would be completed at normal retirement age) of the normal retirement benefit that would be payable if the participant stayed in employment until normal retirement age, based on compensation at the time the determination is made and assuming social security benefits remain constant thereafter?

13. With respect to a participant or beneficiary who is receiving benefit payments from the plan, or a terminated participant with vested rights to receive benefits at a future date, are the plan's benefit provisions designed so that the benefits payable to such persons will *not* be decreased as a result of an increase in the old-age social security wage base taking place after the later of [ERISA: 206(b), 1021(e); IRC: 401(a)(15)]:

(a) 9/2/74, or

(b) The commencement of benefits, or the date of termination, whichever is earlier?

14. If the plan allows immediate commencement of benefits for early retirees, does it allow vested terminations who satisfied the service requirements for early retirement to elect an actuarially reduced benefit commencing at early retirement age? [ERISA: 206(a), 1021(a); IRC: 401(a)(14)]

15. Do benefits under the plan commence not later than the 60th day after the latest of the close of the plan year in which [ERISA: 206(a), 1021(a); IRC: 401(a)(14)]:

(a) The participant reaches normal retirement age, or age 65 if earlier,

(b) Occurs the 10th anniversary of the commencement of the participant's participation in the plan, or

(c) The participant terminates his employment with the employer?

16. Does the plan provide that employer-provided benefits payable to any participant be limited to the maximum annual benefit specified under Section 415(b) of the Internal Revenue Code? [ERISA: 2004(a)(2); IRC: 415; Effective Date: Years beginning after December 31, 1975—ERISA: 2004(d)] (Note 1, page 241)

Note: The maximum employer-provided benefit allowed under Section 415(b) is an amount payable for life equal to the lesser of $75,000 or 100% of the participant's average compensation for his highest three consecutive years. The maximum applies to the aggregate benefit provided under all defined benefit plans of the employer (or of all employers in a controlled group of corporations). The $75,000 limitation is subject to upward adjustments as a result of cost of living increases and downward adjustment where benefits commence prior to age 55. There are also adjustments to the maximum for less than 10 years of service. In any event, the maximum limitations will generally be met if a participant has never participated in a defined contribution plan of the employer and if benefits to such participant under all defined benefit plans of the employer do not exceed $10,000. Benefits for certain participants covered under the plan on 10/2/73 may exceed the maximum limitations pursuant to the transitional rule set forth in ERISA Section 2004(d)(2).

17. If any participant covered by the plan also participates in a defined contribution plan maintained by the employer, does the plan provide that the total of the benefits payable under both plans shall not exceed the maximum benefit limitations specified in Section 415(e) of the Internal Revenue Code, applicable to an employee covered under both a defined contribution plan and a defined benefit plan? [ERISA: 2004; Effective Date: Years beginning after December 31, 1975—ERISA: 2004(d)] (Note 1, page 241)

Note: The limitation provides that the fraction equal to the defined benefit accrued to date over the maximum allowable projected defined benefit accrued at normal retirement age, when added to the fraction equal to the annual additions to date under the defined contribution plan over the maximum annual additions permitted under Section 415(c) of the Internal Revenue Code, shall not exceed 1.4. The 1.4 limitation may be exceeded in certain circumstances pursuant to the special rule set forth in ERISA Section 2004(a)(3). Even if a participant does participate in both kinds of plans, the combined maximum limitation need only appear in one plan. The fact that the combined limitation does not appear in the defined benefit plan will not, by itself, constitute noncompliance, but should cause an examination of the defined contribution plan for such a limitation.

Death Benefits

18. Does the plan offer a participant who has reached the earlier of (a) the earliest retirement age under the plan, or (b) the date 10 years before his normal retirement age, the right to elect a survivor annuity providing payments to his spouse should he die while on active employment prior to his normal retirement age?

(*Note:* The amount of the survivor annuity payments to the spouse must not be less than the payments which would be payable under the joint and survivor annuity described in Question 10, had the participant retired early instead of died.) [ERISA: 205(c)(1), 1021(a); IRC: 401(a)(11)(C); Effective Date: First plan year commencing after 12/31/75—ERISA: 211(b)(1), 1021 (a)(1)]

Forfeiture of Benefits

19. Does the plan limit forfeitures of benefits to the following situations:
    (a) Termination of employment without full vesting [ERISA: 203(a)(2), 1012(a); IRC: 411(a)(2)];
    (b) Death, except where a survivor annuity is payable [ERISA: 203(a)(3)(A), 1012(a); IRC: 411(a)(3)(A)];
    (c) Suspension of benefit payments upon re-employment subsequent to commencement of benefits, but only for the period of re-employment [ERISA: 203(a)(3)(B), 1012(a); IRC: 411(a)(3)(B)];
    (d) Reduction of accrued benefits pursuant to certain retroactive amendments approved by the Secretary of Labor [ERISA: 203(a)(3)(C), 1012(a); IRC: 411(a)(3)(C)]; and
    (e) Certain withdrawals of mandatory employee contributions [ERISA: 203(a)(3)(D), 1012(a); IRC: 411(a)(3)(D)]?
20. Does the plan limit the forfeiture of employer-provided benefits because of withdrawal of mandatory employee contributions to the following situations:
    (a) Where the participant is less than 50% vested in his accrued benefit [ERISA: 203(a)(3)(D)(i), 1012(a); IRC: 411(a) (3)(D)(i)]; or
    (b) Where the forfeited benefit accrued before 9/2/74, but only if no mandatory contributions are made under the plan after 9/2/74 and only if the forfeited amount is proportional to the amount withdrawn [ERISA: 203(a)(3)(D)(iii), 1012(a); IRC: 411(a)(3)(D)(iii)]?
21. If the plan provides for forfeiture of employer-provided benefit as a result of withdrawal of mandatory employee contributions by a participant who is less than 50% vested, does it allow the participant to repay the full amount of his withdrawal with interest and thereby restore the forfeited benefit? [ERISA: 203(a) (3)(D)(ii), 1012(a); IRC: 411(a)(3)(D)(ii)]

Amendments

22. Does the plan provide that no amendment may decrease the benefit previously accrued by a participant? (*Note:* Certain retroactive amendments approved by the Secretary of Labor may

decrease previously accrued benefits without violating the provisions of the law.) [ERISA: 204(g), 1012(a); IRC: 411(d)
(6)]

23. Does the plan provide that no amendment may decrease a participant's nonforfeitable percentage (vesting percentage) in his
accrued benefit? [ERISA: 203(c)(1)(A), 1012(a); IRC: 411(a)
(10)(A)]

24. Does the plan provide that if an amendment to the plan changes
the vesting schedule, participants having not less than five years
of service will be permitted to elect to have their vesting computed without regard to the amendment? [ERISA: 203(c)(1)
(B), 1012(a); IRC: 411(a)(10)(B)]

Termination of the Plan

25. Does the plan provide that participants become fully vested
upon termination of the plan? [ERISA: 1012(a); IRC: 411(d)
(3)] (Note 1, page 241)

26. Does the plan provide that upon termination assets held under
the plan will be allocated in a manner that complies with the
allocation priorities set forth in ERISA Section 4044? (*Note:* The
plan should not actually specify allocation priorities contrary to
those specified in ERISA Section 4044. It is not certain whether
reference in the plan to ERISA Section 4044 will be sufficient or
whether the actual allocation priorities will have to be specified.
Consult ERISA Section 4044 for the specific provisions.)

Miscellaneous Provisions

27. Does the plan provide that benefits under the plan may not be
alienated or assigned? (*Note:* A plan may allow for a voluntary
and revocable assignment of up to 10% of each benefit payment
and may provide for assignment or alienation of vested benefits
to secure a loan from the plan, without violating the prohibition
against alienation or assignment.) [ERISA: 206(d), 1021(c);
IRC: 401(a)(13); Effective Date: First plan year commencing
after 12/31/75—ERISA: 211(b)(1)]

28. Does the plan provide that in the event it merges or consolidates
with, or transfers any assets or liabilities to, another plan, each
participant in the plan would (if the plan then terminated) receive a benefit immediately after the merger, consolidation, or
transfer which is equal to or greater than the benefit he would
have been entitled to receive immediately before the merger,
consolidation, or transfer (if the plan had then terminated)?
[ERISA: 208, 1021(b); IRC: 401(a)(12); Effective Date: First
plan year commencing after 12/31/75—ERISA: 211(b)(1), 1021
(b)]

29. Does the plan provide for, or specify, a claims procedure whereby a participant is notified in writing of a denial of benefits and afforded an opportunity for a full and fair review of the decision denying benefits? (ERISA: 503)
30. Does the plan provide separate accounting for voluntary employee contributions, or for the accrued benefit attributable thereto? [ERISA: 204(b)(2)(A), 1012(a); IRC: 411(b)(2)(A)]

Note 1: Questions which refer only to IRC sections or to ERISA sections which amend IRC sections are applicable only to tax-qualified plans. With the advent of ERISA's funding and vesting requirements it is unlikely that nonqualified pension plans subject to those requirements will continue to be maintained, since participants thereunder will be currently taxed on employer contributions made to fund vested benefits.

Part II—Funding

Effective Date: First plan year beginning after 9/2/74 for plans not in existence on 1/1/74; first plan year beginning after 12/31/75 for plans in existence on 1/1/74; but for certain collectively bargained plans in existence on 1/1/74 which provide certain supplementary or special plan provisions [see ERISA: 211(c)(2) and 1017(c)(1)(D)], the first plan year beginning after the earlier of termination of the collective bargaining agreement (but not earlier than 12/31/75) or 12/31/80. [ERISA: 306, 1017(c)(2)(A)]

The funding requirements are not applicable to certain tax-qualified plans or to insured plans funded exclusively by individual insurance contracts or group insurance contracts having the characteristics of individual insurance contracts. [ERISA: 301, 1013(a); IRC: 412(h)]

31. Has a funding standard account (and an alternative minimum funding standard account where applicable) been established and is it being maintained? [ERISA: 302(b)(1), 1013(a); IRC: 412(b)(1)]
32. Are either of the above account balances in a zero or credit position? [ERISA: 302(a)(1), 1013(a); IRC: 412(a)]
33. Were the following charges and credits made to the funding standard account [ERISA: 302(b), 1013(a); IRC: 412(b)] (Note 1, page 244):
    (a) Charges:
        (1) Normal cost of the plan for the plan year?

(2) The amount necessary to amortize in equal annual installments, until fully amortized (Note 2, page 244):

    a. Unfunded past service liability as of the first day of first plan year subject to ERISA, over 40 years if Single Employer ("SE") plan in existence on 1/1/74 or Multi-Employer ("ME") plan regardless of when established, or over 30 years if SE plan coming into existence after 1/1/74?

    b. Net increase (if any), in any plan year, in unfunded past service liability from plan amendments adopted in such year, over 30 years (SE) or 40 years (ME)?

    c. Net experience loss (if any), in any plan year, over 15 years (SE) or 20 years (ME)?

    d. Net loss (if any), in any plan year, resulting from changes in actuarial assumptions, over 30 years (SE, ME)?

    e. Waived funding deficiency for each prior plan year, over 15 years (SE, ME) (Note 3, page 244)?

(b) Credits:

  (1) Employer contribution considered made for the plan year (Note 4, page 244)?

  (2) The amount necessary to amortize in equal annual installments, until fully amortized (Note 2, page 244):

    a. Net decrease (if any), in any plan year, in unfunded past service liability from plan amendments adopted in such year, over 30 years (SE) or 40 years (ME)?

    b. Net experience gain (if any), in any plan year, over 15 years (SE) or 20 years (ME)?

    c. Net gain (if any), in any plan year, from changes in actuarial assumptions, over 30 years (SE, ME)?

  (3) Waived funding deficiency (if any) for the plan year (Note 3, page 244)?

Note: Additional credits or charges may have to be made to the funding standard account in two instances: (1) Where the full funding limitation provision is applicable [ERISA: 302(c)(6) and (7), 1013(a); IRC: 412(c)(6) and (7)]; and (2) in certain instances where the alternative minimum funding standard account was used in prior plan years [ERISA: 302(b)(2)(D), 302(b)(3)(D), 1013(a); IRC: 412(b)(2)(D) and 412(b)(3)(D)].

34. If the alternative minimum funding standard account is the one used to determine the current year's contribution, were the following charges and credit made to the account [ERISA: 305(b),

1013(a); IRC: 412(g)] (Note 1, page 244):

(a) Charges:

    (1) Lesser of normal cost as determined under the plan's funding method or the unit credit method?

    (2) Excess, if any, of the present value of the plan's accrued benefits over the fair market value of the assets?

    (3) Excess, if any, of credits over charges to this account for prior plan years, if applicable?

(b) Credit: Employer contribution considered made for the plan year (Note 4, page 244)?

35. Has a valuation of plan liabilities and a determination of experience gains/losses been made at least once within the most recent three-year period, or such shorter period as may be required by the Secretary of the Treasury? [ERISA: 302(c)(9), 1013(a); IRC: 412(c)(2)]

    Note: No determination of experience gains or losses will be required if plan costs are determined by an acceptable actuarial cost method which does not separately determine experience gains or losses. In certain cases an election may be made to value bonds and other evidences of indebtedness on an amortized basis running from initial cost at purchase to par value at maturity or earliest call date. [ERISA: 302(c)(2)(B), 1013(a); IRC: 412(c)(2)(B)]

36. Was the value of plan assets determined on the basis of a reasonable actuarial method of valuation which takes into account fair market value and is permitted under regulations issued by the Secretary of the Treasury? [ERISA: 302(c)(2), 1013(a); IRC: 412(c)(2)]

37. Were all changes in funding method (or plan year) during the current year approved by the Secretary of the Treasury? [ERISA: 302(c)(5), 1013(a); IRC: 412(c)(5)]

38. Are normal costs, accrued liability, past service liabilities, and experience gains and losses determined under the funding method used to determine costs under the plan? [ERISA: 302(c)(1), 1013(a); IRC: 412(c)(1)]

39. Are all costs, liabilities, rates of interest, and other factors under the plan determined on the basis of actuarial assumptions and methods which are, in the *aggregate,* reasonable (taking into account the experience of the plan and reasonable expectations)? [ERISA: 302(c)(3), 1013(a); IRC: 412(c)(3)]

40. Are increases or decreases in accrued liability under the plan resulting from a change in benefits under the social security act or in other retirement benefits under federal or state law, or resulting

from a change in the definition of "wages" for social security purposes, treated as experience gains or losses? [ERISA: 302(c)(4), 1013(a); IRC: 412(c)(4)]

Notes:
1. ERISA requires that the funding standard account and the alternative minimum funding standard account (and items therein) be charged or credited (as determined under regulations prescribed by the Secretary of the Treasury) with interest at the appropriate rate consistent with the rate or rates of interest used under the plan to determine costs. [ERISA: 302(b)(5), 1013(a); IRC: 412(b)(5)]
2. Amounts required to be amortized may be combined or offset against each other, with the resulting amount amortized over a period determined on the basis of the remaining amortization periods for the appropriate items entering into such combined or offset amounts, pursuant to regulations to be issued by the Secretary of the Treasury. [ERISA: 302(b)(4), 1013(a); IRC: 412(b)(4)]
3. Waivers of all or part of the minimum funding requirements may be granted by the Secretary of the Treasury in certain cases of substantial business hardship and are limited to not more than five years out of any consecutive 15 years. [ERISA: 303, 1013(a); IRC: 412(d)]
4. This employer contribution can only be credited herein where the employer pays the contribution within two and one half months after the end of the plan year. The Secretary of the Treasury may extend this period up to an additional six months. [ERISA: 302(c)(10), 1013(a); IRC: 412(c)(10)]

Part III—Reporting and Disclosure Requirements

Filings With the Secretary of Labor. Effective Date: 1/1/75 except that proposed regulations postpone the effective date for non-calendar year plans to the first plan year beginning after 1/1/75 (see Table 5–2 for further details). [ERISA: 111(b)]

41. If the plan was in existence on or before January 31, 1976, has the plan administrator filed a "short form plan description" with the Secretary of Labor by the later of 120 days of the date the plan was established or August 31, 1975? (*Note:* A "short form plan description" consists of the first two pages of Department of Labor Form EBS–1, without the schedules referred to therein, and the signature page with only item 38 completed.) [ERISA: 104(a)(1)(B) and proposed regulation Section 2520.104–3]

42. Has the plan administrator filed a plan description (Department of Labor Form EBS–1) and a summary plan description with the Secretary of Labor by the later of 120 days of the date the plan was established or May 30, 1976? [ERISA: 104(a)(1)(B) and proposed regulation Section 2520.104–3]

43. Did the summary plan description contain the following information [ERISA: 102(b)]:

    (a) The name and type of administration of the plan?

    (b) The name and address of the person designated as agent for service of legal process, if such person is not the plan administrator?

    (c) The name and address of the plan administrator?

    (d) Names, titles, and addresses of any trustee or trustees?

    (e) A description of the relevant provisions of any applicable collective bargaining agreement?

    (f) The plan's requirements respecting eligibility for participation and benefits?

    (g) A description of the provisions providing for nonforfeitable benefits?

    (h) Circumstances which may result in disqualification, ineligibility, or denial or loss of benefits?

    (i) The source of financing of the plan and the identity of any organization through which benefits are provided?

    (j) The date of the plan year end and whether the records of the plan are kept on a calendar, policy, or fiscal year basis?

    (k) The procedures for applying for benefits and the remedies available for denial of benefits?

44. Is the summary plan description written in a manner calculated to be understood by the average plan participant and sufficiently accurate and comprehensive to reasonably apprise participants and their beneficiaries of their rights and obligations under the plan? [ERISA: 102(a)(1)]

45. Has the plan administrator filed an updated plan description with the Secretary of Labor every five years, or such longer interval as may be prescribed by the Secretary of Labor? [ERISA: 104(a)(1)(B)]

46. Has the plan administrator filed an updated summary plan description with the Secretary of Labor every fifth year integrating all plan amendments made within such five-year period or, if no amendments were made, every 10th year? [ERISA: 104(a) (1)(C), 104(b)(1)(B)]

47. If there has been any material modification in the terms of the plan or any change in the information described in Question 43, has the plan administrator filed such modification or change with

the Secretary of Labor within 60 days after such modification or change was adopted or occurred? (*Note:* No filing is required if the information is included in the summary plan description filed on or before May 30, 1976.) [ERISA: 104(a)(1)(D)]

48. Has an annual report been filed with the Secretary of Labor (ERISA: 103):
   (a) Within 210 days (or such other period prescribed by regulations) after the close of the plan year? [ERISA: 104(a)(1)(A)] [*Note:* Proposed Form 5500 provides that it is to be filed on or before (a) the 15th day of the fifth month following the close of the employer's taxable year, for a single-employer plan whose plan year ends either with the employer's taxable year or within four months before the end of such taxable year, or (b) 135 days following the close of the plan year, for all other plans; effective with plan years beginning on or after January 1, 1975.]
   (b) With accompanying financial statements and schedules audited by an independent accountant [as defined in ERISA: 103(a)(3)(D); see Question 49]?
   (c) With an accompanying actuarial statement prepared by an enrolled actuary (as defined), including his opinion thereon (based on an actuarial valuation of the plan for at least every third plan year) as to whether the matters contained in such statement are reasonably based on the plan's experience and reasonable expectations, and represent his best estimate of anticipated experience (see Question 50)?
   (d) If *no* to (b) or (c) above, has audit of such material and/or actuary's involvement been waived by the Secretary of Labor?

49. Are the following items, included (except as noted) in the annual report [see Question 48(b)], covered by the accountant's opinion (ERISA: 103):
   (a) Financial statements:
      (1) Assets and liabilities?
      (2) Changes in net assets available for plan benefits?
      (3) Required disclosures in notes to financial statements [ERISA: 103(b)(2)]?
   (b) Supplemental schedules:
      (1) Assets and liabilities by categories and valued at their current value, in comparative form with the prior year's figures?

(2) Receipts and disbursements during year, aggregated by general sources and applications?

(3) Assets held for investment?

(4) Transactions with parties in interest?

(5) Loans or fixed income obligations in default or uncollectible?

(6) Leases in default or uncollectible?

(7) Most recent annual statement of assets and liabilities of a common or collective trust, or in the case of a separate account or trust, certain other information, where plan assets are held by a bank or similar institution or insurance carrier? (*Note:* Generally need not be covered by accountant's opinion, and need not be filed with annual report where Secretary of Labor permits omission.)

(8) Reportable transactions, generally those exceeding 3% of the current value (generally fair market value) of the plan's assets?

(c) Summary of annual report (not required to be filed with annual report) and supplemental schedules referred to in (b)(1) and (b)(2) above (see Question 66)?

Note: See Chapter 5 for discussion of proposed Form 5500.

50. Is the following information, included in the annual report [see Question 48(c)], covered by the actuary's opinion (ERISA: 103):

(a) The date of the plan year, and the date of the actuarial valuation applicable to the plan for which the report is filed?

(b) The date and amount of the contribution (or contributions) received by the plan for the plan year for which the report is filed and contributions for prior plan years not previously reported?

(c) The following information applicable to the plan year for which the report is filed: the normal costs, the accrued liabilities, an identification of benefits not included in the calculation; a statement of the other facts and actuarial assumptions and methods used to determine costs, and a justification for any change in actuarial assumptions or cost methods; and the minimum contribution required under the minimum funding standards?

(d) The number of participants and beneficiaries, both retired and nonretired, covered by the plan?

(e) The current value of the assets accumulated in the plan, and the present value of the assets of the plan used by the actuary in any computation of the amount of contributions to the plan required under ERISA Section 302 and a statement explaining the basis of such valuation of present value of assets?

(f) The present value of all of the plan's liabilities for nonforfeitable pension benefits allocated by the termination priority categories as set forth in ERISA Section 4044, and the actuarial assumptions used in these computations? (*Note:* These requirements may be waived or modified by the Secretary of Labor in certain instances.)

(g) A certification of the contribution necessary to reduce the accumulated funding deficiency to zero?

(h) A statement by the enrolled actuary:
  (1) That to the best of his knowledge the report is complete and accurate?
  (2) The requirements of ERISA Section 302(c)(3) (relating to reasonable actuarial assumptions and methods) have been complied with?

(i) Such other information regarding the plan as the Secretary of Labor may by regulation require?

(j) Such other information as may be necessary to fully and fairly disclose the actuarial position of the plan?

51. Does the plan administrator retain, for at least six years, records on matters on which disclosure is required under Title I of ERISA (filings with the Secretary of Labor and any items of disclosure to participants required by ERISA Sections 104 and 105)? (ERISA: 107)

Filings With the Secretary of the Treasury. Effective Date: Except as otherwise noted, plan years commencing after 12/31/75. [ERISA: 1034(2)]

52. If the plan is subject to the vesting standards, has the plan administrator filed an annual registration statement with the Secretary of the Treasury within the period prescribed by regulations? [ERISA: 1031(a); IRC: 6057(a)]

53. Does the annual registration statement referred to in Question 52 contain the following information [ERISA: 1031(a); IRC: 6057(a)(2)]:
  (a) The name of the plan?
  (b) The name and address of the plan administrator?
  (c) The name and taxpayer identification number of each participant who left covered employment during the plan year with a right to a deferred vested benefit which has not commenced at the end of the plan year?

(d) The nature, amount, and form of deferred vested benefit to which such participant is entitled?

54. Did the plan administrator submit evidence to the Secretary of the Treasury that participants were furnished individual statements of the information contained in the annual registration statement? [ERISA: 1031(a); IRC: 6057(a)]

55. Has the plan administrator notified the Secretary of the Treasury, within the time prescribed by regulations, of [ERISA: 1031(a); IRC: 6057(b)]:

(a) Any change in the name of the plan?

(b) Any change in the name and address of the plan administrator?

(c) The termination of the plan?

(d) The merger or consolidation of the plan with any other plan or its division into two or more plans?

56. Has the plan administrator filed an annual return with the Secretary of the Treasury? [ERISA: 1031(a); IRC: 6058(a); Effective Date: Plan years beginning after 9/2/74—ERISA: 1034(3)] [*Note:* Proposed Form 5500 (which replaces the prior Form 4848, 4849 filings) provides that it is to be filed on or before the 15th day of the fifth month following the close of (a) the employer's taxable year, in the case of a single-employer plan, or (b) the plan year, in the case of a plan with more than one employer; effective with plan years ending in taxable years ending on or after December 31, 1975 (except for industry or area-wide union-negotiated plans for which the effective date is for plan years ending on or after December 31, 1975).]

57. If there was a merger, consolidation, or transfer of assets or liabilities during the plan year, did the plan administrator file, at least 30 days before such event, an actuarial statement of valuation evidencing compliance with the requirements of IRC Section 401(a)(12)? [ERISA: 1031(a); IRC: 6058(b); Effective Date: 9/2/74—ERISA: 1034]

58. Has the plan administrator filed an actuarial report with the Secretary of the Treasury for the first plan year for which the minimum funding standards of IRC Section 412 apply (see Part II for effective date) and for each third plan year thereafter? [ERISA: 1033(a); IRC: 6059(a)]

59. Is the actuarial report filed with the Secretary of the Treasury signed by an enrolled actuary and does it contain the following information [ERISA: 1033(a); IRC: 6059(b)]:

(a) A description of the funding method and actuarial assumptions used to determine costs under the plan?

(b) A certification of the contribution necessary to reduce the accumulated funding deficiency [as defined in IRC: 412(a)] to zero?

(c) A statement:

    (1) That to the best of the actuary's knowledge the report is complete and accurate, and

    (2) That the requirements of IRC Section 412(c) relating to reasonable actuarial assumptions have been complied with?

(d) Such other information as may be required by regulations or which may be necessary to fully and fairly disclose the actuarial position of the plan?

Filings With the Pension Benefit Guaranty Corporation. Effective Date: 9/2/74. [ERISA: 4082(a)]

60. Has the plan administrator filed a premium payment declaration with the Pension Benefit Guaranty Corporation and paid the premium due, all within 30 days of the commencement of the plan year? [ERISA: 4007(a)]

61. Were all reportable events specified in ERISA Section 4043(b) reported to the Pension Benefit Guaranty Corporation within 30 days after the plan administrator knew or had reason to know they had occurred? [ERISA: 4043(a)]

62. Has the plan administrator filed an annual report with the Pension Benefit Guaranty Corporation within six months of the close of the plan year? [ERISA: 4065]

63. If more than one employer makes contributions under the plan and a substantial employer withdrew from the plan during the plan year, has the plan administrator notified the Pension Benefit Guaranty Corporation within 60 days of such withdrawal? (*Note:* See ERISA Section 4001(a)(2) for definition of substantial employer.) [ERISA: 4063(a)(1)]

Reporting to Participants and Beneficiaries. Effective Date: 1/1/75, except that proposed regulations postpone the effective date for non-calendar year plans to the first plan year beginning after 1/1/75 (see Table 5–2 for further details). [ERISA: 111(b)]

64. Has the plan administrator, at least every 10 years (five years if plan amended), and the latest of 120 days after the plan is established, or 90 days after participation or benefits commence, or May 30, 1976, made provision to furnish to participants and/or beneficiaries, a summary plan description which encompasses the topics described in Question 43? [ERISA: 101, 102, 104(b)]

65. Has the plan administrator made copies of the plan description and the latest annual report and the bargaining agreement, trust agreements, and other documents by which the plan was established and operated available for examination by participants and beneficiaries in the principal office of the plan administrator and such other places as may be required by regulations? [ERISA: 104(b)(2)]

66. Has provision been made for participants and beneficiaries to be provided with a summary of the plan's annual report and the required supplemental schedules [see Questions 49(b)(1) and (2)] within 210 days (or such other period prescribed by regulations) after the close of the plan year? [ERISA: 104(b)(3)]

67. If there has been a material modification in the terms of the plan or a change in the information contained in the summary plan description, has the plan administrator made provision to furnish participants, and beneficiaries receiving benefits, with a summary description of such modification or change within 210 days after the end of the plan year in which the change is adopted or occurs? (*Note:* See Note to Question 47.) [ERISA: 104(b)(1)]

68. Has the plan administrator made provision to furnish to participants and beneficiaries, upon written request, copies of the latest updated summary plan description, plan description, the latest annual report, any terminal report, and any documents under which the plan was established or operated (for which a reasonable charge may be made)? [ERISA: 104(b)(4)]

69. Has the plan administrator made provision to furnish to participants and beneficiaries upon written request, at least once every 12 months, a statement indicating on the basis of the latest available information the total benefits accrued, and the nonforfeitable pension benefits, if any, accrued, or the earliest date on which benefits will become nonforfeitable? [ERISA: 105(a), 105(b)]

70. Has the plan administrator made provision to furnish individual statements to all participants reported in the annual registration statement filed with the Secretary of the Treasury, setting forth the nature, amount, and form of the deferred vested benefit to which each such participant is entitled and such other information as is contained in the annual registration statement? [ERISA: 105(c); IRC: 6057(e)]

Part IV—Fiduciary Responsibilities

Effective Date: Except as otherwise noted below, 1/1/75. Postponements of the application of certain of the fiduciary requirements have been applied for and obtained by some employers. The postponements end 12/31/75. (ERISA: 414)

Establishment of Plan and Trust

71. Does the plan document [ERISA: 402(b)]:
    (a) Provide that one or more fiduciaries be named and be given authority to control and manage the operation and administration of the plan?
    (b) Provide a procedure for establishing and implementing a funding policy?
    (c) Provide a procedure for amending the plan and identify the persons who have authority to amend?
    (d) Specify the basis on which payments are made to and from the plan?
72. Are all assets of the plan held in trust by one or more trustees named in the trust instrument or appointed by a named fiduciary? (*Note:* This requirement does not apply to a plan funded by insurance contracts or policies.) [ERISA: 403(a) and (b)]
73. Does the trustee have exclusive discretion to manage and control plan assets, unless the plan expressly provides that the trustee is subject to the fiduciary's direction or if the management responsibility is delegated to an investment manager by the fiduciary? [ERISA: 403(a)]
74. Does the plan provide that the assets of the plan shall never inure to the benefit of any employer and shall be held for the exclusive purpose of providing benefits to participants in the plan and their beneficiaries and defraying reasonable expenses of administering the plan? (*Note:* This requirement does not prevent the return of a contribution made as a mistake of fact; the return of contributions conditioned on qualification of the plan which are returned within one year of denial of qualification of the plan; the return within one year of the portion of contributions for which a deduction was disallowed; or certain correcting distributions made by self-employed individuals.) [ERISA: 403(c)]

Fiduciary Duties

75. Are all plan assets held within the United States unless specifically authorized by the Secretary of Labor? [ERISA: 404(b), 1021(a); IRC: 401(a)]
76. Have the plan assets been invested prudently and are they diversified so as to minimize the risks of large losses, unless clearly prudent not to do so? [ERISA: 404(a)(1), (B) and (C)]

Prohibited Transactions. See ERISA Sections 408, 414, and 2003 (a) and IRC Section 4975(d) for exemptions from and deferrals of certain prohibited transactions.

77. Have the fiduciaries with respect to the plan refrained from causing the plan to engage in any of the following transactions [ERISA: 406(a)(1), 2003(a); IRC: 4975(c)]:
    (a) A sale or exchange, or leasing, of any property between the plan and a party in interest, except to the extent allowed (see Questions 81 and 82)?
    (b) The lending of money or other extension of credit between the plan and a party in interest?
    (c) The furnishing of goods, services, or facilities between the plan and a party in interest?
    (d) The transfer to, or use by or for the benefit of, a party in interest, of any assets of the plan?
    (e) The acquisition, on behalf of the plan, of employer securities or employer real property, except to the extent allowed (see Questions 81 and 82)?
    Note: See ERISA Sections 3(14) and 3(21) and IRC Sections 4975(e)(2) and (3) for definitions of party in interest (disqualified person) and fiduciary.
78. Have the fiduciaries with respect to the plan refrained from dealing with plan assets in their own interests or for their own accounts? [ERISA: 406(b)(1), 2003(a); IRC: 4975(c)(1)(E)]
79. Have the fiduciaries with respect to the plan refrained from acting in any transaction involving the plan on behalf of a party whose interests are adverse to the interests of the plan or participants or beneficiaries? [ERISA: 406(b)(2)]
80. Have the fiduciaries with respect to the plan refrained from accepting any considerations for their own personal accounts from any party dealing with the plan in connection with a transaction involving the assets of the plan? [ERISA: 406(b)(3), 2003(a); IRC: 4975(c)(1)(F)]

Employer Securities and Employer Real Property

81. If any investments are held in employer securities or employer real property, do such investments comprise no more than 10% (less than 10%, if required by the diversification and prudence rules) of the fair market value of plan assets (Note 1, page 254)? (ERISA: 407, 408)
82. Do all employer securities and employer real property held under the plan meet the requirements of "qualifying employer securities

(stock and marketable obligations (as defined))" or "qualifying employer real property" (Notes 2 and 3, below)? [ERISA: 407(a)(1)]

Exculpatory Provisions; Insurance

83. Has the plan eliminated any provision which purports to relieve a fiduciary from responsibility or liability for any fiduciary duty imposed by ERISA? [ERISA: 410(a)]
84. If any fiduciary insurance is being provided to fiduciaries under the plan, are all premiums paid from sources other than plan assets (unless the policy allows recourse against the fiduciary)? [ERISA: 410(b)]

Bonding

85. Are all individuals who handle funds of a plan and all fiduciaries [other than those individuals and fiduciaries exempted by ERISA Section 412(a)(2)] bonded? [Note: Bond must be equal to at least 10% of the amount of funds handled subject to a minimum of $1,000 and a maximum of $500,000 (unless maximum is increased by Secretary of Labor).] (ERISA: 412)

Notes:
1. This provision is effective 1/1/75, but the plan is allowed a 10-year transition period within which to comply with this requirement [ERISA: 407(a)(3)]. By 12/31/79, the plan must meet the divestment schedule specified in regulations to be issued under ERISA Section 407(a)(4)(B). Acquisition or holding by a plan of certain employer debt securities such as bonds, notes, etc., is limited to certain percentages [ERISA: 407(e)].
2. Qualifying employer real property is defined as parcels of real property and related personal property which are leased to an employer or its affiliate and (a) a substantial number of the parcels are dispersed geographically and (b) each parcel of real property and the improvements thereon are suitable (or adaptable without excessive cost) for more than one use. [ERISA: 407(d)(4)]
3. Holding or acquiring employer securities or employer real property other than "qualifying employer securities" or "qualifying employer real property" constitutes a prohibited transaction under ERISA Sections 406(a)(1)(E) and 406(a)(2). The application of these prohibited transaction rules are deferred under certain circumstances until 6/30/84 by ERISA Section 414(c).

Part V—Record-Keeping Requirements

Effective Date: First plan year beginning after 9/2/74 for plans not in existence on 1/1/74; first plan year beginning after 12/31/75 for plans in existence on 1/1/74. (ERISA: 211, 1017)

86. Does the employer or fund administrator maintain records sufficient to determine the benefits due or which may become due to each employee, which records would *probably* have to include the following (ERISA: 209):
    (a) Age?
    (b) Length of service?
    (c) Hours worked?
    (d) Salary?
    (e) Employee contributions?

DEFINED CONTRIBUTION PLANS

Part I—Plan Provisions

Effective Date: Except as otherwise noted below, first plan year beginning after 9/2/74 for plans not in existence on 1/1/74; first plan year beginning after 12/31/75 for plans in existence on 1/1/74. (ERISA: 211, 1017)

Participation

1. If the plan imposes age and/or service requirements on participation eligibility, are employees eligible to participate no later than the later of age 25 or completion of one year of service? (*Note:* If a plan provides for 100% vesting after three years of service, substitute a three-year service requirement for the one-year service requirement. In addition, for plans of certain tax-exempt educational institutions which provide 100% vesting after one year of service, substitute age 30 for age 25.) [ERISA: 202(a)(1), 1011; IRC: 410(a)(1)]
2. If the plan imposes age and/or service requirements on participation eligibility, does actual participation begin no later than the earlier of [ERISA: 202(a)(4), 1011; IRC: 410(a)(4)]:
    (a) The date six months following the date the age and/or service requirements are satisfied, or

(b) The first day of the first plan year beginning after the date the age and/or service requirements are satisfied?

3. Does the plan allow participation without imposing a maximum age limit prohibited by law? [*Note:* A target benefit plan (as defined by regulations) may exclude from participation employees who are hired within five years of normal retirement age. No similar exclusion is allowed under any other defined contribution plan.] [ERISA: 202(a)(2), 1011; IRC: 410(a)(2)]

Vesting

4. Does plan vest employer-provided accrued benefits at a rate which meets or exceeds *at least one* of the following [ERISA: 203(a)(2), 1012(a); IRC: 411(a)(2)]:

(a) Twenty-five per cent vesting after five years of service, increasing 5% for each of the next five years (50% of vesting after 10 years) and at least 10% for each of the next five years (100% after 15 years of service),

(b) Full vesting after 10 years of service (no vesting required prior to completion of 10 years of service), or

(c) Fifty per cent vesting as of earlier of:

(1) Earliest date on which employee has completed at least five years of service and the total of his age and service equals at least 45, or

(2) Completion of 10 years of service

with an additional 10% vesting for each year of service completed thereafter?

5. Is a participant 100% vested at normal retirement age? [ERISA: 203(a), 1012(a); IRC: 411(a)]

6. Are employee contributions 100% vested at all times? [ERISA: 203(a)(1), 1012(a); IRC: 411(a)(1)]

Service

7. Does the plan credit a full year of service for a 12-month period during which the employee or participant completed at least 1,000 hours? [ERISA: 202(a)(3)(A), 203(b)(2)(A), 1011, 1012(a); IRC: 410(a)(3)(A), 411(a)(5)(A)]

8. For participation purposes only, does the 12-month period used for crediting service commence on the employee's date of hire? [ERISA: 202(a)(3)(A), 1011; IRC: 410(a)(3)(A)]

9. Except for those years enumerated below, are all years of employment (whether or not continuous) taken into account in determining service under the plan? [ERISA: 202(b)(1), 203 (b)(1), 1011, 1012(a); IRC: 410(a)(5)(A), 411(a)(4)]

Note: The years of service which may be excluded from consideration are:

(a) Years of service prior to a "one-year break in service" (a specified 12-month period during which the participant or employee does not work more than 500 hours) unless the employee or participant returns to the employ of the employer and completes a year of service. [ERISA: 202(b)(3), 203(b)(3)(B), 1011, 1012(a); IRC: 410(a)(5)(C), 411(a)(6)(B)]

(b) If the participant had no vested rights at the time of a "one-year break in service," all years prior to such break in service, but only if the number of consecutive "one-year breaks in service" equals or exceeds the number of years of service recognized under the plan immediately prior to the "one-year break in service." [ERISA: 202(b)(4), 203(b)(3)(D), 1011, 1012(a); IRC: 410(a)(5)(D), 411(a)(6)(D)]

(c) For participation purposes only, if the plan provides for 100% vesting after three years and requires three years of service for participation and if an employee has a one-year break in service before meeting the service requirement, all service prior to such break in service. [ERISA: 202(b)(2), 1011; IRC: 410(a)(5)(B)]

(d) For vesting purposes only [ERISA: 203(b)(1), 1012(a); IRC: 411(a)(4)]:

    (1) Years of service before age 22 (but if "rule of 45" is used for vesting, years of service during which the employee was a participant may not be disregarded);

    (2) If the plan requires employee contributions, years of service during a period for which the participant declined to make the required contribution;

    (3) Years of service prior to the date the plan was established (but if service for benefits is granted for any such period, such service cannot be excluded for vesting purposes just because it is prior to the date the plan was established);

    (4) Years of service prior to the date ERISA vesting rules become effective with respect to the plan (9/2/74 for plans not in existence on 1/1/74 and first plan year commencing after 12/31/75 for plans in existence on 1/1/74) which would have been disregarded under the rules of the plan with regard to breaks in service as in effect on the applicable date;

(5) If the participant does not have at least three years of service after 12/31/70, all years of service before 1/1/71.

(6) Years of service after a one-year break in service may be excluded from consideration in vesting benefits accrued prior to such one-year break in service.

Retirement Benefits

10. Joint and Survivor Annuity [ERISA: 205, 1021(a); IRC: 401(a) (11); Effective Date: First plan year commencing after 12/31/75 —ERISA: 211(b)(1), 1021(a)(1)]:

(a) If the plan provides for payment in the form of an annuity, is the normal form of annuity payment for married participants a joint and survivor annuity which is the actuarial equivalent of a life annuity to the participant only, and which provides an annuity for the life of the participant and a survivor annuity for the life of the spouse which is not less than one-half of, nor greater than, the amount of annuity payable to the participant?

(b) Does a married participant have a reasonable period before the date his benefits commence during which he may elect in writing not to take the joint and survivor annuity as the normal form of annuity payment?

(c) Does the plan provide that a married participant be supplied with a written explanation of the terms and conditions of the joint and survivor annuity in order to make the election described in (b) above?

11. Is the normal retirement age under the plan no later than the later of age 65 and the 10th anniversary of the participant's commencement of participation in the plan? [ERISA: 2(24), 1012 (a); IRC: 411(a)(8)]

12. Do benefits under the plan commence not later than the 60th day after the latest of the close of the plan year in which [ERISA: 206(a), 1021(a); IRC: 410(a)(14)]:

(a) The participant reaches normal retirement age, or age 65 if earlier,

(b) Occurs the 10th anniversary of the commencement of the participant's participation in the plan, or

(c) The participant terminates his employment with the employer?

13. Does the plan provide that the annual addition for any participant for any year be limited to the lesser of $25,000 or 25% of the

participant's compensation? [ERISA: 2004(a)(2); IRC: 415; Effective Date: Years beginning after December 31, 1975–ERISA: 2004(d)] (Note 1, page 261)

Note: The maximum limitation on annual additions applies to the aggregate annual additions provided under all defined contribution plans of the employer (or of all employers in a controlled group of corporations). The $25,000 limitation is subject to upward adjustment as a result of cost-of-living increases. The term "annual addition" means the sum, for any year, of (a) employer contributions, (b) the lesser of employee contributions in excess of 6% of compensation or one-half of employee contributions, and (c) forfeitures.

14. If any participant covered by the plan also participates in a defined benefit plan maintained by the employer, does the plan provide that the total of the benefits payable under both plans shall not exceed the maximum benefit limitations specified in Section 415(e) of the Internal Revenue Code, applicable to an employee covered under both a defined contribution plan and a defined benefit plan? [ERISA: 2004; Effective Date: Years beginning after December 31, 1975–ERISA: 2004(d)] (Note 1, page 261)

Note: The limitation provides that the fraction equal to the defined benefit accrued to date over the maximum allowable projected defined benefit accrued at normal retirement age, when added to the fraction equal to the annual additions to date under the defined contribution plan over the maximum allowable annual additions, shall not exceed 1.4. The 1.4 limitation may be exceeded in certain circumstances pursuant to the special rule set forth in ERISA Section 2004(a)(3). Even if a participant does participate in both kinds of plans, the combined maximum limitation need appear in only one plan. The fact that the combined limitation does not appear in the defined contribution plan will not, by itself, constitute noncompliance, but should cause an examination of the defined benefit plan for such a limitation.

Death Benefits

15. Does the plan provide that a participant's account becomes fully vested upon his death and payable to his beneficiary? [If not, the survivor annuity provisions of ERISA Sections 205(c)(1) and 1021(a)(1) and IRC Section 401(a)(11)(C) may be applicable; Effective Date: First plan year commencing after 12/31/75–ERISA: 211(b)(1), 1021(a)(1).]

Forfeiture of Benefits

16. Does the plan limit forfeitures of benefits to the following situations:
    (a) Termination of employment without full vesting [ERISA: 203(a)(2), 1012(a); IRC: 411(a)(2)];
    (b) Death, except where a survivor annuity is payable [ERISA: 203(a)(3)(A), 1012(a); IRC: 411(a)(3)(A)];
    (c) Certain withdrawals of mandatory employee contributions [ERISA: 203(a)(3)(D), 1012(a); IRC: 411(a)(3)(D)]?

17. Does the plan limit the forfeiture of employer-provided benefits because of withdrawal of mandatory employee contributions to the following situations:
    (a) Where the participant is less than 50% vested in his accrued benefit [ERISA: 203(a)(3)(D)(i), 1012(a); IRC: 411(a)(3)(D)(i)]; or
    (b) Where the forfeited benefit accrued before 9/2/74, but only if no mandatory contributions are made under the plan after 9/2/74 and only if the forfeited amount is proportional to the amount withdrawn [ERISA: 203(a)(3)(D)(iii), 1012(a); IRC: 411(a)(3)(D)(iii)]?

18. If the plan provides for forfeiture of employer-provided benefit as a result of withdrawal of mandatory employee contributions by a participant who is less than 50% vested, does it allow the participant to repay the full amount of his withdrawal with interest and thereby restore the forfeited benefit? (*Note:* The right of repayment may be limited to the period prior to a one-year break in service following withdrawal.) [ERISA: 203(a)(3)(D)(ii), 1012(a); IRC: 411(a)(e)(D)(ii)]

Amendments

19. Does the plan provide that no amendment may decrease a participant's account? [ERISA: 204(g), 1012(a); IRC: 411(d)(6)]

20. Does the plan provide that no amendment may decrease a participant's nonforfeitable percentage (vesting percentage) in his account? [ERISA: 203(c)(1)(A), 1012(a); IRC: 411(a)(10)(A)]

21. Does the plan provide that if an amendment to the plan changes the vesting schedule, participants having not less than five years of service will be permitted to elect to have their vesting computed without regard to the amendment? [ERISA: 203(c)(1)(B), 1012(a); IRC: 411(a)(10)(B)]

Termination of the Plan

22. Does the plan provide that participants become fully vested upon

termination of the plan? [ERISA: 1012(a); IRC: 411(d)(3)] (Note 1, page 261)

Miscellaneous Provisions

23. Does the plan provide that benefits under the plan may not be alienated or assigned? (*Note:* A plan may allow for a voluntary and revocable assignment of up to 10% of each benefit payment and may provide for assignment or alienation of vested benefits to secure a loan from the plan, without violating the prohibition against alienation or assignment.) [ERISA: 206(d), 1021(c); IRC: 401(a)(13); Effective Date: First plan year commencing after 12/31/75–ERISA: 211(b)(1)]

24. Does the plan provide that in the event it merges or consolidates with, or transfers any assets or liabilities to, another plan, each participant in the plan would (if the plan then terminated) receive a benefit immediately after the merger, consolidation, or transfer which is equal to or greater than the benefit he would have been entitled to receive immediately before the merger, consolidation, or transfer (if the plan had then terminated)? [ERISA: 208, 1021(b); IRC: 401(a)(12); Effective Date: First plan year commencing after 12/31/75–ERISA: 211(b)(1), 1021 (b)]

25. Does the plan provide for, or specify, a claims procedure whereby a participant is notified in writing of a denial of benefits and afforded an opportunity for a full and fair review of the decision denying benefits? (ERISA: 503)

26. Does the plan provide separate accounting for participants' accounts? [ERISA: 204(b)(2)(B), 1012(a); IRC: 411(b)(2) (B)]

Note 1: Questions which refer only to IRC sections or to ERISA sections which amend IRC sections are applicable only to tax-qualified plans. With the advent of ERISA's funding and vesting requirements it is unlikely that nonqualified pension plans subject to those requirements will continue to be maintained, since participants thereunder will be currently taxed on employer contributions made to fund vested benefits.

Part II—Funding

Effective Date: First plan year beginning after 9/2/74 for plans not in existence on 1/1/74; first plan year beginning after 12/31/75 for plans in existence on 1/1/74. (ERISA: 306, 1017)

The funding requirements are only applicable to money-purchase plans (apparently including target benefit plans, as defined by regu-

lations) which are not governmental or church plans. Profit-sharing
and stock bonus plans are excepted from the funding requirements.
[ERISA: 4(b)(1) and (3), 1013(a); IRC: 412(h)]

27. Has a funding standard account been established and is it being
maintained? [ERISA: 302(b)(1), 1013(a); IRC: 412(b)(1)]

28. Is the account balance in a zero or credit position? [ERISA: 302
(a)(1), 1013(a); IRC: 412(a)]

29. Were the following charges and credits made to the account
[ERISA: 302(b), 1013(a); IRC: 412(b)] (Note 1, below):

(a) Charges:

(1) The amount required to be contributed for the plan
year in accordance with the terms of the plan?

(2) The amount necessary to amortize in equal annual installments, over 15 years, the waived funding deficiency
for each prior plan year (Note 2, below)?

(b) Credits:

(1) Employer contribution considered made for the plan
year (Note 3, below)?

(2) Waived funding deficiency (if any) for the plan year
(Note 2, below)?

30. Were all changes in plan year during the current year approved
by the Secretary of the Treasury? [ERISA: 302(c)(5), 1013(a);
IRC: 412(c)(5)]

Notes:

1. ERISA requires that the funding standard account (and items
therein) be charged or credited (as determined under regulations prescribed by the Secretary of the Treasury) with interest
at the appropriate rate consistent with the rate or rates of interest
used under the plan to determine costs. It is not clear whether
this provision should apply to money-purchase plans, and if it
does, what rate should be used, since no interest assumptions are
used to determine costs. [ERISA: 302(b)(5), 1013(a); IRC:
412(b)(5)]

2. Waivers of all or part of the minimum funding requirements may
be granted by the Secretary of the Treasury in certain cases of
substantial business hardship and are limited to not more than
five years out of any consecutive 15 years. This provision may
have been intended only for defined benefit plans and its application to those defined contribution plans subject to the funding
requirements is not clear. [ERISA: 303, 1013(a); IRC: 412(d)]

3. This employer contribution can only be credited herein where
the employer pays the contribution within two and one half

months after the end of the plan year. The Secretary of the Treasury may extend this period up to an additional six months. [ERISA: 302(c)(10), 1013(a); IRC: 412(c)(10)]

Part III—Reporting and Disclosure Requirements

Filings With the Secretary of Labor. Effective Date: 1/1/75, except that proposed regulations postpone the effective date for non-calendar year plans to the first plan year beginning after 1/1/75 (see Table 5–2 for further details). [ERISA: 111(b)]

31. If the plan was in existence on or before January 31, 1976, has the plan administrator filed a "short form plan description" with the Secretary of Labor by the later of 120 days of the date the plan was established or August 31, 1975? (*Note:* A "short form plan description" consists of the first two pages of Department of Labor Form EBS–1, without the schedules referred to therein, and the signature page with only item 38 completed.) [ERISA: 104(a)(1)(B) and proposed regulation Section 2520.104–3]

32. Has the plan administrator filed a plan description (Department of Labor Form EBS–1) and a summary plan description with the Secretary of Labor by the later of 120 days of the date the plan was established or May 30, 1976? [ERISA: 104(a)(1)(B) and proposed regulation Sec. 2520.104–3]

33. Did the summary plan description contain the following information [ERISA: 102(b)]:
    (a) The name and type of administration of the plan?
    (b) The name and address of the person designated as agent for service of legal process, if such person is not the plan administrator?
    (c) The name and address of the plan administrator?
    (d) Names, titles, and addresses of any trustee or trustees?
    (e) A description of the relevant provisions of any applicable collective bargaining agreement?
    (f) The plan's requirements respecting eligibility for participation and benefits?
    (g) A description of the provisions providing for nonforfeitable benefits?
    (h) Circumstances which may result in disqualification, ineligibility, or denial or loss of benefits?
    (i) The source of financing of the plan and the identity of any organization through which benefits are provided?
    (j) The date of the plan year end and whether the records of the plan are kept on a calendar, policy, or fiscal year basis?

(k) The procedures for applying for benefits and the remedies available for denial of benefits?

34. Is the summary plan description written in a manner calculated to be understood by the average plan participant and sufficiently accurate and comprehensive to reasonably apprise participants and their beneficiaries of their rights and obligations under the plan? [ERISA: 102(a)(1)]

35. Has the plan administrator filed an updated plan description with the Secretary of Labor every five years, or such longer interval as may be prescribed by the Secretary of Labor? [ERISA: 104 (a)(1)(B)]

36. Has the plan administrator filed an updated summary plan description with the Secretary of Labor every fifth year integrating all plan amendments made within such five-year period or, if no amendments were made, every 10th year? [ERISA: 104(a)(1) (C), 104(b)(1)(B)]

37. If there has been any material modification in the terms of the plan or any change in the information described in Question 33, has the plan administrator filed such modification or change with the Secretary of Labor within 60 days after such modification or change was adopted or occurred? (*Note:* No filing is required if the information is included in the summary plan description filed on or before May 30, 1976.) [ERISA: 104(a)(1)(D)]

38. Has an annual report been filed with the Secretary of Labor (ERISA: 103):

(a) Within 210 days (or such other period prescribed by regulations) after the close of the plan year? [ERISA: 104(a) (1)(A)] [*Note:* Proposed Form 5500 provides that it is to be filed on or before (a) the 15th day of the fifth month following the close of the employer's taxable year, for a single-employer plan whose plan year ends either with the employer's taxable year or within four months before the end of such taxable year, or (b) 135 days following the close of the plan year, for all other plans; effective with plan years beginning on or after January 1, 1975.]

(b) With accompanying financial statements and schedules audited by an independent accountant [as defined in ERISA: 103(a)(3)(D); see Question 39]? [*Note:* Certain plans (e.g., money-purchase and target benefit plans) are required to file an actuarial statement—proposed Form 5500, Schedule B; for such plans see Question 48(c), page 246.]

(c) If *no* to (b) above, has audit of such material been waived by the Secretary of Labor?

39. Are the following items, included (except as noted) in the annual report [see Question 38(b)], covered by the accountant's opinion (ERISA: 103):
   (a) Financial statements:
      (1) Assets and liabilities?
      (2) Changes in net assets available for plan benefits?
      (3) Required disclosures in notes to financial statements? [ERISA: 103(b)(2)]
   (b) Supplemental schedules:
      (1) Assets and liabilities by categories and valued at their current value, in comparative form with the prior year's figures?
      (2) Receipts and disbursements during year, aggregated by general sources and applications?
      (3) Assets held for investment?
      (4) Transactions with parties in interest?
      (5) Loans or fixed income obligations in default or uncollectible?
      (6) Leases in default or uncollectible?
      (7) Most recent annual statement of assets and liabilities of a common or collective trust, or in the case of a separate account or trust, certain other information, where plan assets are held by a bank or similar institution or insurance carrier? (*Note:* Generally need not be covered by accountant's opinion, and need not be filed with annual report where Secretary of Labor permits omission.)
      (8) Reportable transactions, generally those exceeding 3% of the current value (generally fair market value) of the plan's assets?
   (c) Summary of annual report (not required to be filed with annual report) and supplemental schedules referred to in (b)(1) and (b)(2) above (see Question 49)?
   Note: See Chapter 5 for discussion of proposed Form 5500.

40. Does the plan administrator retain, for at least six years, records on matters on which disclosure is required under Title I of ERISA (filings with the Secretary of Labor and any items of disclosure to participants required by ERISA 104 and 105)? (ERISA: 107)

Filings With the Secretary of the Treasury. Effective Date: Except as otherwise noted, plan years commencing after 12/31/75. [ERISA: 1034(2)]

41. If the plan is subject to the vesting standards, has the plan administrator filed an annual registration statement with the Secretary of the Treasury within the period prescribed by regulations? [ERISA: 1031(a); IRC: 6057(a)]

42. Does the annual registration statement referred to in Question 41 contain the following information [ERISA: 1031(a); IRC: 6057(a)(2)]:
   (a) The name of the plan?
   (b) The name and address of the plan administrator?
   (c) The name and taxpayer identification number of each participant who left covered employment during the plan year with a right to a deferred vested benefit which has not commenced at the end of the plan year?
   (d) The nature, amount, and form of deferred vested benefit to which such participant is entitled?

43. Did the plan administrator submit evidence to the Secretary of the Treasury that participants were furnished individual statements of the information contained in the annual registration statement? [ERISA: 1031(a); IRC: 6057(a)]

44. Has the plan administrator notified the Secretary of the Treasury, within the time prescribed by regulations, of [ERISA: 1031(a); IRC: 6057(b)]:
   (a) Any change in the name of the plan?
   (b) Any change in the name and address of the plan administrator?
   (c) The termination of the plan?
   (d) The merger or consolidation of the plan with any other plan or its division into two or more plans?

45. Has the plan administrator filed an annual return with the Secretary of the Treasury? [ERISA: 1031(a); IRC: 6058(a); Effective Date: Plan years beginning after 9/2/74—ERISA: 1034(3)] [Note: Proposed Form 5500 (which replaces the prior Form 4848, 4849 filings) provides that it is to be filed on or before the 15th day of the fifth month following the close of (a) the employer's taxable year, in the case of a single-employer plan, or (b) the plan year, in the case of a plan with more than one employer; effective with plan years ending in taxable years ending on or after December 31, 1975 (except for industry or area-wide union-negotiated plans for which the effective date is for plan years ending on or after December 31, 1975).]

46. If there was a merger, consolidation, or transfer of assets or liabilities during the plan year, did the plan administrator file, at least 30 days before such event, an actuarial statement of valua-

tion evidencing compliance with the requirements of IRC Section 401(a)(12)? [ERISA: 1031(a); IRC: 6058(b); Effective Date: 9/2/74—ERISA: 1034]

Reporting to Participants and Beneficiaries. Effective Date: 1/1/75, except that proposed regulations postpone the effective date for non-calendar year plans to the first plan year beginning after 1/1/75 (see Table 5–2 for further details). [ERISA: 111(b)]

47. Has the plan administrator, at least every 10 years (five years if plan amended), and the latest of 120 days after the plan is established, or 90 days after participation or benefits commence, or May 30, 1976, made provision to furnish to participants and/or beneficiaries, a summary plan description which encompasses the topics described in Question 33? [ERISA: 101, 102, 104(b)]

48. Has the plan administrator made copies of the plan description and the latest annual report and the bargaining agreement, trust agreements, and other documents by which the plan was established and operated available for examination by participants and beneficiaries in the principal office of the plan administrator and such other places as may be required by regulations? [ERISA: 104(b)(2)]

49. Has provision been made for participants and beneficiaries to be provided with a summary of the plan's annual report and the required supplemental schedules [see Questions 39(b)(1) and (2)] within 210 days (or such other period prescribed by regulations) after the close of the plan year? [ERISA: 104(b)(3)]

50. If there has been a material modification in the terms of the plan or a change in the information contained in the summary plan description, has the plan administrator made provisions to furnish participants, and beneficiaries receiving benefits, with a summary description of such modification or change within 210 days after the end of the plan year in which the change is adopted or occurs? (*Note:* See Note to Question 37.) [ERISA: 104(b)(1)]

51. Has the plan administrator made provision to furnish to participants and beneficiaries, upon written request, copies of the latest updated summary plan description, plan description, the latest annual report, any terminal report, and any documents under which the plan was established or operated (for which a reasonable charge may be made)? [ERISA: 104(b)(4)]

52. Has the plan administrator made provision to furnish to participants and beneficiaries upon written request, at least once every 12 months, a statement indicating on the basis of the latest available information the total benefits accrued, and the non-

forfeitable pension benefits, if any, accrued, or the earliest date on which benefits will become nonforfeitable? [ERISA: 105(a), 105(b)]

53. Has the plan administrator made provision to furnish individual statements to all participants reported in the annual registration statement filed with the Secretary of the Treasury, setting forth the nature, amount, and form of the deferred vested benefit to which each such participant is entitled and such other information as is contained in the annual registration statement? [ERISA: 105(c); IRC: 6057(e)]

Part IV—Fiduciary Responsibilities

Effective Date: Except as otherwise noted below, 1/1/75. Postponements of the application of certain of the fiduciary requirements have been applied for and obtained by some employers. The postponements end 12/31/75. (ERISA: 414)

Establishment of Plan and Trust

54. Does the plan document [ERISA: 402(b)]:
   (a) Provide that one or more fiduciaries be named and be given authority to control and manage the operation and administration of the plan?
   (b) Provide a procedure for establishing and implementing a funding policy?
   (c) Provide a procedure for amending the plan and identify the persons who have authority to amend?
   (d) Specify the basis on which payments are made to and from the plan?

55. Are all assets of the plan held in trust by one or more trustees named in the trust instrument or appointed by a named fiduciary? (*Note:* This requirement does not apply to a plan funded by insurance contracts or policies.) [ERISA: 403(a) and (b)]

56. Does the trustee have exclusive discretion to manage and control plan assets, unless the plan expressly provides that the trustee is subject to the fiduciary's direction or if the management responsibility is delegated to an investment manager by the fiduciary? [ERISA: 403(a)]

57. Does the plan provide that the assets of the plan shall never inure to the benefit of any employer and shall be held for the exclusive purpose of providing benefits to participants in the plan and their beneficiaries and defraying reasonable expenses of administering the plan? (*Note:* This requirement does not prevent the return

of a contribution made as a mistake of fact; the return of contributions conditioned on qualification of the plan which are returned within one year of denial of qualification of the plan; the return within one year of the portion of contributions for which a deduction was disallowed; or certain correcting distributions made by self-employed individuals.) [ERISA: 403(c)]

Fiduciary Duties

58. Are all plan assets held within the United States unless specifically authorized by the Secretary of Labor? [ERISA: 404(b), 1021(a), IRC: 401(a)]
59. Have the plan assets been invested prudently and are they diversified so as to minimize the risks of large losses, unless clearly prudent not to do so. [ERISA: 404(a)(1), (B) and (C)]

Prohibited Transactions. See ERISA Sections 408, 414, and 2003(a) and IRC Section 4975(d) for exemptions from and deferrals of certain prohibited transactions.

60. Have the fiduciaries with respect to the plan refrained from causing the plan to engage in any of the following transactions [ERISA: 406(a)(1), 2003(a); IRC: 4975(c)]:
    (a) A sale or exchange, or leasing, of any property between the plan and a party in interest, except to the extent allowed (see Questions 64 and 65)?
    (b) The lending of money or other extension of credit between the plan and a party in interest?
    (c) The furnishing of goods, services, or facilities between the plan and a party in interest?
    (d) The transfer to, or use by or for the benefit of, a party in interest, of any assets of the plan?
    (e) The acquisition, on behalf of the plan, of employer securities or employer real property, except to the extent allowed (see Questions 64 and 65)?
    Note: See ERISA Sections 3(14) and 3(21) and IRC Sections 4975(e)(2) and (3) for definitions of party in interest (disqualified person) and fiduciary.
61. Have the fiduciaries with respect to the plan refrained from dealing with plan assets in their own interests or for their own accounts? [ERISA: 406(b)(1), 2003(a); IRC: 4975(c)(1)(E)]
62. Have the fiduciaries with respect to the plan refrained from acting in any transaction involving the plan on behalf of a party

whose interests are adverse to the interests of the plan or participants or beneficiaries? [ERISA: 406(b)(2)]

63. Have the fiduciaries with respect to the plan refrained from accepting any considerations for their own personal accounts from any party dealing with the plan in connection with a transaction involving the assets of the plan? [ERISA: 406(b)(3), 2003(a); IRC: 4975(c)(1)(F)]

Employer Securities and Employer Real Property

64. If any investments are held in employer securities or employer real property, do such investments comprise no more than 10% (less than 10%, if required by the diversification and prudence rules) of the fair market value of plan assets (Note 1, below)? (ERISA: 407, 408)

65. Do all employer securities and employer real property held under the plan meet the requirements of "qualifying employer securities (stock and marketable obligations (as defined))" or "qualifying employer real property" (Notes 2 and 3, page 271)? [ERISA: 407(a)(1)]

Exculpatory Provisions; Insurance

66. Has the plan eliminated any provision which purports to relieve a fiduciary from responsibility or liability for any fiduciary duty imposed by ERISA? [ERISA: 410(a)]

67. If any fiduciary insurance is being provided to fiduciaries under the plan, are all premiums paid from sources other than plan assets (unless the policy allows recourse against the fiduciary)? [ERISA: 410(b)]

Bonding

68. Are all individuals who handle funds of a plan and all fiduciaries [other than those individuals and fiduciaries exempted by ERISA Section 412(a)(2)] bonded? [*Note:* Bond must be equal to at least 10% of the amount of funds handled subject to a minimum of $1,000 and a maximum of $500,000 (unless maximum is increased by Secretary of Labor).] (ERISA: 412)

Notes:

1. This provision is effective 1/1/75, but the plan is allowed a 10-year transition period within which to comply with this requirement [ERISA: 407(a)(3)]. By 12/31/79, the plan must meet the divestment schedule specified in regulations to be issued under ERISA Section 407(a)(4)(B). The 10% limitation will not apply to defined contribution plans (other than money-purchase

plans not in existence on 9/2/74 or which did not invest primarily in qualifying employer securities as of such date) if such plan explicitly provides for acquisition and holding of qualifying employer securities or qualifying employer real property. [ERISA: 407(b)(1), 407(d)(3)] Acquisition or holding by a plan of certain employer debt securities such as bonds, notes, etc., is limited to certain percentages. [ERISA: 407(e)]

2. Qualifying employer real property is defined as parcels of real property and related personal property which are leased to an employer or its affiliate and (a) a substantial number of the parcels are dispersed geographically and (b) each parcel of real property and the improvements thereon are suitable (or adaptable without excessive cost) for more than one use. [ERISA: 407 (d)(4)]

3. Holding or acquiring employer securities or employer real property other than "qualifying employer securities" or "qualifying employer real property" constitutes a prohibited transaction under ERISA Sections 406(a)(1)(E) and 406(a)(2). The application of these prohibited transaction rules is deferred under certain circumstances until 6/30/84 by ERISA Section 414(c).

Part V—Record-Keeping Requirements

Effective Date: First plan year beginning after 9/2/74 for plans not in existence on 1/1/74; first plan year beginning after 12/31/75 for plans in existence on 1/1/74. (ERISA: 211, 1017)

69. Does the employer or fund administrator maintain records sufficient to determine the benefits due or which may become due to each employee, which records would *probably* have to include the following (ERISA: 209):
    (a) Age?
    (b) Length of service?
    (c) Hours worked?
    (d) Salary?
    (e) Employee contributions?

APPENDIXES

A

SPECIMEN AUDIT PROGRAM, EMPLOYER COMPANY

Introduction

This specimen audit program is not intended to be all-inclusive, and must be tailored to conditions encountered on a particular engagement. The materiality of pension costs, and the materiality of any possible understatement or overstatement of such costs upon the fairness of presentation of the financial statements, should influence the selection of audit procedures and the extent and depth of the examination, just as materiality is considered in any other audit procedure. As in other areas, however, materiality is not the sole consideration. For example, while penalties for noncompliance with ERISA may be immaterial to the financial statements on a particular engagement, the auditor should nevertheless be alert to instances of noncompliance so as to be in a position to advise clients of a need to consider taking corrective action.

Subject to the foregoing comments, the procedures outlined are intended, unless conditions indicate otherwise, to provide the auditor with a basis for reaching a conclusion that in all material respects the pension expense reported, when considered in relation to the financial statements of an employer company taken as a whole, is fairly stated in conformity with generally accepted accounting principles consistently applied, that the appropriate related disclosures are made, that the pension plan and its operation comply with the requirements of ERISA, and that the accounting-related impact of ERISA requirements is properly reflected in the financial statements. Where departures from generally accepted accounting principles exist, the auditor should refer to "Departures from the Opinion and Interpretation" in Chapter 7 for a discussion of the considerations involved.

General

1. Determine whether a pension plan exists (as defined by APB Opinion No. 8).
2. If a pension plan exists, obtain the following items:
   (a) Copy of plan documents and amendments, including Plan Description and Summary Plan Description required by ERISA.
   (b) Copy of all Internal Revenue Service determination letters (qualified plans only).
3. Determine whether the plan is a defined contribution plan or a defined benefit plan.
   (a) For a defined contribution plan, follow the procedures listed under "Defined Contribution Plans."
   (b) For a defined benefit plan, follow the procedures listed under "Defined Benefit Plans Funded by Insurance Policies" for the portion, if any, funded by insurance policies, and the procedures listed under "Defined Benefit Plans Other Than Those Funded by Insurance Policies" for the remainder.
   Note: Some plans will call for both a prescribed scale of benefits and a fixed rate of employer contributions. In that case, reference should be made to "Defined Contribution Plans" in Chapter 6 for a discussion of the considerations involved.
4. Determine whether the plan complies with Internal Revenue Service regulations. (For this purpose, see procedure 2 under "Audit Procedures Directly Related to ERISA.")
5. Compare the provisions of the plan with prior year to determine whether there are any changes that might affect comparability. An estimate of the effect of such changes on costs should be obtained from the actuary or otherwise determined, as appropriate. Plan amendments materially affecting the financial statements should be disclosed in the footnotes; such changes do not involve consistency of accounting since they stem from altered conditions, and therefore they need not be commented upon in the auditor's report (other than in reports accompanying financial statements

filed with the SEC). Changes resulting from a choice by management where conditions have not changed, however, such as those discussed in procedures 7 to 11 under "Defined Benefit Plans Other Than Those Funded by Insurance Policies," do involve consistency of accounting and therefore normally would require comment in the auditor's report. (See "Comparability and Consistency" in Chapter 7.)

6. Review the period from the date of the latest actuarial or other valuation, as appropriate, to the fiscal year end and beyond for subsequent events which might have a significant impact on pension costs (e.g., plant closings, changes in plan, changes in market value of equity securities). An estimate of the effect on costs of any such events should be obtained from the actuary or otherwise determined, as appropriate. (If deemed desirable, request actuary to confirm date of his most recent actuarial valuation.)

Defined Contribution Plans

1. Obtain copy of latest report of the funding agent (custodian, trustee, or insurance company), showing a summary of receipts and disbursements for the year.
2. Verify that the employer has made the required contributions in accordance with the plan. To do this, test the required contribution against the basis of such contribution [usually the census (and related) data] as follows:
   (a) Test-check salary amounts shown on payroll records against the census data if the contribution is a percentage of salary.
   (b) Test-check hours worked shown on payroll records against the census data if the contribution is per hour.
   (c) Test-check production figures shown on production records against the census data if the contribution is based on production.
   Note: For further details, see "Employer Records" in Appendix B.
3. Ascertain whether there have been any union agreements or board resolutions which change the required contribution level.
4. Ascertain whether the pension footnote is in accordance with paragraph 46 of APB Opinion No. 8.

Defined Benefit Plans Other Than Those Funded by Insurance Policies *

1. Obtain the following items:
   (a) Copy of latest two actuarial valuation reports.

---

* If a defined benefit plan is funded by a combination of insurance policies and a side fund, this section should be used for the portion funded by the side fund and the following section should be used for the portion funded by the insurance policies.

(b) Copy of latest two reports of the funding agent (custodian, trustee, or insurance company), showing assets at book and market value and summarizing receipts and disbursements for the year.

(c) Copy of the latest census and related information used by the actuary to determine costs.

2. Ascertain that the actuary is qualified; this can usually be done by determining that the actuary is a member of a recognized professional actuarial society (e.g., a Fellow of the Society of Actuaries or a member of the American Academy of Actuaries) or by obtaining competent professional advice on the actuary's qualifications from an actuary known by you to be qualified.

3. Determine whether the two actuarial valuation reports obtained in procedure 1(a) above show the following information (any items not included in the report should be obtained from the actuary, if applicable):

(a) Normal cost.

(b) Past service cost plus increases in prior service cost due to plan amendments.

(c) Unfunded prior service cost.

(d) Amortization of unfunded prior service cost.

(e) Amortization of actuarial gains and losses (including unrealized appreciation or depreciation, if applicable).

(f) Amount of actuarial gains and losses arising during the year (including unrealized appreciation or depreciation, if applicable).

(g) Value of vested benefits.

(h) Amount of employee contributions for the year, if any.

(i) Valuation assets used, with explanation if such amount differs from both cost and market value.

(j) Actuarial cost method.

(k) Actuarial assumptions.

(l) Summary of plan provisions considered.

(m) Maximum and minimum contribution for tax purposes.

(n) Appropriate payroll data on which calculations are based (e.g., earnings, number of participants).

Note: See Figure A–1 for further explanation with respect to certain of these procedures.

4. Test the pension census data used by the actuary by test-checking:

(a) The census data to payroll and personnel records to ascertain that individual information is accurate. Determine that all eligible employees are included. See if total payroll used

FIGURE A-1

Actuarial Cost Methods Acceptable Under
APB Opinion No. 8 [1]

1. Aggregate method [2,3]
2. Attained age normal method, with [2] or without frozen initial liability
3. Entry age normal, with [2] or without frozen initial liability
4. Unit credit method
5. Individual level premium method, with or without [3] prior service liability

   1. These methods are acceptable only when the actuarial assumptions are reasonable and the method is applied in accordance with APB Opinion No. 8.
   2. Method automatically spreads employee contributions and actuarial gains and losses, including unrealized appreciation or depreciation, over the present and future years. Hence, procedures 3(e), 3(f), 3(h), and 10 under "Defined Benefit Plans Other Than Those Funded by Insurance Policies" are not relevant when this method is used.
   3. Past service cost plus increase in prior service cost due to plan amendments are not separately determined under this method. Hence, procedures 3(b), 3(c), and 3(d) under "Defined Benefit Plans Other Than Those Funded by Insurance Policies" are not applicable when this method is used.

is reasonable. (Ineligible employees should be included if they may be reasonably expected to receive benefits under the plan; if such employees have been excluded, estimate the maximum effect of the omission upon the provision for pension cost—see paragraphs 34, 35, and 36 of APB Opinion No. 8.)

(b) Retirees and benefit payments to personnel records and to the record of disbursements during year.

Note: For further details, see "Employer Records" in Appendix B.

5. Ascertain that the principal provisions specified in the plan or other agreements are being met (e.g., there may be an agreement to fund past service cost within a certain number of years, or an agreement that assets must be at least as great as the present value of benefits for retired lives).

6. Compare the plan document to the outline of the plan benefits valued, which should appear in the actuary's report. If there is no outline in the actuary's report, it may be necessary to request

one from the actuary or to obtain a confirmation from him indicating the plan document used in his calculations.

7. Determine that the actuarial cost method used by the actuary is acceptable under APB Opinion No. 8 and that it is the same as that used in the preceding year. If changed, obtain an estimate of the cost effect of the change as the auditor's report may have to be modified (if the effect of the change is material). Such a change requires a comment as to consistency in the auditor's report because it results from a choice by management from among two or more accounting methods. (See "Comparability and Consistency" in Chapter 7.)

8. If prior service cost is being expensed separately, determine whether it is being amortized on the same basis as in prior years.

9. With respect to the actuary's asset valuation:
   (a) Reconcile the assets included in the actuarial reports with the assets held by the funding agent. If the actuary is using "adjusted assets," then the method used to adjust assets should be checked.
   (b) If actuary is using book value of assets and there is a substantial difference between book and market value, recognition should be given to unrealized appreciation (depreciation).
   (c) Ascertain whether the asset valuation method used this year was used last year. Use of an asset valuation method different from that used last year resulting in a material effect on the financial statements, without a change in circumstances, would normally require a comment as to consistency in the auditor's report.

10. Determine how actuarial gains and losses, including unrealized appreciation or depreciation, are treated. If the actuarial cost method used does not average or spread gains or losses automatically (see Figure A–1), then gains or losses may have been recognized immediately instead of spread. If this is the case, an adjustment may have to be made. (Actuarial gains or losses arising from a single occurrence and not directly related to the operation of the plan, however, should be recognized immediately as required by paragraph 31 of APB Opinion No. 8.) If the handling of these gains or losses is not consistent with the preceding year, a comment as to consistency in the auditor's report may be needed.

11. Check the actuarial assumptions used in the valuation for the following:
   (a) Comparability with prior year. If not comparable, deter-

mine whether the change (1) is due to changed circumstances, in which case footnote disclosure only is required since such a change does not involve consistency of accounting (except that the auditor must also comment on such a change in his report where it accompanies financial statements filed with the SEC), or (2) is due to a choice by management where conditions have not changed, in which case the auditor should generally include in his report a comment as to lack of consistency.

(b) Reasonableness (the following may be used as a general guide for reasonableness):

(1) An appropriate mortality table should be used.

(2) Interest rates (total investment yields) between 4% and 6% are generally reasonable, but should be supportable.

(3) An estimate of future terminations of employment should be used.

(4) An estimate of future salary increases generally should be made, particularly for a plan whose benefits depend on average salary in a 10-year or lesser period prior to retirement.

(5) An estimate of expenses should be made where expenses of the plan are paid out of the plan's assets.

12. Ascertain whether amounts funded have differed from pension expense; if they differ:

(a) Verify that the proper prepayments or accruals (balance sheet items) have been entered on the books.

(b) Check to see whether an adjustment for interest equivalents has been made on such amounts.

13. If actuary's report does not include the value of vested benefits, request such information from the actuary.

14. Determine the expense provision from Table A-1, A-3, or A-4, as appropriate. (Table A-1 should be used if client is expensing on a minimum basis; Table A-3 should be used if client is expensing on a basis which amortizes prior service cost over a period of years (generally between 15 and 40); Table A-4 should be used if client is expensing on a maximum basis.)

15. Ascertain whether the pension footnote is in accordance with paragraph 46 of APB Opinion No. 8.

Defined Benefit Plans Funded by Insurance Policies

1. Obtain copy of latest premium statement from the insurance company, showing gross premiums, policy dividends credited, and termination credits for the year.

2. Test the pension census data used by the insurance company by test-checking the census data to payroll and personnel records to ascertain that individual information is accurate. Determine that all eligible employees are included. See if total payroll used is reasonable. (Ineligible employees should be included if they may be reasonably expected to receive benefits under the plan; if such employees have been excluded, estimate the maximum effect of the omission upon the provision for pension cost—see paragraphs 34, 35, and 36 of APB Opinion No. 8.)

   Note: For further details, see "Employer Records" in Appendix B.
3. Ascertain that the principal provisions specified in the plan or other agreements are being met.
4. Determine the amount of gross premium less policy dividends. This should serve as the appropriate amount of pension expense, subject to procedures 5, 6, and 7 below.

TABLE A–1. Provision for Pension Expense for the Year (Minimum Basis)

Description	(a) Interest Only	(b) 40-Year Amortization
1. Normal cost	$	$
2. Provision for actuarial (gains) losses [1]		
3. Provision for unrealized (appreciation) depreciation [1]		
4. *Less:* Employee contributions [2]	( )	( )
5. Interest on unfunded, unprovided-for prior service cost		XXXXXXXXXXXX
6. Provision for vested benefits (Table A–2, Item 8)	[3]	XXXXXXXXXXXX
7. Amortization, including interest, of past service cost, and of prior service cost increments [4]	XXXXXXXXXXXX	
8. Interest on excess of prior years' accounting provisions over amounts funded (or credit on excess of amounts funded over provisions)		
9. Total		
10. Minimum pension expense [lesser of Item 9(a) or Item 9(b)]	$	

[1] Only applicable if not recognized in asset valuation method and/or not spread through the routine application of the cost method (see Note 2 in Figure A–1).

[2] Only applicable if included in item 1, normal cost.

[3] If Item 6(a) is "0," Column (b) need not be completed.

[4] Prior service cost increments are increases or decreases in prior service cost which arise when a pension plan is amended and which are analogous to past service cost.

TABLE A–2. Computation of Supplemental Provision for Vested Benefits (Paragraph 17a of APB Opinion No. 8)

Description	(a) At Date of Most Recent Valuation	(b) At Date of Preceding Valuation
1. Actuarial value of vested benefits [1]	$	$
2. Amount of pension fund [2]		
3. Unfunded amount (Item 1 minus Item 2)		
4. Amount of balance sheet pension accruals less pension deferred charges [2]		
5. Actuarial value of unfunded or un-provided-for vested benefits (Item 3 minus Item 4)	[3]	
6. 5% of Item 5(b)	$	
7. Excess of Item 5 for the prior year over Item 5 for the current year, *if any*. [Item 5(b) — Item 5(a)]	$	
8. Excess of Item 6 over Item 7 [provision for vested benefits—to Table A–1, Item 6(a)]	$	

[1] If the plan has changed since the previous year, Items 1(a) and 1(b) should be on a consistent basis.

[2] The dates for Items 2 and 4 may be the end of the company's fiscal year or the actuarial valuation date. Consistency is the primary consideration.

[3] If result in Item 5(a) is "0," Column (b) and Items 6, 7, and 8 need not be completed.

TABLE A–3. Provision for Pension Expense for the Year (__-Year Amortization Basis)

Description	Amount
1. Normal cost	$
2. Provision for actuarial (gains) losses [1]	
3. Provision for unrealized (appreciation) depreciation [1]	
4. *Less:* Employee contributions [2]	( )
5. Amortization, including interest, of past service cost, and of prior service cost increments [3]	
6. Interest on excess of prior years' accounting provisions over amounts funded (or credit on excess of amounts funded over provisions)	
7. Total—Pension expense	$

[1] Only applicable if not recognized in asset valuation method and/or not spread through the routine application of the cost method (see Note 2 in Figure A–1).

[2] Only applicable if included in Item 1, normal cost.

[3] Prior service cost increments are increases or decreases in prior service cost which arise when a pension plan is amended and which are analogous to past service cost.

TABLE A–4. Provision for Pension Expense for the Year (Maximum Basis)

Description	Amount
1. Normal cost	$ _____
2. Provision for actuarial (gains) losses [1]	_____
3. Provision for unrealized (appreciation) depreciation [1]	_____
4. *Less:* Employee contributions [2]	(_____)
5. 10% of past service cost, and of prior service cost increments [3]	_____
6. Interest on excess of prior years' accounting provisions over amounts funded (or credit on excess of amounts funded over provisions)	_____
7. Total—Pension expense	$ _____

[1] Only applicable if not recognized in asset valuation method and/or not spread through the routine application of the cost method (see Note 2 in Figure A–1).

[2] Only applicable if included in item 1, normal cost.

[3] Prior service cost increments are increases or decreases in prior service cost which arise when a pension plan is amended and which are analogous to past service cost.

5. Compare the amount of policy dividends credited this year with amounts credited in prior years. (In the absence of wide year-to-year fluctuations such dividends should generally be recognized in the year credited; where such dividends are not reasonably similar, adjustments may be needed to effect compliance with the requirements of paragraph 30 of APB Opinion No. 8.)

6. Ascertain the amount of termination of employment or death credits arising during the year. (These generally should be averaged with such credits from prior years, with the resulting amount used to reduce the pension expense otherwise determined.)

7. Consider reviewing the method used by the insurance company in making its premium, dividend, and related calculations.

8. Ascertain whether the pension footnote is in accordance with paragraph 46 of APB Opinion No. 8.

Note: This section is applicable only to plans where annuity contracts are purchased prior to employees' retirement and payments of retirement benefits are guaranteed by the insurance company; it is not applicable to plans where retirement benefits are not guaranteed by the insurance company until employees retire (i.e., deposit administration type contracts, such as DA and IPG contracts as discussed in Chapter 3), in which case the auditor should perform the procedures set forth in the preceding section.

Audit Procedures Directly Related to ERISA

1. General:

   (a) Be alert to any evidence of a potential pension plan termination; where deemed appropriate, make inquiries of management. Where a plan termination is more than a remote possibility, ascertain that the financial statements contain appropriate entries or disclosures.

   (b) Where the provision for pension cost is based on the minimum required under APB Opinion No. 8, consider recommending that the company make appropriate modification so that the provision is consistent with the minimum amount required to be funded under ERISA.

   (c) Ascertain that appropriate disclosures (in the footnotes) as required by FASB Interpretation No. 3 are made (such as the future effect that compliance with ERISA will, or may, have on the provision for pension expense, on the funding of pension cost, and on unfunded vested benefits).

   (d) Obtain a representation from management (in the letter of representation) that the client is in compliance with ERISA.

2. Plan Compliance Requirements:

   (a) Ascertain that the terms of the pension plan comply with the requirements of ERISA, as they relate to participation, vesting, etc., as follows:

   (1) In the first year in which the plan is subject to ERISA, perform one of the following procedures:

   a. Examine a tax qualification letter issued by the Internal Revenue Service covering the current plan provisions, determine whether such letter contains any significant caveats with respect to the plan's qualification status, and ascertain whether the plan's provisions are being applied in accordance with Internal Revenue Service requirements.

   b. Obtain a letter from the client's lawyer stating that the plan complies with ERISA.

   (2) In subsequent years:

   a. Be alert to changes in the manner in which plan provisions are applied relative to Internal Revenue Service requirements.

   b. Where plan amendments have occurred, perform procedure 2(a)(1) above.

3. Funding Requirements:
   (a) For money-purchase plans and target benefit plans, ascertain that the (memorandum) funding standard account is being maintained in accordance with the provisions of ERISA, and that the amount required to be funded has been paid or recorded as a liability.
   (b) For defined benefit plans (other than certain tax-qualified or insured plans), check the actuarial report to the (memorandum) funding standard account (and the alternative minimum funding standard account, where applicable), and ascertain that the amount funded meets the minimum funding requirements of ERISA and has been paid or recorded as a liability.

   Note: Payment of required contributions must be made by due date of employer's federal income tax return, including extensions of up to six months.

4. Reporting and Disclosure Requirements:
   (a) Ascertain that an up-to-date plan description (Form EBS–1) has been properly filed with the Secretary of Labor.
   (b) Ascertain that an up-to-date descriptive booklet, or other document which summarizes the provisions of the plan, has also been filed with the Secretary of Labor and distributed to all participants and beneficiaries of the plan. (This summary must be written in language which is "calculated to be understood by the average plan participant.")
   (c) Read the pension fund financial statements, schedules, opinion of qualified accountant, and actuary's report (where appropriate) to determine whether they appear to have been properly prepared and timely filed.
   (d) Review client's procedures for controlling and processing requested and other required distributions of information to plan participants and beneficiaries, and review open files or logs for long outstanding items.

5. Fiduciary Responsibilities:
   (a) Where the company is a fiduciary (as well as a party in interest), as will normally be the case, ascertain whether it has complied with the related ERISA provisions (see "Fiduciary Responsibilities" in Chapter 4).
   (b) Make appropriate inquiries as to the occurrence of any prohibited transactions, and be alert for them during the audit; consider inquiring of the fund auditor as to the occurrence of prohibited transactions.

(c) Obtain a list of all parties in interest, to use as a reference point during the audit; review the company's procedures for identifying parties in interest, and examine related documentation to determine whether the list appears to be complete.

(d) Ascertain whether any prohibited transactions have been disclosed as a result of past IRS or other governmental examinations.

(e) If prohibited transactions have occurred, ascertain whether a liability should be reflected in the financial statements and/or whether disclosure is required.

6. Record-Keeping Requirements:

(a) Ascertain that company is maintaining records of each employee's years of service (including breaks in service) and vesting percentage, and such other records as may be needed to determine each employee's benefits (such as age, hours worked, salary, and employee contributions). (These records are normally tested in conjunction with the auditor's tests of the company's payroll records.)

(b) For multi-employer plans, ascertain that client has furnished the necessary information to the plan administrator. (Such information is normally tested in conjunction with the auditor's tests of the company's payroll records.)

B

SPECIMEN AUDIT PROGRAM, PENSION FUNDS

Introduction

This specimen audit program is designed for a pension fund subject to reporting and disclosure requirements of the Employee Retirement Income Security Act of 1974 (ERISA). It is not intended to be all-inclusive, and should be tailored to conditions encountered on a particular engagement. While this program contains some tests of a procedural nature, it is directed primarily toward validation (substantive) procedures. The auditor is expected to obtain and record an understanding of the fund's system, confirm the correctness of that understanding, and evaluate and test the controls in order to determine the exact nature, extent, and timing of validation procedures to be followed. However, if the auditor does not intend to rely on the system of internal control in determining the nature, extent, and timing of validation procedures he should not engage in extensive procedural testing.

Subject to the foregoing comments, the procedures outlined are intended, unless conditions indicate otherwise, to provide a basis for the expression of a standard opinion on the financial statements being examined, and on the other information covered by the auditor's opinion, as illustrated in the "Illustrative Financial Statements" section of Chapter 10.

In those instances where fund assets are held by a custodian (such as a bank) which maintains accounting records of fund transactions, the fund may not maintain certain books of original entry and/or a general ledger. Rather, the fund may utilize reports prepared by the custodian to serve as its books of account, in part or in their entirety. In such cases the auditor should, for those procedures outlined herein which refer to the books of original entry and/or general ledger, use the appropriate custodian reports in lieu of the specified records. Such procedures are indicated herein by a dagger (†).

Audit procedures that need not be performed where an actuarial information scope limitation exists, as discussed under "Scope Limitations" in Chapter 9, or where actuarial considerations are not present, are indicated herein by an asterisk(*).

General

1. Obtain a copy of the annual report to be filed with the Secretary of Labor, and the summary of the annual report to be furnished to participants and beneficiaries. (The audit of the supplemental schedules and of the summary of the annual report should be integrated with the audit of the basic financial statements to the extent practicable.)
2. Obtain copies, or prepare extracts, of the minutes of the Board of Trustees and Administrative Committee meetings:
   (a) Compare copies with signed minutes.
   (b) Relate all items of accounting significance to the accounting records and audit workpapers.
   (c) Ascertain that any matters mentioned in the minutes which have applicability to the financial statements have been reflected therein.
3. Arrange to obtain the following:
   (a) Letter of representation (see "Letter of Representation" in Chapter 9).
   (b) Lawyer's letter.
   (c) Standard bank confirmations, and cutoff bank statements where appropriate.
   (d) Confirmation of securities held by custodian.
   (e) Confirmation for unsettled trades and/or "fails" from various brokers.
   (f) Actuary's report, where appropriate; ascertain that it contains all the information needed for use in the examination.

(g) Confirmation of actuarial information from the actuary, where appropriate.

(h) Other appropriate confirmations and/or reports (such as from insurance companies, other auditors, etc.), where applicable.

4. Determine that the fund maintains at least the minimum amount of fidelity insurance required by ERISA, and that appropriate performance bonds of employers (where required by terms of the agreement among a multi-employer pension fund and the employers) are in effect.

5. Ascertain whether a tax ruling or determination letter has been obtained.

6. Review the collective bargaining agreement, the declaration of trust, the insurance contract, and other plan documents, and ascertain that any transactions that require the approval of the Board of Trustees or Administrative Committee have such approval and that accounting matters are properly reflected in the accounts.

7. Examine any evidence of a potential pension plan termination; where deemed appropriate, make inquiries of the employer's management.

Cash

Many pension funds maintain a custodian cash account. The operation of this account is governed by the terms of the agreement between the fund and the custodian (bank). The usual agreement provides for the custodian to hold in custody all securities owned by the fund, to receive all proceeds from securities sold and all dividend and interest income, to receive and pay for securities purchased, and to disburse funds for benefit payments and operating expenses. (If checking accounts or other cash accounts are also maintained, audit procedures similar to those used in examinations of financial statements of business entities should be applied.)

1. Review the terms of the agreement between the fund and the custodian.

†2. On a test basis, trace the custodian's advices to the cash receipts and disbursement records, noting proper account distribution; test-foot and crossfoot the cash records and trace to postings in the general ledger.

3. Confirm cash balance with the custodian.

4. Obtain a summary of the monthly totals of cash receipts and cash disbursements for the period under review, analyzed by categories (see procedure 6).

†5. Obtain from client and check (or prepare) a reconciliation of the cash balance with that confirmed by the custodian (see also procedure 7).

6. Reconcile the following totals per the cash summary (procedure 4), taking into consideration related receivables and payables:
   (a) Receipts:
      (1) Dividends received to recorded dividend income for the period.
      (2) Interest received to recorded interest income for the period.
      (3) Proceeds from sales of investment securities to total proceeds of sales recorded on the investment schedule.
      (4) Other items listed by major categories to appropriate account analyses (e.g., contributions).
   (b) Disbursements:
      (1) Investment securities purchased to total cost of purchases recorded on the investment schedule.
      (2) Benefit payments to total amount recorded for the period.
      (3) Other items listed by major categories to appropriate account analyses (e.g., administrative expenses).

7. Obtain and examine a cut-off bank statement for transactions which may require adjustment of the financial statements or footnote disclosure as at the date of the examination.

Contributions Receivable and Received

Multi-Employer Funds: These procedures are directed at non-contributory plans; where a multi-employer fund is based on a contributory plan, the auditor should also consider certain of the procedures shown under "Single-Employer Funds" (e.g., confirming contributions directly with participants).

1. Obtain an official list of contributors as at the beginning and end of the period under examination, showing those added and/ or terminated during the period, and review and test the fund's procedures for maintaining the list on a current basis (this list should be referred to in conjunction with the performance of certain of the following procedures).

†2. Reconcile contribution receipts for a test period from the cash receipts record to (a) the total amount credited to the general ledger contributions accounts, (b) the total amounts posted to the employers' contribution records, and (c) deposits shown by the bank statements. [Reconciliation of aggregate amount of contributions with cash receipts is provided for under cash procedure 6(a).]

†3. Trace selected individual employer contributions payments from the employer's contribution report to (a) the cash receipts record and (b) the amount posted to the individual employer's contribution record.

4. Review and test the fund's procedures for determining that employers' contribution reports have been received from all employers, that they are arithmetically accurate, and that the correct contribution rate was used.

5. Trace selected postings from employers' contribution reports to participants' eligibility records, and trace selected entries on participants' eligibility records to the employers' contribution reports.

6. For a selected period, reconcile the total participants' credits posted to the participants' eligibility records to the total credits shown by employers' contribution reports.

7. Compare the contributions receivable at the statement date to collections received from employers subsequent to the statement date, and review on a test basis the related employer contribution reports to ascertain that such receipts apply to the year under examination; if the fund's books are held open after the year end, ascertain that amounts received in the new year that pertain to the year under examination have been properly recorded as accounts receivable.

8. Confirm contributions recorded as received and receivable during the examination period on a test basis by direct correspondence with selected employers.

9. Ascertain the nature and amount of any delinquent or unrecorded contributions.

10. Review the adequacy of the allowance for doubtful accounts.

11. Perform tests of selected employers' payroll records, as described under "Employer Records" below.

12. For money-purchase plans and target benefit plans, ascertain that the (memorandum) funding standard account is being maintained in accordance with the provisions of ERISA.

13. For defined benefit plans, review the actuary's report to determine that the amounts of contributions are consistent therewith,

and (for other than certain tax-qualified or insured plans) ascertain that the fund is maintaining the (memorandum) funding standard account(s) in accordance with the provisions of ERISA.

Single-Employer Funds:

†14. Trace contributions from the cash receipts book to deposits shown by bank statements and to the general ledger. [Reconciliation of aggregate amount of contributions with cash receipts is provided for under cash procedure 6(a).]

15. Confirm contributions received and receivable by direct correspondence with the employer company or compare to employer company records; consider confirming employee contributions directly with participants on a test basis.

16. Determine the correctness of the contributions received and receivable by a review of amounts received in subsequent months, and reference to the actuary's report where applicable.

17. Review the method used by the fund in accruing employer company contributions to determine that it has been consistently applied and that contribution amounts comply with the provisions of ERISA.

18. Review employer company payroll and other records, as described under "Employer Records" below.

Investments

The following audit procedures pertain to situations where the fund's investments are held either by the fund itself or by a custodian for the account of the fund and the fund maintains supporting documents. Reference should be made to the section "Custodial Relationships" in Chapter 9 for audit procedures to be followed in those instances where investments are held (a) by a custodian/trustee who initiates investment transactions and maintains the records supporting investment-related transactions, (b) by a third-party depository for the account of the fund's custodian, and (c) in pooled or commingled funds or trusts.

1. Obtain an investment schedule showing the activity (e.g., beginning balance, purchases, sales, ending balance, gains and losses, dividends or interest) in each investment owned during the period under examination, and a summary schedule, arranged by major groupings (e.g., U. S. Government bonds, corporate bonds, common stocks, mortgages, real estate).

   (a) Prove footings and crossfootings.

(b) Test market value extensions.

(c) Compare investment schedule with summary schedule, and trace summary schedule to the trial balance.

(d) Trace the opening balances of investments to audit work-papers for the preceding period for both number of shares and cost (and carrying amounts, if different) for stocks, and for related information for bonds.

(e) Trace selected securities held during the period under re-view to a securities publication service to ascertain that all changes in such security holdings for stock splits, stock divi-dends, adjustments for return of capital, name changes, etc., are reflected in the schedule.

†(f) Trace a number of individual investment amounts (activity and ending balances) from the schedule to the investment ledger.

†(g) Trace the aggregate cost of investments owned at the end of the period to the general ledger.

†(h) Scan general ledger investment account and investigate un-usual entries.

(i) For selected purchase and sale transactions (note that rec-onciliation of the aggregate amount of purchases and sales proceeds with cash receipts and disbursements is provided for under cash procedure 6):

(1) Trace to cash records.

(2) Examine brokers' advices and other appropriate docu-ments (e.g., notes, mortgages, and closing statements) for number of shares or principal amount, description of security, trade and settlement dates, interest purchased or sold, commission, net amount, etc.; verify extensions and taxes; check to see that the trade price appears reasonable by reference to published sources.

(3) Ascertain that proper approvals are present (e.g., author-ization of Board of Trustees, approval of Plan Admin-istrator, etc.).

(4) Verify the calculation of realized gains and losses.

2. Verify number of shares or principal amount of securities by in-specting and counting the securities or confirming them with the custodian. Include due bills on hand for stock dividends, stock splits, etc., and determine their collectibility by a review of sub-sequent receipts. Investigate the reputation and financial re-sources of the custodian.

3. Reconcile security positions by comparing information shown on investment schedule (procedure 1) with that shown on list of

securities (procedure 2) and lists of open security positions (procedure 1 under "Receivable for Securities Sold and Payable for Securities Purchased").

4. Confirm the balances and terms of loans and mortgages, and review their collectibility; inspect deeds, title policies, and/or leases covering real property.

5. Test the fair value of investments:

   (a) Price securities owned at the balance sheet date at market quotations by reference to published sources (newspapers, *Bank and Quotation Record,* "pink sheets," etc.).

   (b) In the absence of published quotations, obtain market prices from one or more independent sources. Also, review market prices of such securities for a period prior to and subsequent to the valuation date to identify any large price variations. A large price variation, the unavailability of prices, or a limited number of brokers able to supply price quotations may indicate that the security should be valued at fair value as determined by the Trustees [see procedure 5(c) for elaboration].

   (c) For securities not readily marketable and any other securities or investments valued in good faith by the Administrative Committee or the Trustees, review the fund's procedures for appraisal of such investments and the underlying documentation therefor, and ascertain that such procedures are appropriate and have been followed and that resulting valuations have been reviewed and approved currently by the Trustees (see SEC Accounting Series Releases No. 113 and 118).

6. On a test basis, review the investment activities to determine that the transactions and holdings throughout the year were in accordance with the restrictions and limitations on types of investments imposed by law, plan documents, and policy. (See also "Prohibited Transactions" below.)

7. Where marketable securities are carried at cost and market value is substantially lower than cost, consider whether such securities should be written down to their market values and what disclosures should be made in the financial statements (see the AICPA's Auditing Interpretation on "Evidential matter for the carrying amount of marketable securities" issued in January 1975.)

8. Where investments are carried at a value which recognizes gains and losses over a number of years, verify the manner in which such gains or losses are recognized by reviewing the arithmetic computations and ascertaining that the method is reasonable and consistent with that applied in the prior year.

Assets Held by an Insurance Company

1. Perform the applicable audit procedures listed under "Investments" above.
2. Review the contract between the employer or the fund and the insurance company.
3. Review the experience reports prepared by the insurance company.
4. Confirm the following matters by corresponding directly with the insurance company or its independent auditor:
   (a) Type of contract or contracts.
   (b) Information as to assets, including whether assets are in pooled "separate accounts," individual employer "separate accounts," or in the insurance company's general funds.
   *(c) Assets in other funds or funding media, but requiring consideration for comparison with the actuarially determined present value of vested benefits and prior service cost of the plan.
   (d) Contributions (premium payments) made during the year, including the dates received by the insurance company.
   (e) Interest and dividends, and realized and unrealized gains, earned or credited during the year, plus the basis for crediting investment earnings.
   (f) Annuities purchased and/or benefits paid or payable during the year.
   (g) Refunds and credits paid or payable by insurance company during year due to termination of plan members.
   (h) Amount of asset management fees, commissions, sales fees, premium taxes, and other expenses (sometimes collectively referred to as "retention") charged or chargeable by insurance company during the year.
   *(i) The actuarially determined present value of vested benefits and prior service cost.
   (j) Dividend or rate credit given by insurance company.
   (k) Special conditions applicable upon termination of contract.
5. Test the interest calculation and compliance with the minimum guaranteed interest rate in the insurance contract, if applicable.
6. Test annuity purchases and benefit payments, as described under "Benefit Payments" below.

---

* See page 289.

Dividends Receivable and Dividend Income

1. Obtain an analysis of dividends by security for the period under examination. This information is generally included on the investment schedule (see procedure 1 under "Investments") and should include accrued dividends at the beginning of the period, dividends received, dividend income, and accrued dividends at the end of the period. [Reconciliation of aggregate amount of dividends earned with cash receipts is provided for under cash procedure 6(a).]
2. Trace accrued dividends at the beginning of the period to workpapers for previous period.
3. Foot and crossfoot all dividend columns and agree the totals of dividends receivable at end of year and dividend income to the trial balance.
4. Select a number of securities held during all or part of the examination period and test the income earned for the period and receivable at the end of the period. In connection therewith, the ex-dividend date, payable date, and rate should be obtained from a financial reporting service and the number of shares owned on the ex-dividend date obtained from the investment schedule or the investment ledger.
5. On a test basis, trace dividends received for those securities selected in procedure 4 to the cash record and bank statement.
6. Scan the investment schedule for dividends which should have been received but were not. (Normally, a skip in regular quarterly dividends is indicative of an item to be investigated.)
7. Review dividends receivable at end of period for past due items, giving consideration to the need for an allowance for uncollectible amounts.

Interest Receivable and Interest Income

1. Obtain an analysis of interest or discount by security for the period under examination. This information is generally included on the investment schedule (see procedure 1 under "Investments") and should include amounts accrued at the beginning of the period, interest purchased and sold, amounts received, amounts earned and amounts accrued at the end of the period. [Reconciliation of aggregate amount of interest and discount earned with cash receipts is provided for under cash procedure 6(a).]
2. Trace beginning balances to workpapers for previous period.
3. Foot and crossfoot all interest (discount) columns and agree the

totals of amounts earned and amounts accrued at end of year to the trial balance.

4. Interest purchased or sold should be noted and included in separate totals in order to effect the reconciliations of purchases and sales of securities and interest (discount) earned with cash receipts and disbursements (as provided for under cash procedure 6). For tests of interest purchased or sold, see procedure 1(i) under "Investments."

5. Select a number of interest-bearing securities owned during the year and test interest earned during the period and interest receivable at end of period as follows:

   (a) Check interest earned on those securities held throughout the year and interest receivable at end of the period.

   (b) For securities purchased or sold during the period, test computation of interest earned thereon and, for securities purchased, amounts receivable as at end of period, and compare with amounts listed on summary.

   (c) Discount earned during the period should be substantiated by comparison of cost and face value. With respect to unmatured securities as at end of period, compute discount earned and amount accrued as at end of period and compare with amounts listed on summary.

†6. On a limited test basis, for those securities selected in procedure 5, trace interest received to the cash book and to the bank statement.

7. Scan the investment schedule to ascertain that interest has been collected on each coupon date falling within our examination. Consider propriety of accrual of interest in the case of past due items.

Receivables for Securities Sold and Payable for Securities Purchased

1. Obtain lists of securities sold but not delivered and securities purchased but not received as at the examination date, showing name of broker, description of security, number of shares or principal amount, trade date, normal settlement date, and amount receivable or payable.

2. Foot lists and trace totals to the trial balance.

3. Request confirmation of the unsettled trades from brokers. The confirmation request should include the same data as enumerated in procedure 1. Send second requests, where responses are not received after a reasonable period of time.

4. For the trades for which confirmation is not received, test receipt or payment of cash subsequent to examination date to bank advices or statements, examine brokers' advices and examine evidence of subsequent receipt or delivery of the securities.

Property and Equipment, and Accumulated Depreciation

1. Obtain an analysis of property and equipment and accumulated depreciation accounts for the year, showing beginning balances, activity during the year, and ending balances.
2. Trace beginning balances to workpapers for previous period, and compare ending balances to the trial balance.
3. Check activity to extent deemed appropriate, e.g., vouch selected additions and dispositions, check depreciation calculation, etc.

Accounts Payable and Accrued Liabilities

1. Obtain account analyses showing beginning balances, expense accruals, details of payments charged to account, and the ending balances. [Reconciliation of aggregate payments with cash disbursements is provided for under cash procedure 6(b).]
2. Prove footings, trace beginning balances to workpapers for previous period, and trace ending balances to the trial balance.
3. Vouch significant or unusual payments to approved invoices and to either custodian advices (and/or cash statements) or paid checks, as appropriate.
4. For items contained in ending balances, trace on a test basis to supporting documentation (and to subsequent cash disbursements if paid) and perform other procedures deemed necessary to ascertain reasonableness of ending accruals.
5. Reconcile expense accrual amounts with related expense accounts. Examine approved invoices and either custodian advices (and/or cash statements) or paid checks, as appropriate, for any significant payments charged direct to expense accounts and trace the total of such payments to cash disbursements summary analysis.

Contingencies

1. Ascertain whether there are any contingencies that require disclosure in the financial statements, such as lawsuits or judgments, etc., by making inquiries of the fund's trustees, administrator, and legal counsel.
2. Obtain written representation from fund management and legal counsel as to the existence or absence of any contingencies.

Net Assets Available for Plan Benefits

1. Obtain an analysis of the account for the year.
2. Trace opening balance to audit workpapers for preceding period.
3. Trace closing balance and net change to the trial balance.

Actuarial Considerations

*1. Request a qualified professional, such as an actuary, to review the actuary's report. Alternatively, the auditor may review it himself if he has sufficient technical competence to do so, in which case he should ascertain that the actuary is qualified by determining that the actuary is a member of a recognized professional actuarial society (e.g., a Fellow of the Society of Actuaries or a member of the American Academy of Actuaries) or by obtaining competent professional advice on the actuary's qualifications from an actuary known by the auditor to be qualified. The review should include the following procedures (see appropriate section of Appendix A for further details):

   (a) Determine that the actuary is familiar with the current terms of the plan and that such terms are accorded proper recognition in the calculations.

   (b) Determine that the actuary has employed an appropriate actuarial cost method and ascertain whether the same method was used in the prior period.

   (c) Ascertain that all pertinent factors appear to be included in the actuarial assumptions used and that such assumptions appear reasonable on an overall basis, including the determination that the basis for the investment return and other assumptions appears reasonable in relation to actual experience.

   (d) Determine that the value of fund assets used by the actuary in his calculations appears reasonable.

   (e) Determine that the effect of any changes in actuarial methods and assumptions has been disclosed by the actuary.

   (f) Perform tests to ascertain the reliability of the basic data used by the actuary in his calculations, as described in procedure 7 under "Employer Records."

   (g) Determine that the actuary is aware of and has reflected important events, such as an acquisition, in his assumptions and calculations.

*2. Consider advising the actuary of any changes in conditions that may affect his determinations.

*3. Ascertain whether any material differences exist in the actuarially determined amounts (e.g., present value of vested benefits and prior service cost) between the most recent valuation date and the statement date (and beyond, where appropriate), and obtain from the actuary an estimate of the related dollar effect.

4. Trace actuarially related information contained in the financial statements to the actuary's report.

Employer Records

Procedure 8 below should normally be performed in lieu of procedures 1 to 7 where the auditor is unable to examine the employer company records; otherwise, he should perform procedures 1 to 7.

1. Review pertinent sections of the plan instrument and collective bargaining agreement, where applicable.

2. Reconcile the total gross earnings per the employees' earnings records with total wages shown by the payroll journal and the payroll tax reports.

3. Foot the payroll journal (gross pay) on a test basis.

4. Compare information shown on the employer's contribution reports for a selected number of participant employees with the data shown on the employees' earnings records. Compare a selected group of employees' earnings records with the employer's contribution reports to ascertain that they have been properly included in or excluded from the reports.

5. Compare the data shown in the payroll journal for a selected group of employees to the employee earnings records.

6. Compare the data shown in selected employee earnings records to time records, salary schedules, and other personnel records.

7. Test the reliability of the basic data used by the actuary in his calculations (e.g., size, age distribution, sex, and so forth, of the work force), by tracing data from the actuary's report (if shown therein) or a confirmation letter obtained from the actuary to the client's summary analysis of such data; trace data related to selected employees from the summary analysis to employment applications, salary authorizations, and other supporting personnel records; and test the arithmetic accuracy of the summarization. If contributions are not based on actuarial determinations, as with most defined contribution plans, test the data (e.g., hours worked) used in the calculation of contributions.

8. Where the auditor is unable to examine employer company records, either: (a) obtain appropriate assurances from the employ-

er's auditor, after investigating the independence and professional
reputation of the other auditor and performing such other procedures as considered appropriate in the circumstances, as described
in section 543.04 of SAS No. 1 (the assurances should include a
representation that appropriate auditing procedures have been
performed and should advise his conclusions with respect to the
matters referred to in procedures 1 to 7 above) or (b) perform
such other alternative procedures as described under "Alternative
Procedures for Employer Records" in Chapter 9.

Unrealized Appreciation (Depreciation) of Investments

The following procedures are applicable only where the fund
carries its investments at fair value; similar procedures may need
to be performed where investments are carried at a value which
results in the recognition of gains and losses over a period of time
(see procedure 8 under "Investments").

1. Refer to investment schedule (procedure 1 under "Investments")
   and compute amount of unrealized appreciation (depreciation)
   by deducting aggregate cost of investments from aggregate market
   value at end of period.
2. Deduct opening balance of unrealized appreciation (depreciation)
   from amount determined in procedure 1 and determine the
   amount of increase or decrease for the period; trace to the trial
   balance.

Benefit Payments

1. Obtain a summary schedule of monthly pension benefit payments.
   [Reconciliation of aggregate amount of benefit payments with cash
   disbursements is provided for under cash procedure 6(b).]
   (a) Agree monthly totals to the record of pension benefit pay-
       ments.
   (b) On a test basis, review the changes in the aggregate monthly
       total of pension benefit payments and trace such changes to
       authorizations therefor (such as Trustees' minutes).
   (c) Review client's procedures for recording and controlling
       benefit payments.
2. For a number of persons receiving benefits, as shown on the record
   of pension benefit payments, obtain their files, and review as follows:
   (a) Determine that applications for benefits have been properly
       approved and are properly supported.

(b) Ascertain that the current benefit amounts have been properly approved.

(c) Ascertain that benefit payments to retirees (and benefits for participants with vested benefits separated from the employer's service prior to retirement) have not been decreased due to increases in social security benefits after September 2, 1974 (or, if later, the earlier of a participant's first receipt of plan benefits or separation from service), in accordance with provisions of ERISA.

(d) Check the calculations of the benefit payments by reference to supporting documentation (e.g., worksheet containing salary information, age, length of service, etc.); ascertain that an independent review of the calculations has been made by a responsible individual.

3. For a number of persons dropped from the pension roll during the period under examination, examine documentation in support of the removal. Determine that removal is in accordance with the plan.

4. For a number of persons receiving benefits, as shown on the record of pension benefit payments, examine paid checks for payee, amount, and endorsement and compare such data to the information included in personnel files.

5. Test the footing of the record of pension benefit payments.

6. Ascertain that procedures exist for investigating long-outstanding benefit checks.

7. Confirm on a test basis payments recorded in the record of pension benefit payments as paid during the period under review by direct correspondence with selected participants or beneficiaries.

8. Determine that procedures have been established within the fund to check or test the continued eligibility of participants or beneficiaries to receive benefits. Such procedures should ensure that individuals are removed from the benefit rolls upon death, and that payments made to individuals over an unusually long number of years are still appropriate.

9. Ascertain that the fund maintains a procedure for advising participants or beneficiaries whose claims for benefits are denied of their right to have the decision reviewed, as required by ERISA.

Other Income and Expenses

1. Obtain an analysis of miscellaneous income and expense accounts and any other income or expense account of significance that has not been reviewed in conjunction with audit of investments or

accounts payable and accrued liabilities. (Reconciliation of other income and expense accounts with cash receipts and disbursements is provided for under cash procedure 6.)

2. Prove footings and trace balances to the trial balance.
3. Determine source of the other income and inspect documentation supporting material items.
4. Vouch material items of expense to approved invoices and to either custodian advices (and/or cash statements) or paid checks, as appropriate.
5. Administrative expenses: In addition to those procedures outlined in 1 to 4, perform the following procedures:
   (a) Review the terms of the plan agreement and Trustees' or Administrative Committee's minutes to determine whether administrative expenses were properly authorized.
   (b) When the fund employs a contract administrator, test the basis of the contract payment made to ascertain the propriety and reasonableness of the payments.
   (c) When one office functions as a service organization for several funds and an allocation of administrative expenses not directly associated with a specific fund is required, review such allocation to ascertain that it is equitable and determine that the method of allocation selected was approved by the Trustees.

Subsequent Events

1. Perform appropriate audit procedures relating to subsequent events, as outlined in section 560 of SAS No. 1.
2. Consider whether there have been any material changes in the market value of securities subsequent to the statement date, particularly where the auditor's report is dated near the end of the filing period permitted by ERISA. Where there have been material changes, consider whether there is adequate disclosure in the financial statements (see sections 560.05 and 560.07 of SAS No. 1).

Plan Compliance with ERISA

1. Ascertain that the terms of the pension plan comply with the requirements of ERISA, as they relate to participation, vesting, joint and survivorship coverage, and certain other plan provisions, by performing procedures (a) or (b), as appropriate, or procedure (c):

(a) In the first year in which the plan is subject to ERISA, perform one of the following procedures:

    (1) Examine a tax qualification letter issued by the Internal Revenue Service covering the current plan provisions, and determine whether such letter contains any significant caveats with respect to the plan's qualification status, and ascertain whether the plan's provisions are being applied in accordance with Internal Revenue Service requirements.

    (2) Obtain a letter from the plan's lawyer stating that the plan complies with ERISA.

(b) In subsequent years:

    (1) Be alert to changes in the manner in which plan provisions are applied.

    (2) Where plan amendments have occurred, perform procedure 1(a).

(c) In lieu of procedures (a) or (b) above, the auditor may obtain appropriate assurances from the employer's auditor, after investigating the independence and professional reputation of the other auditor and performing such other procedures as considered appropriate in the circumstances, as described in section 543.04 of SAS No. 1. The assurances should include a representation that appropriate auditing procedures have been performed and should advise his conclusions with respect to compliance of the plan provisions with the requirements of ERISA.

Prohibited Transactions

1. Make appropriate inquiries as to the occurrence of any transactions or activities prohibited by ERISA, and be alert for them during course of audit.

2. Obtain a list of all parties in interest, to use as a reference during the audit; review the fund's procedures for identifying parties in interest, and examine related documentation to determine whether the list appears to be complete.

3. Ascertain whether any prohibited transactions have been disclosed as a result of past IRS or other governmental examinations.

4. Make a special review for significant prohibited transactions, if deemed necessary. (This procedure ordinarily need not be performed, inasmuch as other audit procedures would normally disclose whether such transactions have occurred.)

5. If prohibited transactions have occurred, ascertain whether a re-

ceivable and/or other disclosure should be reflected in the financial statements.

Financial Statements and Reports

†1. Obtain the trial balance, foot it, and agree the balances to the general ledger (where not done in conjunction with other audit procedures).

2. Trace the financial statements to the trial balance; ascertain that statement groupings are comparable with those of the prior year.

3. Ascertain that the notes to the financial statements contain disclosures of all matters necessary to present fairly the fund's financial position (see "Other Financial Statement Requirements and Disclosures" in Chapter 8).

4. Investigate significant account fluctuations from the prior year.

5. Review draft of annual report (to Labor Department as required by ERISA) and summary of the annual report (see procedure 1 under "General"):

(a) Compare information shown therein to financial statements or workpapers, as appropriate.

(b) Perform any additional audit procedures deemed necessary to be satisfied that all appropriate information is properly included therein.

6. Request fund representatives to discuss legal-related audit findings with legal counsel, where deemed appropriate.

SELECTED BIBLIOGRAPHY

AMERICAN INSTITUTE OF CERTIFIED PUBLIC ACCOUNTANTS:

APB Accounting Principles, Volumes 1 and 2. Chicago: Commerce Clearing House, Inc., 1973.

Accounting Trends & Techniques, Twenty-Sixth and Twenty-Seventh Editions. New York: AICPA, 1972 and 1973.

Auditing Standards Division. *Evidential Matter for the Carrying Amount of Marketable Securities.* Auditing Interpretation. New York: AICPA, January 1975.

Auditing Standards Executive Committee. *Proposed Statement on Auditing Standards,* "Using the Work of a Specialist." New York: AICPA, August 15, 1975.

————. *Statement on Auditing Standards No. 2,* "Reports on Audited Financial Statements." New York: AICPA, October 1974.

————. *Statement on Auditing Standards No. 6,* "Related Party Transactions." New York: AICPA, July 1975.

Committee on Auditing Procedure. *Statement on Auditing Standards No. 1,* "Codification of Auditing Standards and Procedures." New York: AICPA, 1973.

Committee on College and University Accounting and Auditing. *Audits of Colleges and Universities.* Industry Audit Guide. New York: AICPA, 1973.

Committee on Finance Companies. *Audits of Finance Companies.* Industry Audit Guide. New York: AICPA, 1973.

Committee on Health, Welfare and Pension Funds. "Audits of Pension Funds." Exposure Draft of Industry Audit Guide. New York: AICPA, March 1973.

————. "Generally Accepted Accounting Principles and Financial Reporting" and "Generally Accepted Auditing Standards" for Pension Funds. Draft Position Papers. New York: AICPA, December 11, 1973.

————. *Audits of Employee Health and Welfare Benefit Funds.* Industry Audit Guide. New York: AICPA, 1972.

Committee on Insurance Accounting and Auditing. *Audits of Stock Life Insurance Companies.* Industry Audit Guide. New York: AICPA, 1972.

Committee on Investment Companies. *Audits of Investment Companies.* Industry Audit Guide. New York: AICPA, 1973.

Committee on Voluntary Health and Welfare Organizations. *Audits of Voluntary Health and Welfare Organizations.* Industry Audit Guide. New York: AICPA, 1974.

Health, Welfare and Pension Fund Task Force, "Generally Accepted Accounting Principles and Financial Reporting for Pension Plans" and "Audit Guide for Pension Plans." Draft Position Papers. New York: AICPA, November 25, 1974.

BNA Pension Reporter. Washington, D. C.: The Bureau of National Affairs, Inc., 1974–1975.

BNA's Daily Reporter System, "Daily Report for Executives—Developments Affecting Taxation and Finance." Washington, D. C.: The Bureau of National Affairs, Inc., 1975.

COMMERCE CLEARING HOUSE, INC. *Pension Reform Act of 1974—Law and Explanation.* New York: Commerce Clearing House, Inc., 1974.

CONFERENCE BOARD, THE. *Financial Management of Company Pension Plans.* New York: The Conference Board, Inc., 1973.

COOPERS & LYBRAND. *Coopers & Lybrand Newsletters, Employee Benefits Supplements,* Vol. 16, No. 9, September 1974 and Vol. 16, No. 12, December 1974.

DEFLIESE, PHILIP L., JOHNSON, KENNETH P., and MACLEOD, RODERICK K. *Montgomery's Auditing,* Ninth Edition. New York: The Ronald Press Co., 1975.

FINANCIAL ACCOUNTING STANDARDS BOARD. *FASB Interpretation No. 3,* "Accounting for the Cost of Pension Plans Subject to the Employee Retirement Income Security Act of 1974." Stamford, Conn.: FASB, December 1974.

GROSS, MALVERN J., JR. *Financial and Accounting Guide for Nonprofit Organizations,* Second Edition. New York: The Ronald Press Co., 1974.

POMERANZ, FELIX, and STEINBERG, RICHARD. *Operational Guidelines for Managing Investment Funds.* C&L Reports to Management. New York: Coopers & Lybrand, 1974.

RAPPAPORT, LOUIS H. *SEC Accounting Practice and Procedure,* Third Edition. New York: The Ronald Press Co., 1972.

SLOAT, FREDERICK P., and BURGETT, DAVID V. *Fundamental Concepts Underlying Pension Plan Financing and Costs.* New York: Coopers & Lybrand, 1970.

U. S. CONGRESS. *Employee Retirement Income Security Act of 1974.* Public Law 93–406, September 2, 1974. Washington, D. C.: Government Printing Office, 1974.

INDEX OF
ERISA SECTIONS

SUBJECT INDEX

organization and management policies, 209–212

outside money managers, 211–212

Potential plan termination, audit considerations, 114, 167

Premium payment declaration, 76

Present value, 16–17
  formula for computing, of future contributions, 25
  of vested benefits, 87, 89, 139–141

Prior service cost, 16; see also Past service cost, Unfunded prior service cost
  disclosing in financial statements, 140

Profit-sharing plans, 6n
  funding standard accounts, 52
  maximum deductible contribution, 55
  vesting, 9n
  vesting benefits, 44

Prohibited transactions, fiduciary responsibilities, 60–64, 253, 269–270; see also Transactions

Projected benefit cost methods, 20–22

Property and equipment, valuation of, 137

Provisions of pension plans, 8–11
  amendments, 239–240, 260
  compliance with ERISA, 116–117, 164–165
  death benefits, 10, 238–239, 259
  defined benefit plans, 233–255
  defined contribution plans, 255–271
  duration of retirement benefits, 10–11
  eligibility requirements, 8
  forfeiture of benefits, 239, 259–260
  miscellaneous, 240–241, 261
  normal retirement benefits, 9–10
  participation, 233–234, 255–256
  retirement benefits, 236–238, 258–259
  retirement dates, 8
  service, 234–236, 256–257
  vesting, 8–9, 234, 256

Qualified pension plans, 6; see also Nonqualified plans
  ERISA requirements, 11
  income tax considerations, 6, 11–12
  maximum deductible contribution, 55

Real estate, fair value of, 132, 154–155

Records and record keeping
  contribution records, 14
  employers' contribution reports, 14
  ERISA requirements, 45, 204–205, 255, 271
  participants' eligibility, 14
  pension fund, 14
  vesting, 45

Registration statement, ERISA requirement, 65, 248–249, 265–266

Regulated companies, accounting for pension costs, 99–100

Reportable events, 76

Reportable transactions, 73, 247, 265

Reporting and disclosure requirements of ERISA
  accountants and actuaries, 69–74
    material covered by accountant's opinion, 70–74
    material covered by actuary's opinion, 74
  actuarial statement, 67, 74, 76
  administrative personnel changes, 67
  annual reports, 67–68, 76–77
    accountant's opinion, 70–74
    actuary's opinion, 74–75
    proposed Form 5500, 69, 71–73
    statement of assets and liabilities, 71–73
    statement of changes in net assets available for plan benefits, 71–72
    statement of income and expenditures, 71–73
    statement of receipts and disbursements, 71–72
  auditing procedures, 117–119, 166–167
  auditor's reports; see Auditor's reports
  benefit information, 68, 77
  claims procedure, 76
  contents of report or disclosure, 76–79
  copies of plan description, 77
  defined benefit plans, 244–251, 255
  defined contribution plans, 263–268, 271
  description of modifications and changes, 77
  filing date and applicable section of law, 76–79
  filings with Pension Benefit Guaranty Corporation, 250
  filings with Secretary of Labor, 67–69, 244–248, 263–265
  filings with Secretary of the Treasury, 248–250, 265–267
  financial and actuarial information, 67–68
  financial statements, 67, 72
  name and address of each fiduciary, 67
  notice of plan termination, 76
  notification of change of status, 77
  number of employees covered, 67
  penalties, 80
  persons to whom report or disclosure furnished, 76–79